DATE DUE

JE 3 '02			
JE 1 0 02			
JE 7 '06			

DEMCO 38-296

Designing State Higher Education Systems for a New Century

Designing State Higher Education Systems for a New Century

by
Richard C. Richardson, Jr.
Kathy Reeves Bracco
Patrick M. Callan
Joni E. Finney

AMERICAN COUNCIL ON EDUCATION ★
ORYX PRESS ★
Series on Higher Education
1999

The rare Arabian Oryx is believed to have inspired the myth of the unicorn. This desert antelope became virtually extinct in the early 1960s. At that time, several groups of international conservationists arranged to have nine animals sent to the Phoenix Zoo to be the nucleus of a captive breeding herd. Today, the Oryx population is over 1,000, and over 500 have been returned to the Middle East.

© 1999 by the American Council on Education and The Oryx Press
Published by The Oryx Press
4041 North Central at Indian School Road
Phoenix, Arizona 85012-3397

Published simultaneously in Canada
Printed and bound in the United States of America

∞ The paper used in this publication meets the minimum requirements of American National Standard for Information Science—Permanence of Paper for Printed Library Materials, ANSI Z39.48, 1984.

Library of Congress Cataloging-in-Publication Data

Designing state higher education systems for a new century / by
   Richard C. Richardson, Jr. ... [et al.].
        p. cm. — (American Council on Education/Oryx Press series on
   higher education)
     Includes bibliographical references and index.
     ISBN 1-57356-174-6 (alk. paper)
     1. Higher education and state—United States—States—Case
   studies. 2. Education, Higher—United States—States—
   —Administration—Case studies. 3. Educational change—United
   States—States—Case studies. I. Richardson, Richard C.
   II. Series.
   LC173.D47 1999
        378.73—dc21
                                                          98-42300
                                                              CIP

CONTENTS

PREFACE

overnors and legislators have shown increasing interest in the performance and adaptability of their higher education systems as their
states have begun to face economic, political, and demographic
changes of a magnitude unseen since the turbulent 1960s. In states such as
Alaska, Illinois, Massachusetts, Minnesota, and New Jersey, the concerns of
elected leaders have translated into system restructuring that has ranged from
discontinuing coordinating or governing boards to creating new ones. While
the challenges of the 1960s led to fairly consistent changes in system design,
there are no clear trends among states that have recently restructured. The
absence of trends or patterns in these changes suggests the need to develop
new understandings of how performance and structure are interrelated.

Our purpose in writing this book is to propose a new and more powerful way
of thinking about how the performance of state higher education systems is
influenced by policy environments, system designs, and leadership. We do not
see our task as an academic exercise. We hope, rather, that improved understanding of the way these variables interact with each other and ultimately
influence performance will lead to better informed public policy. The conclusions we report are based on as much empirical data as we could uncover. At
the same time, our predominantly qualitative design and limited number of
cases require that we caution the reader against accepting our conclusions
without testing them in their own settings. Our findings represent the best
explanation we could devise to describe the relationships we observed in the
systems we studied. We do not argue that the explanations we offer are the

only ways of understanding what we saw. We challenge our readers to develop and test their own explanations in their own settings as one way of driving the discussion of state higher education policy toward better informed decisions.

Our model for explaining performance was drawn from case studies of seven large and diverse state higher education systems (California, Florida, Georgia, Illinois, Michigan, New York, and Texas) conducted between September 1994 and September 1996. We define a *state system of higher education* to include the public and private postsecondary institutions within a state as well as the arrangements for regulating, coordinating, and funding them. Jointly, the seven states encompass the entire range of governance structures. For each state, we collected documents, examined archival data, and conducted interviews to obtain multiple sources of information about context, system design, governance structures, and performance. More than 200 interviews were conducted with state legislators, legislative staff, representatives from governors' offices, representatives from state budget and research agencies, state higher education agency officials, system and institutional presidents, chancellors and board members, and faculty. We examined state budgets, master plans, statistical reports, board agendas, system histories, and newspaper accounts. We wrote individual case reports for each state and asked knowledgeable individuals to review them for accuracy. We developed an explanation of the relationships among policy environments, system designs, leadership, and performance for each state and then tested that explanation against the remaining states, modifying our conclusions until they represented the "best fit" for all seven.

Chapter 1 provides an overview of the evolution of state higher education governance structures and develops the concepts that organized our work. We give special attention to establishing a framework that captures the range of policy environments and system designs found in the states we studied. We also introduce a view of leadership that informs our discussion of elected and professional leadership strategies in chapter 9. The case studies presented in chapters 2 through 8 illustrate the differences in system design and policy environments present in each state. Each of these chapters has been organized to present comparable information under similar headings and in the same sequence. Chapter 9 reports differences in performance observed across the seven systems and relates these differences to system designs and policy environments. Chapter 10 examines the policy implications of our study.

ACKNOWLEDGMENTS

Many individuals contributed to the development of this book. Throughout the project, the research team was guided by the advice of a specially formed national advisory committee comprising 18 experts in higher education governance. The committee members are listed in appendix A. We would like to thank each of them for their valuable assistance. We owe a special debt to Frank Bowen, who assisted with interviews, cowrote the New York case study, reviewed other case studies, and contributed to many phases of the project. Our appreciation also goes to Bill Trombley, Gerardo de los Santos, Mario Martinez, and Yolanda Sanchez-Penley, all of whom assisted with interviews; Mary Ann Diridon, who transcribed most of the interview notes; Will Doyle, who provided research support; and Thad Nodine, who edited the book for the authors. Pat Richardson, Dan Levy, and Jim Bess provided helpful comments and advice at various stages of the project.

We are grateful to those who reviewed drafts of the case studies: Kenneth Ashworth, William Barba, Joseph Burke, Raymond Cardozier, Patrick Dallet, Cameron Fincher, Edward Hines, David Leslie, Marvin Peterson, William Pickens, Stephen Portch, Jack Smart, and Richard Wagner. Staff members from ACE and The Oryx Press encouraged the development of this book, particularly Jim Murray, Susan Slesinger, and Anne Thompson. They have our deepest appreciation. Special thanks go to Christine Davis, who edited the final version of the manuscript. Finally, we wish to thank The Pew Charitable Trusts and The James Irvine Foundation for their financial support of this research project.

CHAPTER 1

The States and Higher Education Governance

Higher education in the United States differs from that in Europe and most other countries in that responsibility for it rests with individual states, rather than with the national government. Despite this dispersion of responsibility for higher education in the United States, American campuses that have similar missions are quite similar in their operations, regardless of the state in which they are located. Although each college or university has its own history and aspirations, faculty members and senior administrators move relatively easily between, say, the Universities of Michigan and Illinois and other major public and private research universities. The same is true among regional universities and colleges. At the same time, state responsibility does make a difference. The unique history, politics, economics, and demography of each state shape the policies and priorities that guide higher education in that state. This comparative study of seven states centers on the ways in which college and university performance is influenced by differences in state policy environments and governance structures.

Past studies of higher education structures have focused on the concept of institutional autonomy and the impact of various state coordinating agencies on that autonomy. The first section of this chapter looks at this traditional concern with autonomy and the taxonomy of state higher education systems that resulted from it—a taxonomy that remains useful for descriptive purposes. The second section briefly reviews the history of state systems in the twentieth century. We define a *state system of higher education* to include the public and private postsecondary institutions within a state as well as the arrangements for regulating, coordinating, and funding them. The third section defines the terms we use in discussing governance structures and introduces the concept that states balance the influences of professional values and market forces. The final section introduces the case studies of seven states and provides a rationale for the order in which they are presented in the following chapters.

THE TRADITIONAL APPROACH TO UNDERSTANDING PERFORMANCE: INSTITUTIONAL AUTONOMY VERSUS STATE REGULATION

Traditionally, scholarship of state governance of higher education has focused on the distinction between coordination and governance, and the extent to which each contributes to or takes away from institutional autonomy. The question has been typically framed as one of institutional autonomy versus state authority, or centralization versus decentralization. Moos and Rourke argue that institutions require autonomy and that only strong, independent lay boards will insulate public institutions from political intrusion and inappropriate budgetary controls.[1] Glenny calls for greater state-level planning and coordination in higher education. He argues that voluntary coordination leads to domination by the oldest and largest institutions, while failing to provide for adequate representation of the public interest or for effective coordination of a large and increasing number of institutions.[2] Berdahl suggests that state agencies are preferable to politicians in resolving such issues as approval of new campuses and new degree programs.[3] Kerr and Gade warn of a "drift" in public higher education toward consolidation and control, and away from the forms of competition and autonomy that characterize trends in American economic policy.[4]

The debate on statewide governance embraces the role and utilization of private as well as public colleges and universities. States vary in their reliance on private higher education, but the presence of a strong independent sector in a state has implications for public institutions and for the overall performance of higher education in that state. To a greater or lesser extent, private institutions may be included in formal state planning for a higher education system. Regardless of formal inclusion in such planning activities, private institutions compete with their public counterparts for students, a competition in which state-funded student financial aid plays a crucial role.

States vary considerably in the approaches they take to organizing their higher education systems. Even the most comprehensive efforts to classify these different approaches fall short of capturing the complexity of the systems in some of the more populous states. These classifications are useful, however, in facilitating comparisons between states. Since World War II, much of the concern about institutional autonomy has focused on the state agencies that were established primarily to manage enrollment growth. The ensuing debate has contributed to the development of generally accepted taxonomies that distinguish three basic types of state structures: consolidated governing boards, coordinating boards, and planning agencies.[5]

In each of the states that have *consolidated governing boards*, a single governing board has legal management and control responsibilities for all public four-year institutions.[6] Twenty-four states have consolidated governing boards that meet this criterion. Nine of these also place community or technical colleges under the same consolidated governing boards that oversee four-year institutions, as in South Dakota and Utah. Fifteen consolidated governing board states, including Arizona and Florida, have separate state-wide boards for community colleges.

In each of the states that have *coordinating boards*, a single agency other than a governing board has responsibility for some or all of nine basic functions (planning, policy leadership, policy analysis, mission definition, academic program review, budgetary processes, student financial assistance, accountability systems, and institutional authorization). Of the 24 states with coordinating boards, 21 (including Illinois, Texas, and New York) have regulatory authority, while the remainder (including California) have advisory authority. A separate community college agency may operate under the auspices of the statewide coordinating board, as in Illinois, or as an independent state agency, as in California.

States that have *planning agencies* have no organization with authority that extends much beyond voluntary planning and convening of higher education. There are two planning agency states, Michigan and Delaware.

Beyond these distinctions, some states, including Pennsylvania and New York, have state boards or agencies with some responsibilities for all levels of education. Coordinating or governing boards may oversee subsystems of institutions with homogeneous missions, as in California, or multicampus subsystems with heterogeneous missions, as in New York. They may also coordinate primarily small subsystems or single campuses, as in Illinois or New Jersey, or mixed single-campus and multicampus institutions, as in Texas. In addition, states vary in the extent to which their higher education governance includes the private sector. States with coordinating boards are more likely than those with consolidated governing boards to recognize and incorporate private higher education in their policy and planning processes.

Under this generally accepted taxonomy, various criteria have been proposed for evaluating higher education system performance. McGuinness suggests buffering political intrusion, avoiding geopolitical problems, maintaining continuity in decision making, sustaining attention to system issues, supporting institutional presidents, articulating an understanding of system mission, facing up to change, and dealing with public policy issues.[7] Schick and his colleagues, in studying governance systems in Maine, Ohio, Pennsylvania, and Tennessee, conclude that effective structures are characterized by lay board members who understand their roles, good working relationships and open communications among internal and external constituencies, sensitive and honest educational leaders who respect and support each other while remaining faithful to institutional vision and needs, accountability to state government, and institutions freed from narrow governmental regulations. They add that effective systems have stable state structures that are perceived by participants as better than whatever they replaced.[8]

While not denying the relevance of these criteria for system performance, we suggest they may shortchange the public interest by relying too heavily on expert "insider" judgment for determining when the criteria are met. What is good for the "General Motors" of higher education may not be good for a particular state or for larger national interests. The assessments of system performance we offer in chapter 9 take into account the judgments of those who run the systems, but they also rely on the perspectives of policy makers outside the academic establishment, and on available quantitative indicators.

THE EVOLUTION OF STATE GOVERNANCE SYSTEMS IN THE TWENTIETH CENTURY

We have grouped structural changes in state higher education systems into three time periods: prior to 1950, 1950 to 1980, and 1980 and beyond.[9] Prior to 1950, centralization in governance structures increased as the role of state government changed from enabling, nurturing, and supporting nascent colleges and universities to building systems. From 1950 to 1980, concerns about the loss of institutional autonomy intensified as states took on more of a regulatory role and continued to move toward more centralized governance models. From 1980 to the present, market influences induced by the growth of student financial aid, as well as the development of statewide management information systems, led states to search for new ways to balance their system structures with changing state needs.

Prior to 1950: The Beginnings of the Autonomy Debate

In 1900, only a small proportion of Americans attended colleges or universities, and most institutions of higher education were controlled and managed by their own governing boards. These institutions developed their own philosophies, programs, and functions, and paid minimal attention to other colleges and universities or to state priorities. The early years of the century saw a continuation of what might be called the institution-building phase of higher education in the United States. There were few public colleges or universities, and these, protected and nurtured by state government, were relatively isolated from one another.

As the century advanced, two developments gradually impinged on this isolation. First, higher education became a more complex and expensive enterprise as additional people went to college for a widening range of purposes. To serve more students and meet more comprehensive purposes, states created new types of public institutions, including two-year colleges, teachers' colleges, and research universities. In the process, traditional beliefs about the meaning of higher learning were transformed. Second, state government itself became more complex, increasing the burden of managing an expanding array of enterprises through executive and legislative direction or oversight. Efficiency-minded legislators asked for better information on projected growth and became uneasy with competing demands for funding. The Great Depression and other periods of resource constraint caused many states, particularly those whose residents were at or below the median per capita income level for the United States, to consider more unified control.[10]

In 1905, Florida became the first state to establish a statewide governing board for four-year institutions. Iowa followed in 1906. In Georgia, a single governing board was established by the legislature in 1931 as part of a larger effort to simplify the operations of the executive branch. The new board brought together 26 institutions, including senior colleges, universities, and two-year colleges. A system board of regents was charged with coordinating the work of the institutions, integrating their educational programs, and freeing the state from wasteful duplication.[11] The board operated under statutory authority until 1943, when the state ratified an amendment conferring constitutional status, largely because of excessive interference on the part of the governor.[12] By 1932, 11 states had adopted statewide governing boards. Oklahoma established the first state-level coordinating board in 1941.

Although most states stopped short of creating statewide governing or coordinating agencies during this period, many states aggregated similar types of institutions under single boards. The City University of New York had its origins in the early 1920s. The economic impact of the Great Depression brought three campuses in North Carolina together in a "shotgun wedding" under the auspices of the University of North Carolina.[13] Many of the earliest multicampus systems aggregated former normal schools or brought agricultural institutes under the same boards that were responsible for land-grant colleges.

By the end of World War II, the trend toward increased state oversight of higher education became well established. The three primary forms of governance or coordination that have been described by traditional taxonomies were in evidence, although no single form had achieved dominance. Some systems acquired their shape in response to specific issues such as excessive political interference. Others evolved as legislators or state officials; and others sought greater efficiency from publicly funded colleges and universities. None of the systems were prepared for the influx of students created by two GI Bills and the post-Sputnik furor over national defense. Most illustrated at least some of the tensions that would frame the state regulation versus institutional autonomy debate for the following 30 years.

1950 to 1980: The Era of Growth and Coordination

During the post-World War II era, higher education in the United States was changed profoundly by two factors. First, there was a phenomenal increase in demand for higher education, caused initially by returning veterans who benefited from the GI Bill, and magnified later by the "baby boomer" children of the veterans. Second, the value of scientific research was established during the war, and the federal government sought to maintain the impetus for peacetime purposes as well as for continuing military ones. Although institutions of higher education were reluctant initially to accept their responsibility for educating older, often less well-prepared, students, they were enthusiastic about receiving federal dollars for research. With the blessings of their states, public colleges and universities underwent explosive growth. State governments considered each of these developments—but enrollment growth in particular—as requiring changes in their posture toward higher education. The role of state government changed from principally that of provider of institutional resources to both provider and regulator of institutional aspirations. With this change in the state's role, the structures of higher education also changed.

During this time period, the major structural change in higher education governance involved a move toward more state-level coordination and control, a nationwide transformation that the Carnegie Foundation for the Advancement of Teaching has documented.[14] In 1940, the majority of states did not have a governing, coordinating, or planning agency with responsibility for all public higher education; by 1979, all states had such an agency. In 1940, only New York State had an agency with planning responsibility that included private colleges and universities; by 1976, all but one state had some type of provision that applied to private colleges and universities. During this period, states continued to shift away from governance arrangements that allowed each campus to have its own board. Approximately 70 percent of public campuses had their own boards in 1940; only 30 percent did in 1976.

States changed their systems for a variety of reasons, but primarily to better manage enrollment growth, minimize institutional conflict over resources, control proliferation of graduate programs, and ensure adequate oversight of new and emerging institutions. State policy leaders also hoped the new transformations would limit institutional lobbying and reduce barriers to transfer and articulation.[15] Millett has argued that state involvement in higher education grew out of two interests: administration/management (arguments about economies and efficiencies) and coordination (attempts to control growth).[16]

Maine, Utah, and West Virginia established consolidated governing boards during the late 1960s. In 1972, North Carolina consolidated all public, four-year institutions under a single board of governors in an effort to "control the competition from below."[17] One year later, a similar system was established in Wisconsin, primarily in response to discontent among state political leaders with increasing competition. By the early 1980s, most of the states that had consolidated governing boards had operated those systems for many years. Many but not all of these states were smaller and less industrialized than those without consolidated governance systems, and only North Carolina and Wisconsin placed a major research university under a consolidated board.

By contrast, states that established coordinating boards were more likely to be urban-industrial with larger demographic and economic bases.[18] As one example, Illinois in the mid-1960s created a "system of systems" by organizing all public four-year institutions into four university systems, each with its own governing board. A statewide coordinating board with substantial formal and informal authority provided oversight for the four systems and for a system of locally governed community colleges with its own statewide coordinating board. Private institutions were integrated into the system of systems through state fiscal and financial aid policies adopted as part of an agreement by the private sector to participate in the statewide planning process conducted by the coordinating board. Texas underwent a similar metamorphosis at about the same time, though the results were not—at least formally—as orderly as in Illinois. Also, private higher education played a less significant role in Texas.

States that had consolidated governing boards eliminated individual campus governing boards and gave authority to the single statewide boards to manage institutions. States with coordinating boards left the governance of individual institutions or subsystems up to their respective boards, but relied on the statewide boards to manage policy areas that required interinstitutional cooperation.[19] Subsystems that developed during this time were created for three primary reasons: (1) as outgrowths to the establishment of branch campuses of major universities; (2) as a way to govern former normal schools, which had been under the authority of state boards of education; and (3) as a vehicle for growth generally.[20]

Statewide agencies created in the context of powerful and entrenched state universities frequently lacked authority to deal effectively with the issues they were asked to address. California, for example, distributed all public institutions among three statewide segments, each with different functions. Two were overseen by governing boards, one of which had constitutional status, and the third was headed by a coordinating board. The 1960 California Master Plan called for a statewide coordinating council controlled by representatives of public and private higher education. In 1974, the council was replaced by the current California Postsecondary Education Commission (CPEC), a coordinating agency with public members but only advisory powers.

New York chose to consolidate its public institutions on the basis of geography rather than mission. In 1948, the state aggregated all four-year institutions outside the city of New York under a single board of trustees as the State University of New York (SUNY). Subsequently, the SUNY trustees also became a coordinating board for upstate community colleges. In 1961, two- and four-year institutions within the city were consolidated under a single governing board as the City University of New York (CUNY). While California tried in the 1970s with limited success to strengthen the authority of a weak coordinating board, New York moved in the opposite direction; the state has gradually constrained the higher education responsibilities of the New York State Board of Regents, which is the coordinating structure for all education in the state.

During this time, some states gave coordinating boards, which had previously exercised only advisory influence, regulatory powers over budgets, new campuses, and academic programs. A growing number of states strengthened the regulatory powers their coordinating agencies already exercised,[21] and these agencies became the primary linkage between institutions and state government.

Michigan was the prominent exception. In 1850, the University of Michigan became the first institution in the country to be accorded constitutional autonomy, a development that grew from many years of political interference in its operations, including legislative and gubernatorial involvement in the selection and removal of faculty.[22] In 1963, Michigan revised its constitution to extend the language on constitutional autonomy to include all public four-year institutions. Glenny and Dalglish suggest that providing higher education institutions with constitutional status is one of the country's most significant legal developments relating to university autonomy.[23] In Michigan and California, policy officials often speak of institutions that have constitutional status as "the fourth branch of government."

In most states, however, governance changes during the 1950s and 1960s, stimulated by the need to manage explosive growth, led to additional bureaucracies to administer new state regulations. During the early 1970s, states increased regulation of higher education as they became more concerned with resource constraints and a projected decline in the number of high school graduates. While the 1972 amendments to the Federal Higher Education Act required states to establish statewide planning commissions (called "1202 commissions"), they had a much more significant effect in strengthening market influences: institutional leaders were confronted with the need to compete for federal dollars by attracting students who were eligible for student aid.

While the marketplace has always been a factor in U.S. higher education,[24] human capital studies in the 1960s furnished an explicit rationale for increased state and federal support for higher education and for the adoption of market forces as a conceptual strategy for achieving governmental policy priorities. The 1972 amendments to the higher education act and the recession of the mid-1970s made federal student aid a critical dimension of state higher education finance, and heightened the importance of these forms of market influences on institutional behavior. By 1980, even those states with a long tradition of low or no tuition were poised to begin the transition to higher tuition and financial aid.

During the late 1970s and early 1980s, states also became more actively involved in higher education policy,[25] partly in response to fiscal restraints and because of the increasing professionalism of their staffs, but also because more sophisticated management information systems made state-level steering activities increasingly feasible. Viewing this pattern with alarm, the Carnegie Foundation for the Advancement of Teaching called for governors to relinquish their seats on higher education boards and for confirmation of gubernatorial appointments by state senates.[26]

By the early 1970s, the basic patterns of contemporary state governance for higher education were in place.[27] Most states had either statewide coordinating boards or consolidated governing boards, with multicampus systems as the dominant institutional form.[28] Structures in different states were more alike than different, in part because they represented relatively common solutions to relatively common problems, but also because policy makers and educators tended to borrow from one another across state lines.[29]

1980 to the Present: Incremental Rebalancing

The changes in state governance during the past 20 years defy simple, one-dimensional explanations. In the early 1980s, Millett argued that policy makers were disillusioned with consolidated governing boards because the boards had become advocates of institutions rather than representatives of state interests.[30] Several states seemed to disprove his thesis, however, by continuing the earlier trend of consolidating institutions and subsystems under single governing boards, usually citing efficiency concerns as they did so. Alaska merged 11 community colleges and three universities into three multicampus systems. Minnesota combined three subsystems involving technical schools, community colleges, and state universities into a single consolidated system.

Other states, however, seemed to confirm Millett's argument by breaking up systems or providing individual institutions with greater decisional authority, albeit within the context of management information systems that assured some reasonable accountability. In the early 1990s, Illinois ended its "system of systems" by providing seven institutions previously organized as two multicampus systems with their own governing boards and making an eighth the third campus of the University of Illinois. Kentucky created an independent community college system out of the branch campuses of its major university while simultaneously providing its state coordinating board with greater powers over the budget. And Massachusetts, which created a "superboard" in 1980, decided in the early 1990s to grant more independence to its major university while retaining statewide governing authority over state colleges and community colleges.

Once again, the role of state government was changing to meet an altered environment. State governments and the public began to shift their attention from simple "inputs" such as state appropriations to "outputs"—that is, to institutional performance. During the 1990s, many states sought improved performance through reforms of governance structures or changes in professional leadership, but they have found that influencing performance in institutions that had been isolated intentionally from political currents requires a policy environment that is supportive of change.

New Jersey provides a current example of a state's attempts to alter its governance structure in response to changing state needs and priorities. Before the 1994 elections, New Jersey had what most acknowledged as the strongest coordinating board of any state in the country. Many believed that its *de jure* role was one more of governance than coordination. Board powers were enhanced by a large staff and a chief executive who served as a member of the governor's cabinet. Under the leadership of a new governor, however, legislation was passed eliminating the board of higher education and its staff. In its place, the state created a commission on higher education to provide general coordination, planning, and policy development. The council was charged with cooperating with a newly formed presidents' council that included representatives from proprietary and religious institutions. In the best federal tradition, responsibilities were carefully divided between the commission and the presidents' council. Institutional governing boards were significantly strengthened.[31] McGuinness has concluded that the New Jersey restructuring has increased the authority of public colleges and universities to govern themselves. The restructuring has also established, according to McGuinness, a flexible state structure that is better aligned with current and future needs and that operates within a framework of accountability and coordination.[32]

While it would be premature to judge the efficacy of the New Jersey experience, the restructuring illustrates the increasingly sophisticated search for designs that alter the balance of influences in the policy environment while remaining sensitive to the importance of institutional vitality and professional leadership. Policy environments and structures are important because they contain incentives and disincentives for performance that may—or may not—effectively reflect state needs and priorities. Although the solutions will vary considerably across the United States, all states will need to balance their systems and the forces acting on them in ways that are responsive to their own needs in the twenty-first century.

INFLUENCES THAT SHAPE STATE HIGHER EDUCATION PERFORMANCE

Prior studies have sought the key to the performance of state higher education systems in the distribution of authority between state agencies and higher education institutions and in the character of the leadership provided by professionals at the institutional and system levels. This approach assumes that the public interest will be served *regardless* of how authority is distributed or how higher education is structured—as long as there is effective leadership. Although this assumption may be true in any one state at a particular time, it is not universally true. Nor is it a firm foundation for assessing either the responsiveness of a higher education system to public policy priorities or its capacity to adapt to societal changes; such as substantial increases or decreases in enrollment demand, pressures for inclusion of heretofore underrepresented groups, technological advances, the emergence of a world market, and competition from proprietary institutions.

Our study suggests that the performance of higher education systems is influenced by at least two primary factors. The first of these is the state policy environment and the role that the state government chooses in balancing the competing influences of professional values and the market. The second is system design, including the way the interface between higher education and state government is structured, and the responsibility for and characteristics of the key work processes. Leadership from elected policy makers and their staffs, and from those who manage higher education systems and institutions, is also an important factor in understanding system performance, as prior studies of this subject have argued.

Performance depends not only on each of these factors considered separately but also upon the degree to which they are mutually complementary. For instance, as suggested in our preceding review of historical developments, states created and revised governance structures in response to how they perceived their own roles in shaping higher education. And each governance structure has particular leadership behaviors associated with it. We now provide a more detailed overview of each of the factors as a conceptual framework for interpreting the case studies. We return to this thesis in chapter 9 as a way of understanding differences in performance.

State Policy Environments for Higher Education

The distribution of authority between states and higher education ultimately reflects the interests articulated by groups inside and outside of government[33] as these are realized in the implementation of public policies and policy priorities. Said somewhat differently, the higher education system in each state operates in a policy environment that is the result of efforts over time to balance the often conflicting interests of academic professionals and, as we define it, the market. Each state, operating within a unique set of circumstances, balances these influences according to its own policies and priorities; there is no ideal or permanent balance.

Academic interests are familiar influences. Our concept of market forces is not. The market, for our purposes, is the broad array of interests and influences that are external to the formal structures of both state government and higher education institutions. Our concept of the market is broader than that of economists. It does include economic influences, such as competitive pressures, user satisfaction, cost and price, and student demand. But it also includes noneconomic forces, some of which are quantifiable, such as demographic characteristics and projections; and some of which are less quantifiable, such as political pressures, public confidence, and the availability of new technologies. Moreover, states can respond to market influences through a wide range of strategies, including promoting institutions (such as the building of community colleges), promulgating regulations, or encouraging competition (such as establishing performance-based budgeting or increasing student aid, thereby enhancing student choice).

Our analysis therefore includes questions that probe beyond institutional vitality and professional satisfaction. What changes are now taking place in society that have implications for colleges and universities? What societal changes are likely in the future? How, if at all, will these changes alter relationships among state government, higher education, and the market? What are the ways that state government and higher education can respond to these changes? Are changing societal conditions creating or widening a gap between state and institutional priorities?

The relationship between state and institutional priorities is a focal point for our study. If there is a gap between these, it may be explained by higher education's traditionally greater independence than that of other state agencies. Shielded by this relative independence, college and university priorities may either lag behind or lead those of state government or the public. Colleges and universities have usually been protected from regulations that affect the rest of state government by state delegation of significant authority to lay governing boards, or by the conferral of constitutional status. They have been protected from transient public influence by these devices, as well as—at least in the past—by the status and deference accorded them because of the professional expertise of their faculty members. Substantial institutional independence has been thought to be essential to the academic freedom of faculty members, and has not, in general, kept colleges and universities from evolving in pace with the larger social system. As valuable as this independence is, however, it may distance institutions from the legitimate concerns of state government and the public.

Our view of the state policy environment springs from the adaptation of ideas proposed by Williams for understanding higher education finance.[34] His model, the work of many minds, and our adaptation of it are best understood, first, in relation to what Clark has called the "triangle of tensions," illustrated in figure 1.1. The line on the left, which represents the tension between higher

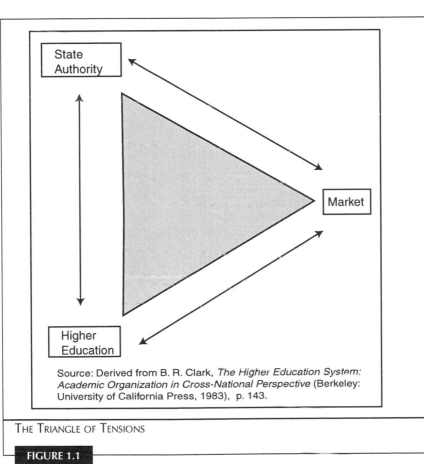

State Authority

Market

Higher Education

Source: Derived from B. R. Clark, *The Higher Education System: Academic Organization in Cross-National Perspective* (Berkeley: University of California Press, 1983), p. 143.

THE TRIANGLE OF TENSIONS

FIGURE 1.1

education and state authority, reflects what we have called the traditional approach to the study of higher education governance.[35] The lower line, which represents the tension between producer domination and consumer sovereignty, provides the basis for the literature on human capital and analyses of rates of return.[36] The triangle was closed when Clark added the line between "state authority" and "market," foreshadowing the possibility of states structuring the market rather than merely providing services directly through public bureaucracies.[37]

Williams has argued that the Clark model is static, and therefore best suited for description. In its place, he proposes a dynamic alternative that allows consideration of the variable roles of government in shaping the relative influence of the market and professional values on the types of services provided and their costs.[38] Under Williams's model, the role of the state changes as the force of the competing claims shifts among state, market, and academic interests. Among the state roles Williams describes are promoter, referee, and consumer supporter. As promoter, the state provides higher education with facilities and operating expenses, and sets the rules for higher education to achieve an overall purpose (such as providing an adequate supply of well-trained workers) that is seen as more important than market forces. As referee, the state mediates between consumers and providers, ensuring fair play. As consumer supporter, the state throws its weight behind users.

Our adaptation of Williams's model, shown in figure 1.2, identifies four policy roles that lie along the continuum from state-provided higher education to the state as playing a steering role. In our model, the state as provider—like Williams's concept of promoter—subsidizes higher education services with little regard for the market. As regulator, the state specifies the relationship between institutions and the market by controlling user charges, constraining administrative discretion in using resources, and eliminating or attenuating the incentives for efficient operation. As consumer advocate, the state redirects some allocations for higher education to students, thereby increasing the influence of their market choices on institutional behavior. Our concept of a steering role has no exact parallel in Williams's model. Popularized by Osborne and Gaebler in their book *Reinventing Government*,[39] states steer by structuring the market for higher education services to produce outcomes consistent with governmental priorities.

Low-tuition, low-aid strategies fall on the provider/regulator end of the scale. High-tuition, high-aid strategies are a good example of the consumer advocacy/steering end of the policy environment continuum. Examples of policies that move beyond consumer advocacy to approach steering include the aggressive inclusion of private institutions in planning to meet public needs, the use of contracts to take advantage of private capacity in lieu of creating or expanding public capacity, the use of targeted vouchers that

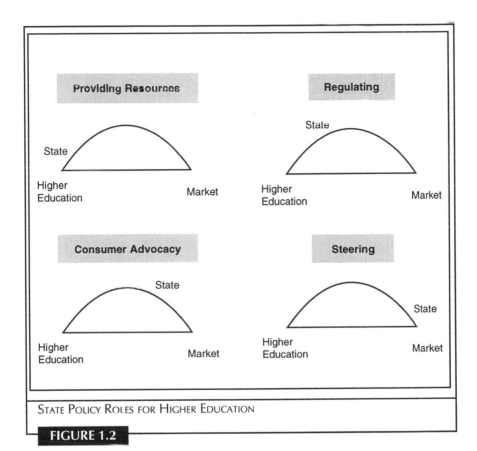

STATE POLICY ROLES FOR HIGHER EDUCATION

FIGURE 1.2

enable students to purchase approved services from any provider, and the appropriation of different levels of funding for some degree programs based on state human resource needs. The key distinction between roles involves the use that a state makes of the market. In a market-dominated environment, price is a function of demand. In the consumer advocacy role, the state concentrates on supporting demand. In the regulating role, the state controls price.

States that fail to establish an appropriate role for managing the conflicting pressures of professional values and the market end up with less satisfying outcomes than those that do. Ignoring the market in favor of state-planned systems of public higher education increases costs and limits responsiveness to emerging state needs and priorities. Excessive state regulation removes institutional incentives for efficiency and quality. Excessive reliance on consumer choice substitutes what people are willing to buy at present for longer term investment strategies. Overzealous market structuring can leave the most expensive tasks to public institutions, while stripping them of critical mass and flexibility. Priorities, economics, and demographics are key factors in determining the policy role most useful to a state at a particular time. States with abundant resources and a stable population have more freedom to ignore market forces than their less affluent and more rapidly growing counterparts. In selecting a policy role, states must make clear choices. A state that increases the importance of the market while maintaining a regulatory posture toward institutions creates a "catch-22" environment for its professional leadership.

Structure: The Design of Higher Education Systems

System design determines the tools policy makers and professional leaders have available to improve or change higher education performance. States make four sets of decisions when they design systems of higher education:

- Decisions about governance structures establish lines of authority and accountability between state governments and providers.
- Decisions about work processes define responsibility for and characteristics of the major work processes: (1) collecting and disseminating information about performance; (2) prescribing the framework for budgeting; (3) allocating responsibilities for monitoring program quality and redundancy; and (4) providing arrangements for encouraging higher education institutions to see themselves as systems and to work together on such tasks as school-to-college transitions and student transfer.
- Decisions about missions divide responsibilities for achieving higher education goals among types of institutions.
- Decisions about capacity determine the availability, quality, and location of educational programs and services.

We characterize state governance structures for higher education systems as *segmented, unified,* or *federal.* In most *segmented systems,* multiple governing boards are each responsible for one or more institutions. There is no effective state agency with meaningful responsibility for all of higher education. State government reserves only the power to determine the appropriation each institution receives each year. Each governing board and its appointed executive represent institutional interests directly to state government through the budgeting process. Four-year institutions and community colleges may have their own separate arrangements for voluntary coordination in dealing with state government and with each other.

In *unified systems,* a single governing board manages all degree-granting higher education institutions and represents them in discussions with governors and legislators. Unified systems are characterized by Handy's principles of twin citizenship, interdependence, common rules, and common ways of communicating and measuring. Twin citizenship involves the degree to which participants feel part of both the larger system and the institution to which they have their primary allegiance.[40]

Federal systems have a statewide board responsible for collecting and distributing information, advising on the budget, planning programs from a statewide perspective, and encouraging articulation. Federal systems, like their unified counterparts, emphasize interdependence, common rules, and common ways of communicating and measuring. To these characteristics, they add separation of powers and subsidiarity. Separation of powers divides responsibilities for representing the public interest (e.g., monitoring inputs, measuring performance, and maintaining institutional accountability) from responsibilities for governing institutions (e.g., strategic direction, management accountability, and institutional advocacy). The former responsibilities are carried out by a statewide board and the latter by institutional or system governing boards. Subsidiarity safeguards the legitimate roles of institutions by limiting the size and influence of central system agencies.

Does it really matter how a state structures its system of higher education? Those who have studied this question, while rejecting the notion that any one arrangement is best under all circumstances, nonetheless agree that governance is important.[41] Our case studies suggest that the level of importance is often understated. Certainly, leadership matters, but even good leaders should not be expected to achieve consistent results in the presence of a system design that inhibits institutional collaboration and system synergy. Leadership can make a system perform better or worse than its structural design, but it cannot compensate for badly designed systems or mismatched policy environments.

Leadership

Heifetz identifies three situations that call for different forms of leadership. In *technical situations*, both the problem and the solution are clearly defined, and the solution lies within previously learned behaviors of system participants. In *strategic situations*, the definition of the problem is clear, but identifying and implementing a solution requires "learning." In *adaptive situations*, neither the problem nor the solution can be defined or addressed in the absence of learning.[42] Each of these circumstances calls for a different type of leadership.

Leaders who founded new institutions and consolidated existing ones between 1900 and 1950 primarily used consensus-building strategies based on the implicit assumption that reasonable solutions were within the capabilities of the existing system and could be reached through the normal give and take of leadership activities that Burns has characterized as "transactional." Transactional leaders achieve their ends by exchanging one thing for another.[43] Even though the 1960 California Master Plan has often been described as "visionary," its chief architect, Clark Kerr, has described the plan more as a compromise among the three segments to achieve a system design that would be acceptable to the legislature. We equate Heifetz's idea of technical leadership with Burns's notion of transactional leadership.

Leaders who designed higher education systems or presided over them in the turbulent 1960s and 1970s could not count on commonly held norms and values to address the problems associated with transforming higher education from meritocratic to open-access institutions in an era of civil rights, student activism, and concerns about gender inequality. Long-serving transactional leaders were displaced by those committed to academic strategy.[44] Strategic leadership is transactional leadership that is goal oriented and creative. To resolve clearly defined problems, strategic leaders seek solutions that require learning from system participants.

The technological and fiscal issues of the current era are more adaptive than transactional or strategic. Many elected leaders are no longer confident that their current higher education systems will be able to produce the outcomes they project as essential to future needs. In adaptive situations, there can be no solution without changes in values and behaviors, a process that requires leadership that Burns labels as "transformational."[45] Adaptive leadership is transformational leadership that has as its most important goal an informed public that knows what it wants and what it should expect from a higher education system. Leaders in adaptive situations—i.e., situations without clearly defined problems and acceptable solutions—search for opportunities to improve the balance between expert and public opinion to promote the learning that is essential for progress. According to Yankelovich, attempting to force a solution developed by experts onto an unprepared public produces "stalemate, divisiveness, and polarization."[46]

According to Burns, most leadership is transactional. Such bureaucracies as higher education institutions and coordinating/governing boards rely almost exclusively on transactional leadership in "moving from routine to creative, responsive activity" but rarely does such activity "play a role in transforming leadership." Legislatures "cannot on their own exercise transforming leadership." Even leadership from the governor "is inadequate for sustained and planned social transformation."[47] This leads us to a pivotal question for this study of whether some governance structures are more likely than others to call forth transformational leadership from elected leaders when circumstances require this approach.

INTRODUCING THE CASE STUDIES

The seven states we studied provide examples of a wide range of policy environments as well as all three of the major governance designs. We also observed technical, strategic, and adaptive leadership in the states as both elected and appointed officials worked to create more synergistic higher education systems out of the institutions they inherited.

Georgia, relatively small and mostly rural when its system was designed in the 1930s, chose a consolidated governing board. When this arrangement proved too susceptible to political intervention, the entire system was granted constitutional status. As one result, higher education institutions in the state have been somewhat insulated from the direct impact of the policy environment, which has most recently exhibited increased emphasis on consumer advocacy as a result of the governor's widely studied HOPE scholarship program. During our visits, the system was experiencing strong strategic leadership from a new chancellor.

Illinois and Texas, larger states with more complex systems of higher education than Georgia, opted in the 1960s for coordinating boards that include federal checks and balances that are similar to those found in the U.S. Constitution. In both states, legislators provide technical leadership and see themselves as watchdogs protecting institutions from excessive central dominance. In Illinois, elected and appointed leaders make use of their federal structure to address adaptive issues in ways that are not visible in Texas. The policy environment in Illinois emphasizes steering, while the one in Texas is much more regulatory.

California, New York, and Florida have created an eclectic mixture of segmented bureaucracies and quasi-federal agencies. California is closer to the segmented end of the continuum, while Florida is closer to a unified model than the other two. The policy environment in all three states is predominantly regulatory. Michigan essentially features a system of segmented institutions in which the policy environment is primarily that of providing resources. Only Florida appears to provide direction to system leaders, at least on short-range issues. Leadership in these states at all levels seems more technical than strategic. We saw no evidence of adaptive leadership on statewide issues in any of these four states.

In Illinois, Texas, and Georgia, the legislature or the state constitution had delegated to an interface agency authority over four central work processes:

- *Information Management*[48] helps states know where they are to help them decide where they need to go. Assessing system performance in relation to state priorities provides information about the extent to which current educational inputs and outcomes reflect state priorities.
- *Budgeting* enables state governments to negotiate with institutions to achieve state priorities. Budget language often calls attention to priorities without changing system arrangements for financing.
- *Program Planning* determines the availability, quality, and location of educational programs and services. Planning done for the entire

system can produce very different results than planning done by each subsystem or institution.

- *Articulation and Collaboration* refer to the extent to which higher education institutions see themselves as systems and work together on such tasks as student transfer. These terms also help to define the extent to which postsecondary institutions work closely with the schools that furnish their incoming students.

In the remaining four states, no single agency has statewide responsibility for these processes. Hearn and Griswold argue that states with central agencies, whether coordinating or governing, are more likely than their segmented counterparts to undertake policy innovations, particularly in academic areas.[49] This seems to be the case in the states we studied.

Figure 1.3 provides our estimates of where the seven states are positioned in relation to their policy roles and system designs.

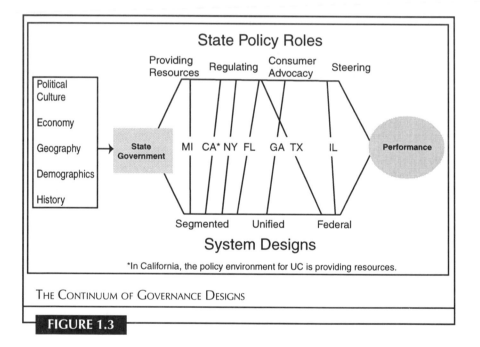

The Continuum of Governance Designs

FIGURE 1.3

The order of the seven case study chapters that follow derives from the design of the respective systems. We begin with Michigan, the most segmented state, and conclude with Illinois, a federal model. In each of these chapters, we begin with a discussion of context to highlight historical, political, economic, demographic, and geographic factors that contribute to the state policy environment for higher education providers. In this section, we give attention to such factors as civil service requirements, collective bargaining, tuition policies, and use of the private sector. A second section details the characteristics and history of the higher education system. A third discusses system design, including the higher education–state government interface. The following four subsections of each chapter describe how key work processes have been implemented in each state as a function of the policy environments and system designs.

NOTES

1. H. D. Graham, "Structure and Governance in American Higher Education: Historical and Comparative Analysis in State Policy," *Journal of Policy History* 1, no. 1 (1989), pp. 80–107.
2. L. A. Glenny, *Autonomy of Public Colleges: The Challenge of Coordination* (New York: McGraw-Hill, 1959).
3. R. O. Berdahl, *Statewide Coordination of Higher Education* (Washington, D.C.: American Council on Education, 1971).
4. C. Kerr and M. Gade, *The Guardians: Boards of Trustees of American Colleges and Universities, What They Do and How Well They Do It* (Washington, D.C.: Association of Governing Boards, 1989).
5. See in particular Berdahl, *Statewide Coordination*; and Education Commission of the States. 1997. *State Postsecondary Education Structures Sourcebook* (Denver, Colo.: Education Commission of the States). The number of states referenced in the following paragraphs do not equal 50 because some states have two types of agencies.
6. R. Novak, "Statewide Governance: Autonomy or Accountability Revisited," *Trusteeship* (March-April 1993), pp. 10–14.
7. E. Schick, R. Novak, J. Norton, and H. Elam. *Shared Visions of Public Higher Education Governance: Structures and Leadership Styles That Work* (Washington, D.C.: American Association of State Colleges and Universities, 1993), p. 23.
8. Ibid., pp. 7–8.
9. See A. C. McGuinness, *Perspectives on the Current Status of and Emerging Policy Issues for Public Multicampus Higher Education Systems* (Washington, D.C.: Association of Governing Boards, 1991); and R. Novak, "Methods, Objectives and Consequences of Restructuring," in T. J. MacTaggart and Associates, *Restructuring Higher Education: What Works and What Doesn't in Reorganizing Governance Systems* (San Francisco: Jossey-Bass, 1996), pp. 16–50.
10. Glenny, *Autonomy of Public Colleges*; and Novak, "Methods, Objectives and Consequences of Restructuring," p. 19.
11. University System of Georgia, *Information Digest, 1994-95* (Atlanta, Ga., 1995), p. 8.
12. C. Fincher, *The Historical Development of the University System of Georgia: 1932–1990* (Athens, Ga.: Institute of Higher Education, 1991), pp. 24–25.
13. E. Lee and F. Bowen, *The Multicampus University* (San Francisco: Jossey-Bass, 1971), p. 3.
14. Carnegie Foundation for the Advancement of Teaching, *The States and Higher Education: A Proud Past and a Vital Future* (San Francisco: Jossey-Bass, 1976).
15. A. C. McGuinness, "The Changing Structure of State Higher Education Leadership," in *State Postsecondary Education Structures Handbook*, ed. A. C. McGuinness, R. M.

Epper, and S. Arredondo (Denver, Colo.: Education Commission of the States, 1994), pp. 19–21; and Novak, "Statewide Governance," p. 12.

16. J. Millett, *Conflict in Higher Education: State Government versus Institutional Independence* (San Francisco: Jossey-Bass, 1984), pp. 58–59.

17. Ibid., p. 89.

18. Ibid., p. 88.

19. P. Callan, *Perspectives on the Current Status of and Emerging Policy Issues for State Coordinating Boards* (Washington, D.C.: Association of Governing Boards, 1991), pp. 6–7.

20. McGuinness, *Perspectives on . . . Multicampus Higher Education Systems*, p. 9.

21. Callan, *Perspectives on . . . State Coordinating Boards*, p. 12.

22. L. A. Glenny and T. K. Dalglish, *Public Universities, State Agencies, and the Law: Constitutional Autonomy in Decline* (Berkeley, Calif.: Center for Research and Development in Higher Education, 1973), p. 17.

23. Ibid., p. 14.

24. See L. L. Leslie and S. A. Slaughter, "The Development and Current Status of Market Mechanisms in United States Postsecondary Education," *Higher Education Policy* 10, no. 3/4, pp. 239–52.

25. McGuinness, "The Changing Structure of State Higher Education Leadership," p. 23.

26. Carnegie Foundation for the Advancement of Teaching, *The States and Higher Education*, p. 19.

27. McGuinness, "The Changing Structure of State Higher Education Leadership," p. 19.

28. Ibid.; and Kerr and Gade, *The Guardians: Boards of Trustees*, p. 25–26.

29. Novak, "Methods, Objectives and Consequences of Restructuring."

30. J. Millett, *Conflict in Higher Education*, pp. 235–65.

31. Commission on Higher Education and the Presidents' Council's Joint Committee on Interim Assessment of Restructuring, *The Restructuring of New Jersey Higher Education: An Interim Report to the Governor and the New Jersey Legislature* (Trenton, N.J., 1996).

32. A. C. McGuinness, *Restructuring State Roles in Higher Education: A Case Study of the 1994 New Jersey Higher Education Restructuring Act* (Denver, Colo.: Education Commission of the States, 1995), p. 11.

33. B. R. Clark, "The Many Pathways of Academic Coordination," *Higher Education* 8, no. 3 (1979), pp. 251–67.

34. G. L. Williams, "The 'Marketization' of Higher Education: Reforms and Potential Reforms in Higher Education Finance," in *Emerging Patterns of Social Demand and University Reform: Through a Glass Darkly*, ed. D. D. Dill and B. Sporn (Tarrytown, N.Y.: Elsevier Science, Inc., 1995), pp. 170–71.

35. See Berdahl, *Statewide Coordination of Higher Education*, and M. Shattock, *The UGC and the Management of British Universities* (Buckingham, United Kingdom: Open University Press, 1994).

36. See B. Johnstone, "Tuition Fees" and "Rate of Return Studies," *The Encyclopedia of Higher Education*, vol. II, ed. B. R. Clark and G. Neave (Oxford: Pergamon Press and Psacharopoulis, 1992), pp. 1501–9, and pp. 999–1003, respectively.

37. B. R. Clark, *The Higher Education System: Academic Organization in Cross-National Perspective* (Berkeley, Calif.: University of California Press, 1983).

38. Williams, "The 'Marketization' of Higher Education," pp. 172–74.

39. D. Osborne and T. Gaebler, *Reinventing Government: How the Entrepreneurial Spirit Is Transforming the Public Sector* (Reading, Mass.: Addison-Wesley, 1992).

40. C. Handy, "Balancing Corporate Power: A New Federalist Paper," *Harvard Business Review* (November-December 1992), pp. 59–72. We draw here upon a modified version of Handy's concepts to distinguish federal from unified systems.
41. See Schick et al., *Shared Visions of Public Higher Education Governance*, pp. 144–46; McGuinness, "The Changing Structure of State Higher Education Leadership"; and Novak, "Statewide Governance."
42. R. Heifetz, *Leadership without Easy Answers* (Cambridge, Mass.: The Belknap Press of Harvard University Press, 1994), p. 76. Heifetz describes the type of leadership we have labeled as "strategic" as a mixture of technical and adaptive.
43. J. M. Burns, *Leadership* (New York: Harper and Row, 1979), p. 4.
44. See G. Keller, *Academic Strategy: The Management Revolution in American Higher Education* (Baltimore, Md.: John Hopkins University Press, 1983).
45. Burns, *Leadership*, p. 24.
46. D. Yankelovich, *Coming to Public Judgment* (Syracuse, N.Y.: Syracuse University Press, 1991), pp. 98, 242–45.
47. Burns, *Leadership*, pp. 307, 368, 396.
48. M. J. Wheatley and M. Kellner-Rogers, "Self Organization: The Irresistible Future of Organizing," *Strategy & Leadership* (July-August 1996), p. 22.
49. J. C. Hearn and C. Griswold, "State Level Centralization and Policy Innovation in U.S. Postsecondary Education," *Educational Evaluation and Policy Analysis* 16 no. 2 (summer 1994), pp. 161–90.

CHAPTER 2

Michigan

T he constitutional status of public colleges and universities in Michigan, combined with weak political oversight and a fairly noninfluential independent sector, places Michigan decidedly on the provider end of our conceptual model of higher education policy environments. Playing the role of provider, the state supports institutions usually with across-the-board increases and with few restrictions on how state money is spent. The state's higher education structure, which is the most highly segmented of any in this study, further reinforces the weight given to institutional interests in this system.

Michigan's governor, who enjoys strong veto and other powers granted by the state constitution, is the state's most influential higher education leader. A historically powerful legislature has been increasingly challenged by shifting political currents. After years of fiscal crisis due to downsizing in the auto industry, Michigan is now experiencing relatively stable economic growth but growing budgetary pressures from corrections (primarily prisons) and Medicaid. The state faces only moderate growth in higher education enrollments.

Elected leaders have been supportive of higher education. While there is no consensus about what the state looks for from its higher education system, those we interviewed mentioned affordability, access, economic development, quality, and relevance. Despite concerns about affordability, Michigan has the nation's highest tuition charges for public institutions, charges that the state, for the most part, does not offset with commensurate levels of financial aid.

Michigan has no statewide agency with significant responsibilities for higher education, and all four-year institutions have constitutional status. Universities are regarded as the "fourth branch" of state government. While the 1963 state constitution charged the state board of education with serving as the general planning and coordinating body for all of higher education, universities have successfully used the courts to resist any coordinating activities as encroachments on their constitutional authority.

A voluntary council of university presidents develops positions on the state budget, monitors legislation, provides limited data collection and dissemination, reviews academic programs, and serves as a vehicle for interacting with state government. Michigan's 29 community colleges are linked together through the voluntary Michigan Community College Association and through the community college board, which advises the state board of education.

Private institutions enroll about 15 percent of the full-time-equivalent (FTE) student enrollment in Michigan. There is no dominant private university. The private sector is included in state policy decisions to the extent that the state provides reimbursements for degrees awarded to Michigan residents. There is also a need-based tuition grant program for students attending private institutions and three other small financial aid programs.

Because of the segmented nature of the structure, no one agency or institution has responsibility for the work processes (information management, budgeting, program planning, and articulation and collaboration) in Michigan. The structure lacks any capacity for statewide planning except through voluntary consensus on distribution of resources. Funding is based primarily on historical patterns. Institutions determine their own missions and decide which programs they will offer and where. Voluntary program review processes serve to allay some policy concerns about program duplication, but they do not prevent a determined institution from doing as it pleases. Institutions in Michigan do not provide information that permits comparisons or judgments about performance, except as it may be required by the legislature as a condition of the budgeting process. Voluntary agreements on articulation are a matter of institutional interpretation and subscription.

STATE CONTEXT

With 9.5 million residents, Michigan is the eighth most populous state in the nation. Although the state is not projected to experience the high levels of population growth that many of the southern and western states will confront over the next decade, the state will face increasing numbers of minorities in its major population centers, and population growth in its western region. In 1995, approximately 41 percent of the population resided in the three largest counties: Wayne, Oakland, and Macomb, which encompass the Detroit metropolitan area and immediate suburbs.[1] This concentration is expected to change somewhat as population growth is now primarily in the western part of the state. Among study states, Michigan has the least diverse population. African Americans, by far the largest minority group in the state, comprise 14.5 percent of the population, a proportion that is expected to grow to almost 20 percent by 2020.[2] The percentage of families who do not speak English in the home is low, as is the high school dropout rate. Michigan is about average in terms of its per capita income, as well as the percentage of its families living in poverty. Its population is below average in educational attainment.[3]

Republican governor John Engler, a veteran of 20 years in the legislature including seven years as majority leader in the senate, narrowly defeated a Democratic incumbent in 1990 by promising to "cut taxes, downsize government, create jobs, improve the business climate, and improve the quality of the public schools."[4] He was reelected in 1994 by the second largest margin in state history. Michigan's constitution grants the governor strong budget and line-item veto authority.[5] The governor also appoints 10 of the 13 university governing boards. Governor Engler's influence has been enhanced by Republican control of both the senate and the house.

Citing financial mismanagement and declining enrollment,[6] the governor used his constitutional powers to close Highland Park Community College, a primarily African-American college in the Detroit area, by vetoing the institution's state appropriation in 1995. He also eliminated 40 to 50 commissions and boards as well as the public relations offices in all state agencies except his own office. Many of those we spoke with believe the governor tried to reduce the influence of elected boards by moving key programs from agencies with elected boards to those without such boards. One example involves the recent transfer of financial aid programs from the Department of Education to the Department of the Treasury. In addition, Engler has been the first governor to hand-pick Republican candidates for the elected boards of the University of Michigan (UM), Michigan State University (MSU), and Wayne State University (WSU).

Republican control of the house and senate has brought significant change to the legislature. For 25 years prior to the 1994 elections, Democrats controlled both chambers, with the balance of power in the Detroit metropolitan area.[7] The 1994 elections shifted the power base to the western part of the state, the home of the governor and several key legislators. Michigan recently enacted an initiative that will limit terms of house members to six years and of senators to eight. The governor is limited to two four-year terms. Those we spoke with were uncertain about the full effects of term limits, but most agreed that the limits will transform the past system, which relied heavily on seniority to socialize leaders to a traditional set of values.

The senate and the house rely on separate, nonpartisan fiscal agencies with very small staffs for information and analysis on higher education and other public issues. The fiscal agencies operate under a confidentiality arrangement that prevents them from disclosing the requests they receive from legislators. The two most powerful legislative committees for higher education are the Senate Subcommittee on Appropriations for Higher Education and the House Appropriations Committee. We were told that funding decisions for higher education depend upon who holds the respective chairs of these committees. A senator described the meetings of his committee as, "congenial hearings on the campuses of institutions," adding that the House Appropriations Committee tends to "bring presidents in and browbeat them." A house member told us that many representatives would like to be more prescriptive about what higher education can and cannot do, but the senate and the more experienced members of the house are unwilling to support such initiatives.

For many years, Michigan's economy was dominated by the American automobile industry. The industry's high-wage jobs, which did not require education beyond high school, contributed to the relatively low educational attainment among residents. Downsizing in the automobile industry reduced the number of such jobs dramatically and contributed to a significant slow-down in the state's economy. Service jobs now outnumber manufacturing jobs for the first time in state history. In the late 1970s, Michigan's per capita income was about 8 percent higher than the national average; in 1993, per capita income was 2 percent below the national average.[8] The state tax structure has historically been dominated by property taxes, but recent changes will make the property tax burden lower and the sales tax burden higher.[9] An income tax increase enacted in 1983 was phased out in 1993.

Budget shifts caused by high unemployment, increased federal require-ments for social services, prison construction, and declining enrollment in elementary and secondary schools have produced a roller coaster effect on educational funding.[10] From 1968 to 1993, K–12 education decreased from about 33 percent of the state budget to 20.5 percent, higher education fell from 11 to 7.4 percent, and social services increased from 17 to 31 percent. Total dollars for higher education, however, increased during the first half of the 1990s. The fiscal year 1996 budget provided $1.31 billion of general fund revenues to universities, an increase of 4.7 percent from fiscal year 1995. Community colleges received $253 million in fiscal year 1996, an increase of 2.1 percent. From 1990 to 1996, general fund/general purpose spending for higher education grew at more than twice the rate of state spending overall.[11]

While there was no consensus among those we interviewed concerning state priorities for higher education, affordability was most frequently men-tioned as a priority, often in tandem with access. Yet Michigan has the highest public tuition charges in the country, and during the 1990s the state has relied increasingly on student and parent contributions. The high percentage of out-of-state undergraduates at UM further complicates policy discussions of affordability and access. Many legislators, including a previous chair of the House Appropriations Committee, believe that the university is doing a disservice to residents by enrolling too many out-of-state students. University officials counter by arguing that UM's increasing national and international status requires a very selective admissions process that inevitably admits large numbers of students outside the state. Several years ago the legislature asked that the university take no more than 30 percent of its undergraduate student body from out-of-state. After the university failed to meet this target, the legislature withheld resources temporarily. The legislature eventually gave the university the money, but the tension over out-of-state enrollment continues.

CHARACTERISTICS AND HISTORY OF HIGHER EDUCATION

There are 109 institutions of higher education in Michigan: 15 public four-year institutions, 30 public two-year institutions (including one tribally controlled community college), 56 private four-year institutions, and 8 private two-year institutions. Enrollments by head count totaled approximately 548,000 students in 1995. Public four-year institutions accounted for 47 percent of this total, public two-year institutions enrolled 37 percent, and the independent colleges and universities enrolled the remainder.[12] From 1991 to 1995, enrollment declined by 1.2 percent at four-year and 6.7 percent at two-year institutions—due primarily to decreasing numbers of high school graduates. The state expects a 13 percent increase in the number of high school graduates between 1996 and 2006, compared to a 20 percent increase nationally.[13] New high school graduates in Michigan participate in higher education at slightly above average rates.[14] The low percentage of the population holding a baccalaureate, combined with relatively high enrollments in four-year institutions, suggests an intergenerational change in educational aspirations, as does the relatively high percentage of the population holding an associate's degree.

The 15 public four-year institutions in Michigan enroll approximately 260,000 students. The "big three"—UM, MSU, and WSU—are large research universities. Each enrolls over 30,000 students and offers a full range of graduate and undergraduate programs. Western Michigan University is a Doctoral I university according to the Carnegie Classification System. Michigan Technological University is specialized with a focus on engineering. The rest are general comprehensive universities although four offer at least one doctoral degree.[15]

Each of Michigan's public institutions, with the exception of UM's two branch campuses at Flint and Dearborn, has its own governing board. Each board has nine members, including the institutional president, who serves as an ex-officio member of the board. Other board members serve eight-year terms. The boards of UM, MSU, and WSU are elected by the public in statewide elections. The governor appoints the board members of the remaining four-year institutions. Each of the public two-year community colleges has a regionally elected governing board.

The "big three" public universities are a cut above the rest in the minds of most Michigan residents. According to one university board member, "Developments at Michigan and Michigan State in particular tend to spill over into public perceptions of higher education generally, due in part to the size of these institutions and the elevating impact on institutional autonomy of elected boards."

All four-year public institutions in Michigan have constitutional autonomy. In 1850, the University of Michigan became the first institution in the country to be granted constitutional autonomy, primarily because of many years of political interference that included legislative and gubernatorial involvement in the selection and removal of faculty.[16] The language granting constitutional autonomy can be found in all subsequent state constitutions. The intent was to keep the legislature from getting involved in areas considered to be the domain of the faculty and university administration. In the most recent 1963 version, Article VIII, Section III, states, "The power of the institutions of higher education provided in this constitution to supervise their respective institutions and control and direct the expenditures of the institution's funds shall not be limited to this section."[17] Based on this language, individual boards have acquired the power to set tuition and to determine how their state appropriations will be spent.

The University of Michigan, the "flagship" institution, is considered one of the best public research institutions in the country. It enrolls more than 36,000 students in highly selective undergraduate and graduate programs, attracting students from across the state, country, and world. In fiscal year 1996, the university received about $288 million from state appropriations, which comprise 10 to 37 percent of the institution's total revenues depending on whether auxiliary enterprises are included.[18] The University of Michigan has spearheaded many of the court battles over, as one respondent from higher education said, "long-standing, substantive issues of conflict between the university and the state." During our study, the university was involved in a suit challenging the state's open meetings act for the "big three" institutions.

Michigan State University, located just outside Lansing, is the largest institution in the state, with more than 30,000 undergraduates and 40,000 total students in 1995. As the state's land-grant institution, MSU provides a wide array of undergraduate, master's, and doctoral programs, including several programs in agriculture and natural resources. In 1995, MSU's president, concerned with rising costs to students, instituted a guarantee that tuition would not increase by more than the rate of inflation, as long as state appropriations kept pace with inflation. Michigan State University received approximately $256 million in state funding in fiscal year 1996.[19]

Wayne State University differs from the other two research universities because of its urban Detroit location and the diversity of its more than 30,000 students. Among four-year institutions in the state, WSU has the largest percentage of students from low-income and minority backgrounds. Tuition at WSU is lower than at the other research institutions, and lower than in some of the comprehensive institutions as well. Wayne State University's president has argued that if tuition increases too rapidly, the institution will lose enrollments and, ultimately, revenues. Unlike the other "big three" institutions, Wayne State has a unionized faculty. Relations between the administration and faculty have been a constant source of tension. Wayne State University received approximately $205 million in state appropriations in fiscal year 1996.[20]

Michigan's 10 doctoral, comprehensive, and liberal arts regional universities have enrollments ranging from more than 26,000 at Western Michigan to about 3,500 at Lake Superior State. All receive significantly less state funding than the "big three." In 1996, state appropriations to the regional institutions ranged from $98 million at Western Michigan to $11 million at Lake Superior.[21]

Many interviewees told us that the Michigan higher education system and especially its regional universities are creative and responsive in serving the needs of the educational market because of the autonomy of individual institutions. One person said, "Individual institutions have been able to develop their own character, to cultivate their own mission" in response to student and economic needs. Another argued that competition for students among regional institutions makes them better institutions. A university administrator added, "We don't want to keep an institution from getting out of a category" (moving up a level in the Carnegie institutional classification system) because of artificial constraints.

In keeping with this perspective, universities have begun developing centers beyond traditional geographic service areas with the intention of extending the range of opportunities for the bachelor of science degree and for master's level work. In some cases, it is possible to earn a bachelor's degree without attending the main campus of the institution granting the degree. This development is viewed by some as a significant benefit and by others as evidence of the need for greater coordination. Supporters of this practice told us that universities are extending services into communities where the programs have not been offered and therefore are providing a key statewide benefit. While not denying the potential for program duplication and waste, most of those we spoke with said that relying on market forces is less costly and more effective than creating a bureaucratic structure. A key senator on the higher education appropriations subcommittee added that Michigan does not expect efficiency from its universities.

Critics said they are concerned about competition developing into a free-for-all, where public four-year institutions would expand all over the state, regardless of need, with every institution wanting to emulate UM or MSU. They also said that relying on the budget as the sole mechanism for preventing mission creep is wasteful and produces institutions that have no real focus and no real expertise. An example cited by both supporters and critics involves the establishment of an evening M.B.A. program in Lansing by Western Michigan during a period when MSU resisted offering its day M.B.A. program in a format suitable for employed adults. Student demand for the Western Michigan program changed MSU's posture. Now there are two publicly supported evening M.B.A. programs in the Lansing area, one offered by an institution located 75 miles away in Kalamazoo.

The constitutional status of universities in Michigan gives institutional presidents a great deal of power. A legislator told us the institutions have been able to attract very qualified candidates because of their relative independence. It is important, he said, that the presidents "know that they are essentially the boss, that they don't have to report to a higher, system-level agency or to more than one board." Some presidents told us, however, that they feel more vulnerable and more at risk in Michigan because of the absence of any insulating system office or board. "There is no place to hide," said one.

With the exception of the University of Michigan, Michigan State University, and Grand Valley State University, four-year faculties are unionized.

Community college districts currently serve about 80 percent of the state's population and enroll approximately 208,000 students. Each community college has its own regionally elected governing board. While percentages vary across districts, community colleges receive about 30 percent of their funding from local property taxes, about 34 percent from state funds, and about 32 percent from tuition.[22] Faculties of most community colleges are organized for collective bargaining.

Private institutions do not present a significant market force in Michigan. Private colleges and universities enroll about 15 percent of the FTE student enrollment in the state, with almost 19 percent from underrepresented groups. There is no dominant private university, and few of the colleges are nationally visible or very large. Many of the private institutions are credited with being creative in finding niches not occupied by the public sector.

Tuition at each level of public higher education in Michigan is well above the national average. The percentage of tuition paid by students and their families relative to total funding (measured by state and local appropriations plus student tuition) rose from 34.4 percent in 1986 to 44.5 percent in 1995. The national average for 1995 was 31.4 percent.[23] Many of those we spoke with worry that students are being priced out of the market. Others argue that the state has not yet reached its tuition threshold even though many of the smaller regional institutions may have reached their limits.

Michigan offers several financial aid programs aimed at making college more affordable. The two largest state financial aid programs include competitive scholarships for students at public and private institutions and tuition grants for students attending private colleges and universities. Competitive scholarships, which have need- and merit-based components, award a maximum of $1,200 per student. Approximately 26,500 scholarships totaling $32 million were awarded in 1994-95, with 78 percent of the grants going to students at public institutions.[24] The Tuition Grant Program is need-based and was designed to promote choice. The maximum grant under this program in 1994-95 was $1,975. Because of large numbers of eligible students, the maximum award is lower than in most states. In 1994-95, this program awarded approximately $45 million to over 31,000 students.[25]

Michigan Educational Opportunity Grants provide public institutions with discretionary financial aid money. Approximately $1.7 million was given for 5,000 awards under this program in 1994-95.[26] A tuition incentive entitlement program guarantees the first two years of college tuition (equal to the average of two-year public tuition in the state) to welfare families whose children stay in school. The governor has proposed eliminating a second entitlement program, the Indian Tuition Waiver Program.

DESIGN OF THE HIGHER EDUCATION–STATE GOVERNMENT INTERFACE

Michigan differs from the other six states in this study in that it has no statewide agency, board, or commission responsible for the coordination of higher education, and all four-year institutions have constitutional autonomy. During the 1960s, when many states were creating coordinating agencies, Michigan resisted. The closest Michigan comes to a system-wide agency for higher education is the state board of education. The 1963 constitutional revisions attempted to address concerns about public accountability for higher education by expanding the board's responsibilities to include "planning and coordinating" of the educational policies of institutions in ways that do not impinge on constitutional status. The 1963 constitution also gave the state board responsibility for leadership and *general* supervision of community colleges without altering the supervisory or control authority of their locally elected boards.[27] Beyond expanding state board authority, the legislature was to be given an annual accounting of all income and expenditures; the governor could reduce institutional expenditures in the event state revenues fell short of estimates on which the appropriations were based; formal meetings of the institutional governing boards would be open to the public; and the state auditor would be given the power to audit the books of universities that were accorded constitutional status.[28]

Following adoption of the 1963 constitution, the state board tried to gather information about the number of out-of-state students and to monitor program duplication. In response, the institutions challenged state board actions as violations of their constitutional status. The frequently cited 1975 *Salman* decision held that the University of Michigan did not need approval from the state board to expand or establish programs or departments, or to expand branch campuses. As a result of *Salman* and similar decisions, the authority of the state board was gradually confined to advising the legislature on requests for funds. The limited authority the board has exercised has been further constrained by the actions of Governor Engler and the Republican legislature. As part of the governor's initiative to eliminate bureaucracy, the budget appropriation for the board was cut by almost 60 percent in fiscal year 1995.

Interestingly, the state board has more authority over independent institutions than it does over public colleges and universities because the former operate under charters from the state. When an independent institution wants to change its charter to add a degree level, it must petition the state board. Public institutions do not need to go through this procedure.

In the absence of formal state coordination, the four-year public institutions established the voluntary Presidents' Council in 1952. While presidents provide overall direction, the council is supported by an extensive committee structure through which provosts, academic deans, business officers, governmental relations officers, and others gather to discuss issues involving policy and programs. The council's activities include: developing positions on the state budget for higher education; reviewing and monitoring legislation affecting higher education; collecting and disseminating data; reviewing academic programs; and interacting with state agencies and organizations.[29] The council serves as a referee among institutions that want to offer services in the same locale. Through its lobbying efforts, the council tries to ensure that community colleges do not become upper division institutions.

Observers differ on the role and effectiveness of the council. One president described it as a "forum" but not much else. We were also told that the council is most effective in dealing with such issues as State Postsecondary Review Entities (SPRE) and grants for Native-American students, where institutional competition is not a factor. It is not a structure through which higher education can address contentious issues such as the allocation of funding, largely because of the absence of common ground among council members. A legislative staff member told us that universities use the Presidents' Council for those issues that benefit them, but prefer to stand alone on most issues. All institutions have a substantial lobbying presence in Lansing. None rely exclusively on the council to speak for them.

Advocates for voluntary coordination argued that the council has been successful as a vehicle for communication among presidents, particularly when there have been plentiful resources and when the institutional pecking order has been maintained. Some also described the council as an important vehicle for bringing institutions together on key issues and, most importantly, for presenting a united front to the legislature on the budget.

Constitutional autonomy vests exclusive management of each institution in a governing board.[30] At the "big three" institutions (UM, MSU, and WSU), boards are selected through statewide elections. While we heard some concerns that elected board members can be captives of special interests, most of those we spoke with said that, once elected, members have set partisan politics aside and served as "statesmen" for their institutions. One prominent exception occurred after the 1994 elections, which produced a UM board consisting of four Republican representatives of the far right and four Democrats backed by unions. The resulting gridlock left the board unable to elect a chair for more than a year. Many speculated that board infighting and lack of movement on key issues contributed to the surprise resignation of the UM president in October 1995. The governor took the president's resignation as a sign of problems with elected boards, and called for the appointment of all higher education boards.

We were told by some respondents that constitutional status and the lack of any statewide governing mechanism have enhanced faculty influence over higher education policy, and that there have been fewer "end runs" because of the absence of statewide boards or executives. On the other hand, faculty groups seem to have limited visibility at the state level. Several legislators argued that while faculty unions have the opportunity to present information to the House and Senate Appropriations Committees, their influence has declined, perhaps because of the shift in control of the legislature from Democrats to Republicans. In today's environment, said one legislator, unions "do not have as much clout."

The community college board, created in the 1963 constitution as an advisory body to the state board of education, has the power to approve programs that receive federal funding. Still, the board's role, according to one community college president, is "minimal at best," and, he added, "That is best." The board may be losing the little influence it has had. Prior to 1978, the board was responsible for portioning out the lump-sum state appropriation to each community college. Institutional funding is now based on a formula that is outside board jurisdiction. During our study, the board experienced severe funding cuts, and the governor eliminated all per diem expenses for board members. In response, the board reduced its number of yearly meetings to three and was contemplating further reductions. At the time of our visit there were three vacancies on the eight-member board.

The Michigan Community College Association, funded by institutional dues, provides legislative advocacy, facilitates information sharing, and provides in-service professional development programs for trustees. According to one college president, the association fosters voluntary coordination among colleges even though there is no formal mechanism for collaboration and communication. The limited resources of the state, he said, force colleges to coordinate services. In 1996, the state appropriation for total community colleges was less than the state appropriation for MSU. Community college representatives told us that they enhance their political clout by negotiating with the legislature as a group instead of lobbying on their own.

The state has made several efforts to address the affordability issue. In the late 1980s, a previous governor tried to use the threat of financial sanctions to persuade governing boards to hold down tuition; he suggested that tuition increases would result in cuts in the executive budget the following year. Constitutional status notwithstanding, a tuition freeze was in effect from 1987 to 1989 due to political pressures. After tuition increased dramatically over a four-year period in the early 1990s,[31] Governor Engler developed a tuition tax credit plan designed to hold down tuition. Students attending institutions where tuition increases were held below the rate of inflation for the previous year received a tax credit equal to 4 percent of that institution's tuition. Four public universities—Michigan State, Grand Valley State, Western Michigan, and Lake Superior State—were able to hold tuition increases below the inflation level, and thus their students were eligible.

The legislation that established this incentive plan was not popular with most four-year institutions. Presidents and their representatives argued that the state should have provided more money to help institutions keep tuition increases down. The legislation was also viewed by some as a violation of constitutional status, which grants to individual boards the right to set tuition. Several legislators who were early supporters of the tax credit told us they were reconsidering their position. The tax credit was not continued in the 1996-97 budget.

The Association of Independent Colleges and Universities, which represents private institutions, focuses primarily on lobbying for financial aid and degree reimbursement programs. A general degree reimbursement program awarded $425 to private institutions in 1994-95 for each bachelor's or master's degree that they granted to a Michigan resident in the preceding year, and half that amount for each associate's degree except in areas such as theology and divinity. A second program provided $2,325 in 1994-95 for each bachelor's or master's degree awarded to a Michigan resident in allied health fields requiring clinical experience or state licensing. A third program provided a flat grant of $4 million to the private University of Detroit's Mercy Dental School as a less expensive alternative to opening another dental school at a public university.

Need-based aid awarded by the state grew from $70 million in 1989-90 to more than $89 million in 1994-95, an increase of 15 percent. During this same period, however, tuition increased by more than 44 percent. While financial aid programs are seen by some as serving poor students in Michigan well, working class students must borrow to attend. We were told by several respondents that the general public believes that price increases, without offsetting increases in financial aid, will result in a system that cannot provide the access it once did.

WORK PROCESSES

There is no one agency responsible for coordinating the work processes in Michigan. Institutions are not linked to one another or to state government through the work processes, except through the budget or those processes that they establish voluntarily. Information in Michigan is poor and institutions fight any development of a stronger statewide information system. The budget process is the main link between the state and the institutions, with funding based on historical patterns and preservation of an institutional pecking order. While there are voluntary efforts to improve articulation and program planning, these do not require any actions by the institutions.

Information Management

The Department of Management and Budget (DMB) collects and analyzes data on institutional expenditure and faculty compensation through the Higher Education Information Data Inventory (HEIDI). Many policy officials told us they are dissatisfied with HEIDI data. "We cannot use it to measure performance," said one. The database is "woefully inaccurate," according to another. It is not kept up well, added a third. The HEIDI database is used primarily by house and senate fiscal agencies. Analysts in these agencies told us the database is sufficient for the kinds of requests they receive. They are rarely asked to provide information on faculty workload, the progress of minority students, or the performance of students in remedial education—all of which are beyond HEIDI's capacity.

The Department of Education maintains the Integrated Postsecondary Education Data System (IPEDS) database, which in theory could be used to address questions beyond the scope of HEIDI. However, HEIDI is not compatible with IPEDS and institutions seem to prefer this arrangement even though it means they must report data to two different systems. When the department tried on several occasions to get funding and authorization for studies of minority participation, remediation, and institutional performance, they were turned down by the legislature, reportedly under pressure from the Presidents' Council. One president told us four-year institutions have been adamant about keeping information out of the hands of the Department of Education. When the department did succeed one year in getting funding for information collection ("because we weren't paying attention," said a president), institutions were able to get it removed the following year. Four-year institutions prefer to have the DMB collecting information because that is where budget decisions are made. Community colleges collect and report to the Department of Education all data needed to preserve eligibility for federally funded programs.

While there was consensus among those we interviewed that Michigan has no adequate system for collecting and reporting information about higher education performance, there were differences of opinion about whether this is problematic. To some, the lack of information means that no one has any idea how state funding is being spent, or what the state gets for its investment. "The state has no clue about what universities do," said one. Another person questioned the capacity of the state to address the needs of minorities and women, since the state has not collected or reported information on their participation or progress for many years. Others told us, however, that no one worries about the lack of information, because, they said, no one would trust its accuracy or use it rationally, even if it were available.

Budget Process

In Michigan, "The power to influence public university policies resides primarily in the appropriations process," said a university board member. The budget process begins when the DMB solicits annual requests from colleges and universities. Budget requests include information on current and prior year FTE positions, faculty salaries, enrollments, tuition, and fee rates. A second part of the budget development request requires justifications for changes to the prior year's base. "Once we get the requests," said a budget official, "we proceed to ignore them" because, he said, they are always way too high. In 1995-96, UM and MSU asked for more than the entire budget for higher education in the state.

In a process that parallels submission of budget requests, the Presidents' Council works to develop consensus among its members concerning key priorities and then presents these major issues to the state's executive branch. In fiscal years 1996 and 1997, the council focused on three priorities: increases in appropriations at least at the level of inflation; a minimum level of funding for each student, with different floors for general comprehensive, Doctoral I, and Research I institutions; and budget appropriations that recognize changes in institutional role and mission.

The DMB begins the process of developing the governor's budget by looking at revenue growth expected in the state during the coming year. This growth determines the level of increase higher education will receive. After the governor's budget is introduced in the legislature, it serves as the base budget, or point of departure, from which the legislature works. The legislature is very attentive to the governor's recommendations because the threat of a veto is taken seriously. Each year, initial work on the budget alternates between the house and senate. As legislators work, the Presidents' Council continues to push for consensus among its members in as many areas as possible, and individual institutions lobby for their own priorities in a process described to us as "dynamic."

Allocation of funds is based primarily on historical funding patterns, which tend to reflect institutional power bases in the legislature over the past 20 to 30 years. Equitable treatment in the budget process in Michigan has come to mean that each institution will receive the same percentage increase, regardless of their base budget. A university president described the political process in Michigan as one that maintains the status quo to ensure each institution's share of funding. Across-the-board increases lock in the base funding for institutions. A formula that took enrollment and program data into account was abandoned in 1980.

There are some exceptions to across-the-board treatment for institutions. Grand Valley State received a 19 percent budget increase in 1994-95 because past enrollment growth had not been adequately recognized in previous funding. Most other institutions received a 5 percent increase. And in spring 1995, the governor's budget recommendation called for a $10 million increase in appropriations to MSU for technology initiatives, significantly more than the increases recommended for any other institution in the state. In contrast to the increase at Grand Valley State, which the Presidents' Council supported, the additional appropriation for MSU was seen as political favoritism. Michigan State University's president attributed the increase to the progress his institution had made in addressing such state priorities as affordability, undergraduate education, and cost. A legislator represented the increase as an attempt to close the gap between funding for UM and MSU. Regardless of rationale, the larger increase did not sit well with the heads of many four-year institutions, who were particularly incensed because the MSU president reportedly lobbied lawmakers to reject across-the-board increases in favor of extra money for his institution.[32] From their perspective, these actions violated the common mode of operation in Michigan, where presidents are collegial and fight for increases for all universities—not just their own institutions. The president of MSU argued that the Presidents' Council was "effectively neutered" that year by his actions. During the fiscal year 1997 budget process, the state returned to essentially across-the-board increases.

In the past, the DMB invited institutions to request special-item funding for new facilities and program revisions, in addition to their regular appropriations. Special-item appropriations represented an opportunity for powerful legislators to channel additional funding to institutions in their districts or to reward programs they favored. If an institution built a new facility, it was entitled to request special-item funding in the subsequent year's budget for its operation. Many institutions, however, began to build faculty line-items into their requests. Now, if institutions build new facilities, they must fund their operations from their regular appropriations. The amount of money appropriated for program revisions has also decreased significantly under a new chair of the Senate Appropriations Subcommittee.

Four-year institutions each receive a lump-sum appropriation. While the legislature includes intent language in the budget bill, it is not binding. We were told by a legislative staff member that legislators like this approach because it relieves them of responsibility for tasks they would rather not perform, like monitoring institutional performance.

Community colleges are funded by an enrollment-driven formula developed by the House Appropriations Committee in 1984. The formula determines the gross amount needed by each institution to operate its programs. The state then subtracts the level of funding each is projected to raise through local taxes and tuition revenues. The formula has never been fully funded. Non-formula factors such as inflation are often inserted by the governor and the legislature. Institutions typically receive a 2 percent increase across the board and an additional 1 or 2 percent increase based on the formulas. In the 1997 budget, the governor called for a 5 percent increase with one-half allocated across the board and the rest distributed through the formula.

Capital outlay projects are funded through bonds. The DMB asks universities to list projects for new construction, major renovation, and repair in order of priority. After negotiations are held between the DMB and the institutions, requests are submitted to the joint House and Senate Capital Outlay Committee. Typically, by the time the requests reach the legislature, universities have reached consensus among themselves. The general rule of thumb is that when money is available, every campus will get one project. Community colleges are required to provide a 50 percent match of state support for capital outlay, because it is assumed that they can get local tax dollars to cover the match. There is no matching requirement for four-year institutions.

Program Planning and Review

Constitutional status is a source of considerable pride to those we interviewed. Most said they believe that formally coordinated systems do not work, and that Michigan is much better off without the added layer of bureaucracy. Others said they were not so sure. The president of a comprehensive university, while agreeing that constitutional status might be valuable for the "big three," described the arrangement as somewhat dysfunctional for other institutions. "The state cannot control growth of programs," he argued, "and this is problematic from a statewide perspective." Autonomy can lead to inefficiencies and to many duplicative programs. The proliferation of programs is most problematic in the area of doctoral degrees; there used to be four public institutions in the state that offered doctorates, and now there are eight. The legislature could stop this, either through intent language in the budget bill or funding directed toward undergraduate education, but they do not. Institutions are free to develop and offer new programs as they wish, and the only limits on implementing new programs are those that are driven by student demand.

Most of those we met seemed to be "true believers" in the power of the market to take care of such inefficiencies as unnecessary program duplication. A legislative staff member echoed the sentiments of many when he told us, "Market forces in Michigan control both enrollment and the number of programs; if there is no need for a program, students will not come and the program will be eliminated." At the same time, most concede the existence of more program duplication than desirable. Yet no one seemed concerned about the possible relationship between duplication and higher costs.

In the absence of state regulation, each institution is free to change its missions or program offerings in response to whatever it defines as market needs. Program review for four-year institutions takes place on a voluntary basis, under the auspices of the Presidents' Council. Through this peer review process, institutions can endorse or not endorse proposals for new programs. This process was described to us as beneficial because it strengthens the hands of campus academic administrators, who can reject or discourage new programs that are not ready to be critically reviewed by peers. The process was said to require institutions to develop a strong case for new programs and to encourage recommendations for improving programs.

If a program is not endorsed by the Presidents' Council, it will not be added to the list of approved offerings in the legislature's boiler plate language in the appropriations bill. However, this is not always a deterrent. Ferris State established a pharmacy school even though the program was not endorsed through the program review process. The legislature attempted to prevent the institution from offering the program, but to no avail; the program is still in operation. Likewise, Grand Valley State began an engineering program even though it was not initially endorsed by the council.

System Articulation

An agreement developed in 1973 by the Michigan Association of Collegiate Registrars and Admissions Officers (MACRAO) establishes the courses acceptable to each signatory for fulfilling general education requirements. The MACRAO agreement is supplemented by individual arrangements between institutions. Not all of the state's four-year institutions participate in the agreement. One notable holdout is UM. Beyond MACRAO, there is no agency with the responsibility or authority to promote articulation and transfer. Students are dependent for the most part on local arrangements.

One observer described the linkages between K–12 reform activities and university priorities as weak. There are dual enrollment programs that allow high school seniors to enroll in college or university courses for credit, with the state covering the cost of tuition. The intent, according to one legislator, is to prevent students from wasting the senior year, rather than to graduate students early. The 1995-96 appropriations bill included language calling on colleges and universities to provide high schools with information on the performance of their graduates. While some pointed to this as an example of better communication, others doubt that anything will ever come of it. Legislative language is not binding on institutions that have constitutional status.

CONCLUSION

While many observers of higher education consider Michigan's higher education system to provide an example of a market model, there are a number of characteristics of a market model that it lacks. Although the state's decentralized governance of its colleges and universities provides some characteristics of a market structure, the financing mechanisms do not rely on market forces, as institutional funding typically involves incremental, across-the-board increases. Independent colleges and universities play a relatively small role in the state. The state uses financial aid in very limited ways to provide choice to students. And there are no mechanisms for holding institutions accountable for performance.

The dominance of institutional forces in Michigan's higher education system leads to a system that equates the interests of higher education institutions with that of the public interest. This system has produced a fair amount of satisfaction among higher education and political leaders. Signs of dissatisfaction within both groups are appearing on the horizon. Concerns about affordability on the part of political leaders and some dissatisfaction with the established pecking order among public institutions may upset the balance of these forces in the future. However, forces to counter the powerful status of constitutional autonomy do not seem to be present in Michigan, and the capacity for change seems limited by the interests of institutions in preventing such change.

NOTES

1.   Michigan Senate Fiscal Agency, *Study of Michigan Public University Enrollment Patterns by County and Institution* (Lansing, Mich., 1996), p. 1.

2. American Association of Community Colleges, *1996-97 Annual: A State-by-State Analysis of Community College Trends and Statistics* (Washington, D.C., 1996), p. 44.
3. *Chronicle of Higher Education Almanac* 43, no. 1 (September 1996), pp. 67–68.
4. Michigan Office of the Governor, "Profile of Governor John Engler" (www.migov.state.mi.us), not paginated.
5. J. M. Burns, J. W. Peltason, and T. E. Cronin, *State and Local Politics: Government by the People* (Englewood Cliffs, N.J.: Prentice Hall, 1990), p. 113.
6. *Chronicle of Higher Education Almanac* 42, no. 1 (September 1995), p. 64.
7. Multistate Associates, Inc., *Legislative Outlook 1996* (Alexandria, Va., 1996), pp. 33–34.
8. R. Kleine, "Michigan: Rethinking Fiscal Priorities," *The Fiscal Crisis of the States*, ed. S. D. Gold (Washington, D.C.: Georgetown University Press, 1995), p. 302.
9. Ibid., p. 303.
10. Ibid., p. 298.
11. Michigan Department of Management and Budget, "Fiscal Year 1997 Executive Budget" (www.michigan.state.mi.us), not paginated.
12. *Chronicle of Higher Education Almanac* 44, no. 1 (August 1997), p. 72.
13. *Chronicle of Higher Education Almanac* 43, p. 67.
14. K. Halstead, *Higher Education Report Card 1995* (Washington, D.C.: Research Associates of Washington, 1996), p. 61.
15. J. Minter Assoc., Boulder, Colo., 1996 (www.edmin.com/jma/cohort/carnegie.html). Doctoral I institutions offer a full range of baccalaureate programs and are committed to graduate education through the doctorate. Research I institutions offer a similar range of services but also place a high priority on research. General comprehensive universities offer a full range of baccalaureate programs and are committed to graduate education through the master's degree.
16. L. A. Glenny and T. Dalglish, *Public Universities, State Agencies and the Law: Constitutional Autonomy in Decline* (Berkeley, Calif.: Center for Research and Development in Higher Education, 1973), p. 17.
17. State of Michigan, *Constitution of the State of Michigan of 1963* (Lansing, Mich., 1963), Article 8, Section 3, p. 93.
18. G. Rosine and E. Jeffries, *Fiscal Year 1995-96 Higher Education Appropriations Report* (Lansing, Mich.: Senate and House Fiscal Agencies, 1996), p. 13.
19. Ibid.
20 Ibid.
21. Ibid.
22. Michigan Board of Education, *Michigan Community Colleges: Activities Classification Structure, 1993-94 Data Book* (Lansing, Mich., 1995), p. 51.
23. K. Halstead, *State Profiles for Higher Education 1978 to 1996: Trend Data* (Washington, D.C.: Research Associates of Washington, 1996), pp. 47, 104.
24. National Association of State Student Grant and Aid Programs, *NASSGAP 26th Annual Survey Report* (Albany, N.Y.: New York State Higher Education Services Corporation, 1996), pp. 13, 19.
25. Ibid.
26. Ibid.
27. State of Michigan, *Constitution of the State of Michigan of 1963*, Article 8, Section 3.
28. Glenny and Dalglish, *Public Universities, State Agencies and the Law*, p. 24.
29. Presidents' Council, *State Universities of Michigan 1992-93 Directory* (Lansing, Mich., 1992), p. 1.

30. For a detailed discussion of the origins of constitutional autonomy, see Glenny and Dalglish, *Public Universities, State Agencies and the Law.*

31. G. Rosine, *Profiles of Michigan's Public Universities 1995* (Lansing, Mich.: House Fiscal Agency, 1995), p. 3.

32. P. Healy, "Michigan State University's Political Coups Provoke Anger," *Chronicle of Higher Education* (August 18, 1995), p. A25.

CHAPTER 3

California

In addressing public needs regarding higher education, California relies primarily on institutional forces, combined with limited state regulation of some of its higher education segments. The state's role is primarily that of provider and regulator. The 1960 California Master Plan for Higher Education recognized three public segments—or subsystems—of higher education, each with its own clientele and specific program authority. The nine-campus University of California (UC), which has constitutional autonomy, has been described by many as "the fourth branch of state government" because of its independence. The 22-campus California State University (CSU) and the California Community Colleges, on the other hand, experience various degrees of state oversight, from micromanagement by state agencies on some issues to segment-wide or local governance in other areas. A strong independent sector provides some market influence in higher education, though the size of the private sector is dwarfed by that of the public sector.

During recent decades, the political environment has sent few clear messages to higher education regarding public needs. The governor, who is granted strong veto and other powers by the state constitution, has the power to influence higher education in pivotal ways, but recent governors have not prioritized higher education issues. During the recession that hit California in the early 1990s, state legislative leaders opted to make across-the-board cuts and reduce student enrollments rather than promoting specific state priorities and confronting strong institutional forces in doing so. Meanwhile, voter initiatives (including property tax limitations, income and inheritance tax limitations, set-asides for public schools and community colleges, term limits for legislators, and the ending of affirmative action) have limited the discretion of elected officials.

The statewide coordinating agency, the California Postsecondary Education Commission (CPEC), has weak statutory authority and must rely on subsystem sources for data. A voluntary coordinating committee created by the public institutions, the California Education Roundtable, has been inconsistent in providing statewide leadership on articulation and transfer.

Student enrollment in higher education is expected to increase by more than 450,000 students over the next decade, an increase of about 28 percent. Opinion is divided on the range of appropriate responses that would prepare California's institutions of higher education to meet this demand. Many leaders within each of the public subsystems believe that the sum of their individual responses will provide for increased state enrollment needs—so long as there is sufficient funding. Many leaders outside of higher education have little confidence that change in higher education can be addressed with real purposefulness within the existing system. Private institutions have not been fully included in planning to meet the state's enrollment needs, even though estimates suggest that the private sector might be able to supply about 10 percent of the projected enrollment surge.

Thus, California represents a segmented governance model with three large public subsystems operating fairly independently of one another, with few mechanisms for addressing statewide priorities that might differ from institutional priorities. The work processes in California are designed to maintain the present balance of forces. The budget process is the only mechanism around which the state can assert its priorities, but it is a process that emphasizes short-term solutions. Program approval processes, including those approving new campuses, have proven ineffective, and statewide information on higher education is dependent on institutional approval.

Relatively few forces exist in California to balance the dominant institutional influences in higher education. As California continues its impressive recovery from its worst recession since the Great Depression, its system of higher education faces a series of unique challenges. An ongoing question concerns how effectively higher education can meet public needs in a state system that features formidable institutional independence, weak statewide coordination, and few clear messages from the political or policy environment.

STATE CONTEXT

California, with 31.5 million residents, is more than one-half again the size of the next largest study state. It is also the most diverse state in our study, with close to one-third of its population from non-white groups.[1] Hispanics are the largest and fastest growing minority in the state. The Asian-American population is also growing rapidly. Four out of every five new Californians in the twenty-first century will be either Hispanic or Asian American. Shortly after the turn of the century, a majority of all Californians will be other than white. The state has the most highly educated population among the seven study states, although a somewhat higher percentage of New York residents hold graduate and professional degrees. At the same time, California has a young population that is less likely to speak English in the home. The per capita income is only average and the potential tax revenue per student is less than in other study states.[2]

California voters have established significant constraints on policy decisions. Proposition 13, approved by voters in 1978, reduced local property taxes overnight by 57 percent and effectively destroyed the power of local governments to raise ad valorem taxes. Hard on the heels of Proposition 13 came other initiatives indexing the income tax and abolishing the state inheritance tax. Next came Proposition 98, which required at least 40 percent of general fund revenues to go to public schools with part set aside for the California Community Colleges. Six-year term limits for members of the state assembly and eight-year limits for state senators were passed in 1990. In 1994, voters passed a "Three Strikes" initiative, which placed additional demands on the state general fund. The most recent voter initiatives have allowed homeowners whose property taxes were frozen at 1975 values to pass their homes on to their children without reassessment,[3] and have ended the use of race or ethnicity in admissions, hiring, and contracting in public agencies.

Governor and Legislature

California's governor is granted strong veto and other powers by the state constitution, making his influence on higher education pivotal.[4] A legislative staff member told us, "The governor really runs the show. Between the power of budget and the power of appointment, there is no one else who has his influence over higher education." Actual influence has not always equaled potential influence, however. The last governor to change higher education in significant ways was Pat Brown (governor from 1959 to 1967). Many, but not all of those we interviewed told us that Governor Pete Wilson, a Republican in his second term, is not particularly interested in higher education. Until 1994-95, both the state senate and the state assembly held Democratic majorities. Recent governors, on the other hand, have been Republicans. Despite differences in political parties, a governor's veto has not been overridden in the funding process for higher education during the last 13 years.

Shifting political philosophies, uncertainties about term limits, and a highly autonomous system contribute to a political environment that sends few clear messages to higher education. When asked about political leaders' goals regarding higher education, a legislative staff member said, "There are the classic answers of quality and access. Access tends to be important primarily because of anecdotes they hear from constituents who are unable to get into one of the colleges or universities. Quality may be less important."

As concern about the impact of term limits rises, there is heightened interest in appointments to governing boards. A former UC executive told us that the governor had made two appointments to the UC Board of Regents within a month and that it was highly unlikely that the "Democrat-controlled" senate would approve either. In the history of the UC system there have been only two instances in which the appointment of a regent by a governor was not confirmed. Current resistance to gubernatorial appointments is also seen as a protest against such controversial actions as the regents' vote ending affirmative action within the UC system, a vote that was strongly supported by the governor.

State Economy and Support for Higher Education

The state is now recovering from one of its worst recessions since the Great Depression. Between 1990 and 1994, California lost 868,000 jobs, equivalent to firing the entire workforces of Nevada and Alaska. More than 43,000 businesses went under. California's recovery from the recession has been slower than elsewhere in the United States, due primarily to a relatively high unemployment rate; more low-paying and fewer high-paying jobs; a slippage in educational levels of some segments of the labor force; and growth in the younger, non-working population.[5] Along with these problems, California has impressive strengths. The size of the state economy is equal to those of Argentina, Mexico, and Australia combined. The civilian labor force dwarfs that of Canada. California has more new and fast-growing companies than any other state, nearly double its closest competitors. Its agricultural industry is more than 50 percent larger than its nearest U.S. competitor, Texas. California also has the nation's largest manufacturing base, with particular strength in aerospace and electronics.

In 1994, state spending on health and welfare, corrections, higher education, and K–12 education accounted for more than 90 percent of general fund expenditures. Allocations for health and welfare and for corrections have been increasing with few interruptions over the past 25 years, while allocations for higher education have been decreasing. According to one estimate, if current trends continue, by 2002 CSU would have to turn away 200,000 to 300,000 students it would otherwise have admitted.[6]

From 1991 to 1994, the state gave block grants to institutions without any consideration of enrollment changes. For 1995 and 1996, appropriations have been based on a four-year compact the governor negotiated with UC and CSU. The compact provides for increases in annual appropriations of approximately 4 percent and for other state guarantees in return for university guarantees of enrollment growth, limits on student fee increases, increased portability of courses, continued increases in productivity and efficiency, and improved graduation rates.

In summer 1996, higher education was preparing to enter the second year of the compact. Already the governor had "bought out" one year of student fee increases with an additional $57 million of state appropriations. A senior legislative staff member told us that during the recession, there were some opportunities to look at new ways of doing business, at new ways of working together for higher education, but with the pressure off because of two good budgets, people will go back to business as usual. Nonetheless, many of those we interviewed expressed particular concern about the extreme disparities in per student allocations to the three public segments, especially since changes in affirmative action may result in an even greater proportion of the least affluent and least well-prepared students attending the community colleges. Most of our respondents also said that the community colleges are underfunded.

CHARACTERISTICS AND HISTORY OF HIGHER EDUCATION

The 1960 California Master Plan for Higher Education recognized three public segments of higher education in the state: UC, CSU, and the California Community Colleges. The master plan established differential functions and enrollment pools for each of the public segments, and called for the establishment of a statewide coordinating council for higher education that would include representation of the independent colleges and universities.

During our study, higher education in California consisted of:

- UC, with eight general campuses, one health science campus, and numerous research facilities. In 1995, the UC system served 163,256 full- or part-time students, 39,519 of whom were postbaccalaureate.
- CSU, with 22 campuses. In 1995, the CSU system served 325,976 full- or part-time students, all but 61,581 of whom were undergraduates.
- The California Community Colleges, with 71 locally governed districts operating 107 colleges. In 1995, these colleges enrolled 1.1 million full- or part-time students.
- 147 private, four-year institutions and 36 private, two-year institutions. In 1995, these institutions collectively enrolled 231,337 full- or part-time students, 47,580 of whom were graduate students.[7]

California ranks high among study states in the percentage of students in public institutions, the percentage of full-time-equivalent (FTE) students per 1,000 population, and the percentage of high school graduates going on anywhere—reflecting the extraordinary commitment California has made to public higher education.[8] The system operates at a lower than average per student cost by requiring most high school graduates to begin their college careers at lower-cost community colleges, which many believe to be seriously underfunded.

The University of California and the independent colleges and universities experienced enrollment increases from 1985 to 1995. Enrollments at CSU and the community colleges, however, were almost the same in 1995 as they were in 1985, primarily because significant enrollment declines in the early 1990s negated enrollment increases in the late 1980s.

The issues facing higher education are wide-ranging. Perhaps the most visible challenge is a projected enrollment surge that has been called "Tidal Wave II": an estimated 455,000 Californians beyond those already enrolled in the state's colleges and universities who will seek access to higher education in the next decade. Access for these students is threatened by limited space in existing institutions as well as by disagreements among the three public segments about how many students each should serve and how.[9] Access is also threatened by growing student indebtedness and lack of consensus about the appropriate purposes and amounts of student aid.

California Postsecondary Education Commission

The California Postsecondary Education Commission (CPEC) was founded in 1974 as an advisory group to the legislature, the governor, and postsecondary institutions. The commission is composed of 17 members, nine of whom are appointed from the general public: three by the governor, three by the Senate Rules Committee, and three by the speaker of the assembly. Six members represent various segments of education, including the UC Board of Regents, the CSU Board of Trustees, the statewide community college board of governors, the state board of education, and the California Postsecondary and Vocational Education Commission. One member is appointed by the governor to represent independent institutions. The remaining two members are students, both appointed by the governor. The commission's executive officer is appointed by the commission and serves at its pleasure.[10] The commission has statutory authority to establish a statewide database, to review institutional budgets, to advise on the need for and location of new campuses, and to review all proposals for new academic programs in the public sector. The commission's primary purpose is to prevent unnecessary duplication and to coordinate efforts among the segments.

University of California

The University of California, a premier research university, admits only the top 12.5 percent of high school graduates and has exclusive responsibility among the public institutions for doctoral degrees and professional programs beyond the master's degree. The University of California is governed by 26 regents (18 of whom are appointed by the governor to 12-year terms after confirmation by the senate) and a student member appointed by the regents for a one-year term. The 1879 ratification of the state constitution granted to the UC Board of Regents powers that lead some to describe the university as "the fourth branch of government." When the state legislature passes bills affecting the university, lawmakers usually include a clause explaining that the statute will go into effect only if the board of regents passes a comparable resolution. During the 1970s a series of court decisions laid out the separation of powers implied by constitutional status in terms of tuition, academics, and other areas of board responsibility. The university has its own retirement system, an asset that was used to fund one major campus strategy for responding to the state's fiscal crisis of the 1990s. The university has the capacity to shift funds among accounts, an element of flexibility that also helped the university preserve student numbers and services during the recent fiscal cutbacks. While the state can prescribe the proportion of CSU's fees to be used for student aid, they have only an unwritten agreement with the UC system.

The academic senate is the umbrella for faculty governance in UC. The academic council serves as the executive committee of the academic senate. The chair and vice chair of the academic council attend board of regents' meetings and regularly participate in discussions, although they cannot vote. The source of power of the academic senate, including its authority over academic programs and admissions, is found in the standing orders of the board of regents and dates to a faculty revolt of 1919. Faculty view the authority of the academic senate as constitutionally established. The senate must be consulted on appointments, promotions, and tenure. Divisions make recommendations on academic personnel that chancellors are unlikely to contravene, although technically they could. A regent told us that tenure and curriculum decisions never get to the board, adding that while the president's office gets involved on a policy level, most decisions are made at the campus level.

Depending upon whose perspective is valued, the academic senate is either the reason why UC became as great as it did or the principal barrier to fundamental change. In reality, it may be both. A former regent told us, "The strengths of the senate are the strengths of the university, but it makes analysis and change more difficult." A chancellor described the academic senate as "the principal barrier to change because it insists that UC is one university, that all faculty must be treated the same at all campuses, and that all campuses must be comprehensive." A former system executive said, on the other hand, "Chancellors complain more about the senate than is justified."

California State University

California State University, the largest four-year higher education system in the nation, admits the top one-third of high school graduates and has authority to offer master's degrees across the board. Doctoral degrees must be offered in cooperation with UC or a private university. California State University is primarily a system for commuting students. Campuses such as CSU Los Angeles and CSU Dominguez Hills are at the cutting edge of the demographic changes taking place in California.

California State University is governed by trustees who are appointed by the governor for eight-year terms and who are subject to senate confirmation. A trustee compared CSU to a large corporation with 22 branch offices. He continued by describing the presidents as "managers" and the board's most important responsibility as that of hiring and evaluating system management, including the chancellor, principal staff in the chancellor's office, and the presidents. Every six years, each president is formally evaluated against written standards by a committee (comprised of at least one trustee and two or three additional people) that conducts a series of interviews on the campus.

Faculty involvement in CSU is governed by the Higher Education Employee Relations Act, which divided the turf between the union and the academic senate. There are gray areas that might have led to conflict but have not. While the system-wide senate has generally stayed out of hard-cash issues, every campus senate wants to be seen as a serious player in budget development. Campus finance, however, has traditionally been a process that belongs to the president. Opening up the budget process has been used by some presidents as a trade-off for greater flexibility in dealing with such issues as technology and recommendations regarding tenure and promotion. Negotiations for collective bargaining are done centrally by a team that includes employee relations' staff and one campus president. A support team made up of senior systems' staff and a handful of presidents sets major directions for the negotiations. The involvement of presidents in the negotiating process is new.

Relationships among faculty, presidents, and trustees have a troubled history in CSU. While relationships are better now, there are still tensions. A president described the union as the major barrier to change and added, "Campus senates run the union a close second. They are still in the mode of, 'We should run everything and who the hell are the presidents?'" He then qualified his comment: "The senate isn't all wrong. They correctly perceive that new presidents are very different from previous ones." In contrast, the system-wide academic senate was described as a "pretty constructive force partly because of the time the chancellor spends working with them."

Community Colleges

Locally governed community college districts are loosely overseen by a 16-member statewide board of governors, five of whom (two local trustees, two faculty members, and one student) represent local colleges. While the board was given responsibility for fiscal oversight, accountability, program review, and a management information system, most perceive actual authority as more coordinating than governing.

Local governing boards consist of five members who serve four-year staggered terms. Because local board members negotiate collective bargaining agreements but are not responsible for levying the taxes to pay for them, employees spend money and time to ensure those favorable to their interests are elected. A faculty union representative noted that in the Los Angeles district, the union typically contributes about $100,000 to the candidates it backs in board races, and that this amounts to more money than anyone else has—which could be one reason why union candidates usually win. But, he argued, "You don't buy them; you don't even rent them for very long."[11]

Faculty dominate local governance through the combination of collective bargaining, the election of faculty-friendly local trustees, and the confusion surrounding shared governance created by Assembly Bill 1725 (enacted by the legislature in 1988). Community colleges in some districts were described as almost entirely "provider-driven in that faculty fill in when and what they want to teach, not what students want or when they are available to take classes." Faculty leaders see the situation differently. According to one, shared governance has allowed the faculty "to take back the curriculum" from administrators, and it has made the academic senate "a player at the table" with regard to campus budget decisions.

Despite governance controversies, community colleges get high ratings. A UC regent told us that community college transfers do very well and that community colleges are the best bargain for taxpayers. A senior UC staff member echoed this assessment, noting that 88 percent of the system's transfer students are not initially UC-eligible. A member of the state board of governors described the community colleges as "the sole savior for California," adding that community colleges are also taking on California economic needs and doing so very successfully. A legislative aide described the community college system as a real strength because it provides students with the opportunity to have a second chance. A former system chancellor praised their hard work to retrain the workforce, and to satisfy other needs despite the fiscal constraints they faced during the recessionary years.

Independent Colleges and Universities

Private institutions occupy a distinctive niche in California higher education that has not been fully utilized, partly because the California constitution prohibits direct support to private entities. Private institutions enroll 22 percent of all undergraduates in four-year institutions, 48 percent of master's degree students, 60 percent of doctoral students, and 67 percent of those seeking first professional degrees. In terms of statistical averages, private institutions appear less important than those in other states because of the skewing effects of community college enrollments.

DESIGN OF THE HIGHER EDUCATION–STATE GOVERNMENT INTERFACE

Many of those we interviewed questioned whether California's higher education institutions add up to a system. There are no structural arrangements that encourage institutions to work together or to keep track of examples of collaboration and report them. The separate systems go their own ways, negotiating their own deals with the governor and the legislature, with higher education as a whole presumably guided by the invisible hand of the 1960 master plan for higher education. A state senator told us, "You really have to ask what system means. If a system means that institutions help one another and share resources then we do not really have a system in California." A second senator described the master plan as "a jurisdictional agreement disguised as an ideal arrangement based on assumptions about how you can carve up the territory." A CSU senior executive said the California system was designed to maximize the influence of professionals and minimize external intrusion. A former consultant to the state senate told us, "The arrangement assumes that state needs are coterminous with the sum of what the systems are willing to deliver." A member of the UC Board of Regents added, "There is a disconnect across all units." A community college spokesman said, "Instead of a single system of education, California has five independent and autonomous systems." A writer for *Harper's Magazine* has suggested that "anarchy" in higher education is the consequence of institutional disconnects and voter interventions.[12]

The California Postsecondary Education Commission was designed to be an independent voice in higher education, but its authority is limited. A legislative staff member said, "While their statutory role is a coordinating body, they are too captive of the segments." A UC chancellor said, "We have coordination when we want it but not when we don't." Few insiders want CPEC to play a stronger role. A CSU executive told us, "If the governor or the legislature had a fundamental interest in higher education, they wouldn't think of CPEC as an instrument for implementing their interest. When the legislature wants to study the master plan, they appoint a lay commission and a blue-ribbon citizens' commission. They do not rely on CPEC." The absence of any close relationship between CPEC and the governor and legislature is evidenced by recent cutbacks that have cost the commission one-third of its staff.

In the past, the legislature has considered establishing a statewide agency with greater regulatory powers over higher education. Partly to fend off such future efforts, segmental heads have recently reenergized the Education Roundtable, a voluntary organization that includes a representative from the private sector, the superintendent of schools, and representatives from the segments. First organized in 1979 to address student outreach and teacher preparation issues, the roundtable has also focused on issues such as articulation and transfer, the interface between K–12 and higher education, and teacher preparation. Its initiatives are carried out largely through the Intersegmental Coordinating Committee (ICC), its operating arm. The roundtable is independent of CPEC, although the executive director of CPEC participates as a member.

The most controversial agenda item under consideration by the roundtable at the time of our interviews was a study funded by the Hewlett Foundation and conducted by the Rand Corporation. The study focused on student flow and enrollment demand, innovative responses to change, and long-term funding. To some degree, these issues duplicate what CPEC has already done or is doing. A state senator described the study as "sending foxes to guard the hen coop," and considered it a possible strategy to reduce student demand to what segment heads believe the market ought to be. Since roundtable members do not want the organization seen as an attempt to supplant CPEC, they have planned to bring their recommendations from the Rand study to CPEC. Educational leaders have done little to draw attention to the Rand study since it was completed.

Student Aid Commission

The Student Aid Commission administers three forms of state grants. Cal Grant A was the first state scholarship program and was originally designed to be based on merit. It is now need-based but also incorporates measures of scholastic capacity as measured by grade point average. Most grants are awarded to students attending UC or private institutions. Cal Grant B focuses on disadvantaged students, with most awards going to students attending CSU or community colleges. Cal Grant C is for vocational education. Originally, 90 percent of Cal Grant funds went to students attending private institutions. By 1994, UC students were receiving slightly more funds than their private sector counterparts. In 1994, the share awarded to CSU students was less than 20 percent. Community college and proprietary students each receive less than 5 percent of student aid funds.[13] Because so few of the eligible students receive state grants, institutions have had some proportion of their fees set aside from tuition revenues for financial aid. Recycled fees in public institutions now account for more aid than the state provides directly to students. Part of the governor's agreement on budget increases for UC and CSU is that 30 percent of any increase in fees will be used for financial aid.

University of California

There are significant differences of opinion both within and outside the UC Board of Regents concerning its appropriate role. A chancellor told us, "The regents' role is to set policy, to set the rules and regulations for the university at large. They are then supposed to delegate operations to the president, who in turn delegates to the chancellors, who in turn delegate to vice chancellors and so on." New regents, who tend to be activist, are not particularly happy with this definition. One expressed frustration with "the love-hate relationship" among the board, the administration, and the rest of the university: "Regents come to the board with particular interests but the establishment doesn't want the regents involved. The regents then lose interest and simply follow administrative recommendations." He described the question of how to channel regents' interests for the best use of the university as "a major issue."

Regents seem disengaged from many of the decisions an outsider might ordinarily expect them to consider. They don't evaluate chancellors. They don't evaluate the president and they don't receive information on the relative performance of campuses. In the absence of any formal evaluation process, a regent told us the board relies on national rankings of graduate programs, adding, "When the rankings came out last fall, it gave everybody a lift." Regents do not get involved in actions involving academic personnel. Curriculum decisions typically do not come to the board either. A regent who had served on the board for well over half of his total term had very little information about the regents' role with respect to graduate programs. He asked rhetorically, "Why do five universities have medical schools?" He thought the regents should be involved in approving new doctoral programs but was not sure if this was the case.

The UC president's office maintains at least a minimum level of coordination and consistency across the system in relation to issues where there is legal exposure. It manages the processes that define and sustain an organizational culture (academic personnel, admissions, and the curriculum), which keeps individual campuses from moving into their own orbits. The president's office also negotiates the annual budget with the legislature and the governor, ideally with the support of the board of regents. Part of the challenge here is to reconcile the campus budget process, which largely faces inward, with the system budget process, which is focused outward. Established procedures for relating the system budget to academic planning are, in the words of one system administrator, "enormously cumbersome and do not accomplish much."

California State University

While the California State University does not have constitutional status, the practical differences between CSU's and UC's relationships with state government were less significant during our study than they have been in the past. This was partly because the CSU chancellor has, in the words of a UC campus executive, "been successful in fuzzing the line-item budget and UC has given up prerogatives upon which it might otherwise have insisted." A CSU executive used similar language to note that UC, with constitutional autonomy, has been less willing than CSU to test the legitimacy of policy decisions by state government. The executive added that when UC chooses to compromise about policy issues involving budget language, it becomes more difficult for CSU to speak out.

Although CSU may be subject to less state regulation than in the past, its lack of constitutional status leads to greater control by state government than UC has to tolerate. A senior system executive described a "tendency in Sacramento to micromanage." California State University's efforts to achieve greater managerial flexibility at the campus level have been supported by the director of the state Department of Finance and by the state Department of General Services, under the direction of the governor. These efforts have been opposed by the elected state comptroller (described by one interviewee as "never having seen a regulation he didn't like") and they have been opposed by some middle-management staff in the state Departments of Finance and General Services.

The job of the central office, in the words of one CSU executive, is "creating synergy so that the whole is greater than the sum of the parts." This takes place "through persuasion, information sharing, and overarching strategic goals." The state university we saw was described as having changed significantly in the past five years. A CSU executive described the old CSU as "the most bureaucratic system I had ever encountered—wrapped up like a mummy in red tape and collective bargaining." We heard often about the profound change underway. We were also told that despite having to take $300 million out of the budget over 18 months, CSU had avoided a "bunker mentality" by providing greater management flexibility for campuses so they could be creative in responding to difficult circumstances. "Now," the official continued, "for the first time, campuses perceive that someone up there is fighting for them."

The positive view that central staff have of CSU performance was widely shared among others we interviewed. The president of a private university described the state university as "much better managed than other public segments," as well as "wiser in decision-making and in sticking to mission." A CSU campus president told us that the system structure works well for the campuses: "I am surprised at the extent to which I am really left alone to run the campus." A colleague who had recently joined CSU from a well-regarded system in a different state said that the state university is doing a better job of considering workforce development and the implications of technology for teaching than any other public university in the country.

The CSU executive council, composed of campus presidents and the chancellor, meets 10 times a year. In such meetings, participants create agendas for board meetings and discuss major issues of collaboration. When the trustees engage in protracted discussions concerning policies, the chancellor convenes a task force of presidents to work with them. The board policy on remedial education developed from this approach. Because executive council discussions are probing, the trustees have confidence in the chancellor's reports on presidential views. The work of the council is augmented by a long-standing academic vice presidents' council, as well as by a newer group involving business vice presidents. There is a presidential task force on synergy and there are many ad hoc groups in areas such as technology. Those we interviewed suggested that there is a climate of openness, that all major decisions within the system are on paper.

Community Colleges

Community colleges cannot easily be understood as a subsystem. A CSU faculty leader said, "The community college system is not a system at all." A senior staff member of the statewide board of governors told us that the community colleges were never set up to be a system, adding, "It is better to think of the community colleges as a federation." A CSU official told us that the story going around about the vacancy for the position of chancellor of the California Community Colleges was a reprise of the Groucho Marx joke: "Anyone who wants the job is unqualified." One participant said simply, "The system doesn't work."

A community college president described the state chancellor's office as "weak," and added, "To some degree, the presidents like that. The state board flip-flops between governance and coordination. Governance attempts are not very warmly welcomed." A second president argued, "The governance process in its present form traps colleges and [local] trustees. If local governance is to be maintained, the chancellor's office must take a hard line on such issues as the amount of resources to be devoted to operation, maintenance, and technology, as opposed to collective bargaining agreements." A third president reported that local boards are saying to district administrators, "We don't want you spending time with the state board; they have just created a lot of chaos and conflict."

Local resistance to leadership attempts by the state board of governors contributes to the appearance of chaos—as does the high turnover rate of senior executives at state and local levels. During our study, the system chancellor resigned after being subjected by a majority of the board of governors to such humiliations as a prohibition against out-of-state travel without specific advance authorization. A local trustee described a recent decision of his board as "pro-student and pro-faculty" and therefore not disposed to pay much attention to administrators. He added, "It's very difficult to fire a chancellor, but board members can make his life miserable."

The state legislature is often seen as providing an arena for granting requests or resolving disputes regarding the community colleges. Community college CEOs, local trustees, administrators, students, and classified staff all have statewide organizations that come together under the umbrella of the Community College League of California to develop lobbying strategies. Faculty members are represented in Sacramento by their respective unions as well as by the statewide academic senate. Beyond these agencies, a president told us that regional organizations and presidents are beginning to hire their own lobbyists as well.

The combination of high partisan interest and lack of confidence in governance invites frequent legislative intervention. After CPEC told a district that it could not start a new campus, a bill was introduced in the legislature to authorize one. After the board of governors denied a request by a community college district to place funds in high-risk investments, the legislature passed a bill granting such authority. Legislators are said to emphasize local control when they want to be perceived as district supporters, and to focus on the chancellor's office when they want to get something done.

Leadership and Structure

Most of those we interviewed attributed higher education problems to poor leadership. Virtually no one identified a need to change the structure. A member of the state assembly argued that changing the structure would not change the way people behaved. A former member of the UC Board of Regents described a need for improved collaboration, but added that he would oppose altering the tiered character of the system in order to achieve better collaboration. And the legislature recently rejected a bill that would have added a regional structure for higher education. One respondent said, "California has a very fine public system, a world-class system at unbelievably low prices to consumers. It wouldn't be realistic to break up a system with which people are reasonably comfortable." The paradox is that few believe the current system can respond to the larger issues it will confront in the next century.

WORK PROCESSES

In California, the use of work processes and the links to state government are different for each higher education segment, or subsystem. The state does not appear to have the capacity to engage in significant statewide strategic planning, even though it has a coordinating structure charged with that responsibility. Statewide program review procedures are often more of a formality than an actual barrier to program duplication. Each subsystem negotiates its own budget with the governor and the legislature. Often such negotiations are the primary or only way for state government to influence institutional performance. Where subsystems lack constitutional autonomy, the legislature may exercise direct statutory control of some operations.

Each of the public segments in California is responsible for coordinating the activities and services of its own institutions. California State University is credited with doing the best job of such coordination, the community colleges with the worst. The University of California lies somewhere between the two extremes. Within this scheme of things, CPEC is not so much a coordinating agency as a source of information and a mediator of last resort for disputes that are not resolved elsewhere. The Education Roundtable, with very few formal meetings per year, provides some voluntary coordination, as does the Intersegmental Coordinating Committee on issues related to transfer. Most of the people we talked with recognized problems with this arrangement but preferred it to the constraints of a tighter structure. The absence of a credible coordinating structure for higher education shifts the statewide action on such work processes as budgeting and articulation to state government.

Information Management

Providing information may be CPEC's most important current function. Annual commission reports focus on such issues as faculty salaries, executive compensation, and higher education performance. There are fact books on fiscal profiles and student profiles as well as topical reports in such areas as: "Three Strikes" legislation; planning for projected increases in student enrollment; improved outcomes; and community college student charges. Most policy makers, however, believe these reports raise only those issues that institutions want to have raised. A community college spokesman told us, "The amount of staff time spent looking at CPEC studies or responding to them is very small. They are not central players." A CSU executive said, "CSU and UC work closely with CPEC to be sure that the organization doesn't tell a different story to the legislature than the one being told by their organizations." A senator described the "contradiction between official word and truth. You go to CPEC for a version but you expect them to put a spin on it." A UC regent said that so far as he knew, CPEC has no influence on the regents.

If CPEC reports have marginal impact, the fault may not lie solely with CPEC. A CSU executive told us the state makes policy by anecdote. If an executive summary of a CPEC report reaches a conclusion that is counter-intuitive, legislators will pay attention. Otherwise little attention is given to reports. A senator confirmed that legislators most often get information by anecdote, by personal experiences, and through cocktail party talk. He added, "There are a series of reports that are available to legislators such as those put out by CPEC and the legislative analyst. While these are important, their impact is really overrated. Unless someone has a real interest in an area and takes the extra time to wade through some of these reports, they are not likely to pay them much attention."

Beyond the reports provided by CPEC, the Legislative Analyst's Office, which is a nonpartisan body, raises issues that systems must respond to as part of the budget process. The legislative analyst focuses primarily on questions of efficiency, including such issues as deferred maintenance and the weight of faculty salaries. A senator described the legislative analyst's work as helpful but limited in the sense that analyses don't start with any vision for higher education or occur within a mission framework. A representative told us that over the past year the legislative analyst's recommendations had been all over the map. The credibility of the state Department of Finance is limited by its role as compiler and advocate for the governor's budget. There is need for a longer range focus in providing analyses and recommendations, particularly on such sensitive issues as student fee increases.

The legislature has also contracted special studies on faculty workload and other issues. We were told by a legislative staff member that some analysis occurs in these studies, but not at a very high level. The reports are primarily anecdotal and include very little longitudinal data or original research. A Democratic senator said that the situation would get worse rather than better as the legislature increasingly relies on a weaker and more partisan staff that will bring ideological agendas to any analysis they do. He added that if Republicans continue to gain control there will be much more emphasis on student aid and privatization issues with a voucher system for higher education as a real possibility.

University of California

Most respondents criticized UC for its slow turnaround in providing information to the public, and for a lack of quality in the information it does provide. A state senator told us that the university needs to do a much better job of outreach and information dissemination in describing its mission and its importance to the state and the communities that it serves. A regent characterized the university as "elitist and detached in the past," and added, "This is a luxury we can no longer afford."

University of California administrators expressed high levels of satisfaction with the information system. A senior executive told us, "Information is abundant and fine. If there is not enough information out there, it is certainly not the fault of the system. There is simply too much information for any one person to understand but certainly the university does all that it needs to do to provide information." University of California faculty members disagreed, however. An academic senate leader reported: "The information system doesn't work well because it is imbedded in so much junk. A large part of the problem has to do with the way the university manages information to support positions and please constituencies. We try to provide information that conceals differences between campuses."

California State University

Perspectives on CSU information services vary. A senior CSU executive described information capabilities as "good," adding, "If someone asks CSU a question, they will get an answer." He described a decision by CSU to stop providing information on student retention because UC refused to do so as "atypical." A former state official said, "Systems do not make an effort to provide information that might put them in a bad light." California State University central staff members were said to be anxious about giving out information, suspicious about a "data dump," and afraid of people misusing information. The University of California and CSU remain as competing systems, so administrators are careful about what information is furnished to whom. Most of those we interviewed indicated, however, that CSU has been better about furnishing information than UC.

A CSU trustee described the information he received as a board member as "very good." He added, "The chancellor knows how to work with the board; his approach is full disclosure. When you ask him for things they are there." A campus president told us that information is available within the CSU system, but it is not collected systematically, so budget people have to make a special effort to get it. The president added that since the system's student, payroll, and personnel data are separate, there is no easy way they can be combined to provide information to policy makers.

Community Colleges

While the community college board of governors is charged with maintaining a management information system, board members have chosen to emphasize the governing rather than coordinating aspects of their duties. Recently, the legislature charged the board with developing a set of performance indicators for community colleges, an assignment on which little progress has been made. As part of the budget process, the chancellor's office collects information related to enrollment growth, inflation, and other indicators of fiscal need. There is little use of this information, however, beyond the development of the estimate of operating costs that is sent to the state Department of Finance.

Information and the Policy Environment

In the current policy environment, it is not clear that more or better information would necessarily have much impact on decisions. The governor vetoed a student information system passed by the legislature. It is easier to cut deals with system heads on the basis of political philosophy and available resources than to try to make sense out of data pried from reluctant systems. Perhaps Californians prefer this arrangement; higher education leaders seem to.

Budget Process

The three public segments and the California Student Aid Commission (CSAC) submit budget requests to the Department of Finance in the form of budget change proposals in September. In late November, the governor meets with the system heads, who support their requests. A veteran of many of these sessions described the meetings as "characterized by glazed eyes and few questions." Based on these and other meetings, the governor develops line items for the public systems of higher education and CSAC within his overall executive budget, which is introduced to the legislature in January.

Budget and finance committees in the senate and assembly consider higher education as part of the single central budget that includes all state expenditures. Very seldom is there a policy debate on the policy implications of the budget. No one looks at the big picture. Discussions in subcommittees are very political and focus on meeting the individual requests of the various interests. This process usually does not produce an acceptable budget.

On May 15, the state Department of Finance revises the governor's proposed budget, based on new estimates of the state of the economy. The real budgetary decisions are then made behind closed doors among the "big five" (the governor's representative and the majority and minority leaders of both chambers of the legislature). These leaders often introduce the results of the compromises on the floor of the legislature late at night and, according to legislative staff members, "try to ram the budget through." There is never a final budget until after the 15th of June. Within this process, the Legislative Analyst's Office is the nonpartisan body that has responsibility for looking closely at budgets and asking questions about what they contain.

Capital projects are considered through the same budget process but funded in a different way, largely through revenue bonds or general obligation bonds that have to be acted upon by the voters. The projects included in either of these funding methods are determined by the governor's office and the legislature. Unlike the operating budget, the capital outlay budget is designated by campus.

After the governor's budget has been acted upon by the assembly and the senate, a conference committee consisting of three members from each chamber issues a supplemental report, which provides a statement of legislative intentions. As with a joint resolution, the supplemental report does not have the force of law, though it does advise recipients that they will incur disfavor if the instructions are ignored. The supplemental report, which is incorporated as a part of the official budget when it is finally adopted, is one of the primary ways the legislature formally sends messages to higher education.

Prior to the election of Governor Wilson, there was often proviso language in the budget that specifically directed the segments as to how they should spend state funds. Democrats generally favor this control language. Governor Wilson's philosophy is to provide block grants and maximum flexibility. His policy is to veto regulatory language in the budget or from the legislature. In California the governor can use line-item vetoes to delete control language in appropriations bills without affecting appropriation levels. In non-appropriation bills, the governor must either veto the entire bill or none of it.

In response to the governor's use of line-item vetoes for control language, the legislature has used "trailer bills" more frequently as a basis for providing direction. As one example, a trailer bill established a duplicate degree charge in 1992, providing that someone who had already earned a bachelor's degree and enrolled for another undergraduate degree would be charged the full tuition established for an out-of-state student. Since trailer bills make long-term changes, most often in response to a short-term problem, they usually contain a sunset clause. The duplicate degree charge expired in 1997.

University of California

The UC president's office coordinates the development of a unified budget for the University of California. The UC request for state funds for capital improvements is submitted in a separate volume and is projected on a five-year time line. In the past, the budget was based on annual negotiations, but the compact with the governor negotiated in 1995 has changed that. The compact represents a four-year plan that guarantees funding increases averaging approximately 4 percent per year, in addition to funds provided for state debt service. In return, the university guarantees limited enrollment growth, increased portability of courses, continued increases in productivity and efficiency, and improved graduation rates.

Once the legislature has made its lump sum appropriation to the university, the university divides the funds among campuses. A faculty member told us that this task used to be accomplished by yelling and screaming. Under a previous president, a formula was devised that weighted graduate students more than undergraduates. A new president is now reconsidering that formula. A proposal under consideration during our study would provide equal compensation for undergraduate and graduate students for new resources above the current base. Neither the president nor anyone else can take away from one campus to give to another. The most that can be done is to redistribute the increment.

Campuses have substantial latitude over the funds they receive. However, funds that flow to the campuses are watched very carefully by internal constituencies, thus limiting what chancellors can do in the absence of consensus about expenditures. Funds appropriated for salaries are held sacred. Funds related to workload have much greater flexibility. Most student fees return to the campuses where they are generated, but some of the funds are redistributed among campuses to take into account different economic profiles and differing kinds of students.

California State University

Historically, California State University depended upon an extremely complex array of formulas to produce its annual budget requests to the legislature. In 1994, a redesign of the internal process eliminated the formulas. Concurrently, the governor's compact guaranteed CSU a 4 percent average annual increase in general fund operational support, annual funding of $150 million for capital renewal, and support for modest fee increases to help stabilize funding and strengthen growth. In return, CSU agreed to accommodate average annual enrollment growth of approximately 1 percent and to increase financial aid for qualified but financially needy students.[14]

Internally, the CSU budget process begins when the chancellor articulates the priorities that have previously been discussed with the CSU executive council. The allocation process is heavily enrollment driven, with a base for each campus to which incremental changes are made. Most of the budget is in the form of salaries. If campuses have enrollment gains or losses, changes can be made. However, the system can also decide to preserve an institution's budget in the face of enrollment losses, as in the case of CSU Northridge, which lost 10 percent of its enrollment following serious earthquake damage in 1995. Apart from special circumstances, institutions can gain or lose 2 percent in enrollment without affecting their base levels of funding. Campus presidents negotiate with the chancellor for additional monies that may be available.

Community Colleges

The budget process for community colleges begins when the state chancellor's office collects from local districts information related to enrollment growth, inflation, and other indicators of fiscal need. From this information the board of governors determines the full cost of operating the community college system and submits this estimate to the Department of Finance as a budget change proposal.[15] This budget process is largely incremental, since the amount of funding for enrollments is capped. Tuition and fees are set by the state.

While capital projects are funded through general obligation or revenue bonds (rather than by the general fund), they must still be approved by the governor. The state also has about 20 categorical programs that affect community college funding, including services for disabled students, economic development programs, and programs to increase transfer rates. Together these programs represent from 10 to 15 percent of the total appropriation to the community colleges. Categorical programs are subject to cuts in the budget process, however, and are particularly vulnerable to the political process.

Legislators cannot be certain that monies appropriated for a specific purpose will be used for that purpose. This problem is apparent at both system and local levels. In 1993, the state identified $90 million for enrollment increases in the community college budget. The chancellor, however, used the money to fill in gaps in community college funding rather than to fund enrollment increases. The money the legislature thought it was appropriating for enrollment increases went to collective bargaining agreements and other purposes, an arrangement that created a furor when it was pointed out to legislators.

Program Planning and Review

The 1960 master plan dominates most discussions of California higher education. The plan represented a compact among citizens, the institutions, and state government promising an orderly system of higher education where institutions had clear missions and where planning in the public interest would determine the location of new facilities and services. For every qualified adult citizen, an undergraduate space would be available with the cost for instruction paid by the state. Public institutions were promised that the state would support a first-rate system of higher education with faculty, equipment, and facilities among the very best in the nation. Independent institutions were offered a state program of student financial aid. Over time, additional elements with fiscal implications became identified with the original master plan, including: faculty salaries at public institutions competitive with similar public and private institutions; special assistance for the disadvantaged, the underrepresented, and those with special needs; geographically convenient opportunities; and employee collective bargaining.

A senior CSU executive described to us three current perspectives on the master plan: "The public treats the master plan as 10 commandments, asking only 'Are desired services available?' The power structure is so taken with the mythology of the master plan that for them it has outrun the plan's reality.

Institutions believe their self-interests are best served if no one is doing anything to them." A legislative staff member, after describing the system as "self-contained," noted that the governor and legislature have been fairly deferential. A CPEC official described the difficulties of planning when all of the issues that might be addressed are enshrined in the master plan: "It is difficult to have policy discussions with the legislature and the governor. Everything is dominated by the annual budget. Considerations are short-term. There are no long-term issues raised."

In the more than 30 years since the provisions of the master plan became law, the master plan has been revisited no fewer than five times, most recently in 1986. Among the more important changes resulting from these restudies has been the creation of the CPEC, with strengthened authority and a majority of public members compared to the original, institutionally dominated coordinating council. There have also been a number of attempts to reform community college governance.

Planning is not much in evidence among any of the three public segments. The budget approach for UC addresses issues on an annual basis and therefore does not feature significant long-term planning. The most publicized planning decision made by the CSU board during our case study involved ending remedial education over a seven-year period. The decision was taken in relation to political realities rather than planning priorities.

According to the 1960 master plan, community colleges were supposed to be located throughout the state but to remain locally governed and financed. In 1977-78, just prior to the passage of Proposition 13, community colleges received 39.6 percent of their funding from the state and 60.3 percent from local revenues. A year later, the funding mix was 69.2 percent from the state and 28.9 percent from local sources. Both the state money and the local funding are appropriated through the state, leading some to describe "local property tax" as a misnomer since there is little local control over it. Local community colleges are required to submit facilities' plans and master plans to the state chancellor's office.

While the 1960 master plan mentioned private higher education only in the context of student financial aid, the private institutions were influential in the development of the master plan.[16] Yet from 1960 to the 1986 master plan revisions, private higher education was largely ignored in policy discussions. Until 1985, student demand and available resources created an environment in which higher education was one big happy family. There was, for practical purposes, no market competition. Between 1985 and 1990, tuition costs increased rapidly. Private institutions, in competition with the public sector, engaged in tuition discounting, leading to financial problems for many of these institutions. To address these problems, language was inserted in the 1986 master plan revision requiring the state to consider the capacity and utilization of the private sector in making planning decisions. Current estimates suggest that the private sector might be able to supply from 10,000 to 40,000 seats— or about 10 percent of the projected demand for "Tidal Wave II."

The academic program review process is primarily campus-based, but the system offices do provide a fairly serious review of new programs and of those programs considered for discontinuation. The California Postsecondary Education Commission maintains an inventory of programs and must review new majors, new programs (the School of Public Administration, for example), or joint doctoral programs. While CPEC cannot prevent a degree or program from being offered, systems typically work with CPEC to negotiate around any controversies.

University of California

The most serious program issue for the University of California is duplication at the graduate level, with five graduate programs in Scandinavian studies and the five teaching hospitals cited most frequently. But the issue is extraordinarily complex. A campus provost who acknowledged an overproduction of Ph.D.s in the nation was not sure that UC, with its reputation for high-quality departments, was the right place to begin addressing the problem.

Some UC provosts no longer believe all campuses must replicate Berkeley. They have been meeting for the past two years to study ways to get faculty to engage in cooperative planning. Like many activities within the university, this one has been largely invisible, in part because of concerns that if administrators are perceived to be too visibly involved, they run the risk of offending the academic senate and alienating people whose collaboration is essential. Provosts are also concerned about appearing to promise more than they can deliver, perhaps wisely since their efforts to date seem to have achieved very mixed results.

The budget provides the primary incentives for collaboration among faculty. The system is trying to hold some central discretionary money to encourage collaboration that will lead to greater efficiencies, but most of the examples we were able to uncover underscore the extreme difficulty of working through system processes and safeguards in matters involving university faculty. Absent exceptional fiscal stress, collaboration is very problematic, particularly if it has connotations for ending a program at a particular campus. We found, however, that cooperation among faculty is more successful in research, where state and national laboratory money create the possibility of funding at the system level. Cooperation is much more difficult to obtain in areas such as history and foreign languages, although faculty in both of these fields have been involved in discussions.

California State University

Every new major or degree at CSU must come through the central office as well as CPEC for approval. There are two primary criteria in the review: Does the proposal meet central office standards? And will the proposal get past CPEC? Because every campus has its own system of arriving at which programs should be offered, central office involvement tends to be routine and more directed to facilitating CPEC approval than constraining campus initiatives.

A routine review of existing academic programs happens on each campus every five or six years. Campuses report the outcomes of these reviews, but the central office does not mandate specific responses to the reviews. The process is much less centralized and directive than in the past. Not all presidents believe such campus reviews have much to offer. One told us that the process had been captured by the faculty and did not produce reports with any value for decision makers.

System initiatives related to the curriculum tend to be broadly strategic rather than focused on specific programs or majors. Project 2001 is an example. This study builds on collaborative relationships with the Department of Finance and asks four questions: (1) From the state's perspective, why do people need to be in college in the year 2001? (2) Who is likely to be in college and what are their needs? (3) What curricula will be required to match state needs to student characteristics and needs? (4) What modes of instruction will be most effective? The hope for Project 2001 and related initiatives is that they will lay out the strategic directions CSU intends to follow. Strategic directions will not require campuses to act, but it will define priorities that will be reflected in such other processes as presidential evaluation and budgeting.

Community Colleges

At the community colleges, program review, like budget development, reflects the fissures and cracks in governance. Districts can offer courses without approval of the board of governors, but they must have board approval for new programs. The chancellor's office did not review a gay and lesbian program started by the Community College of San Francisco. When state legislators criticized this program, it became apparent that the college had simply put some courses together and given them a name. This type of arrangement is not covered by the program review process. In approving programs, the chancellor's office looks only at duplication with the offerings at nearby community colleges and does not consider the impact on other parts of California higher education.

Several current and former chancellors told us that sound academic planning in the local community college district is the rare exception. One added, "Curricular changes in general come from retirement." The same chancellor described program review as "nonexistent." A trustee described the problems that administrators encountered in his district in developing a board-mandated program-review process. When asked if the process might lead to any program closures, he said, "I hope so." In a different district, a former administrator said, "The power of unions has cannibalized the educational program." A superintendent and president decried the adverse impact of faculty resistance to entrepreneurial activity, noting that his district has experienced no real curriculum development in 16 years.

System Articulation

California provides many examples of collaborative activity among individual institutions. California State University is involved with UC and several private institutions in offering joint doctoral programs, such as a collaboration between UC Davis and Fresno State. But for the most part, observers told us that cooperation between CSU and UC as intended by the master plan has never really occurred. Restraints on CSU doctoral and professional programs remain a source of irritation to those at CSU.

There are several examples of four-year institutions working with community colleges to coordinate services or collaborate on programs. There is, however, no single authority with responsibility for articulation, despite the importance of transfer to the state's plan for universal access to upper division work.

The legislature has tried to fill the gap by initiating transfer centers, course articulation numbering systems, and, most recently, a common course numbering system. Legislators also established a general education core of 34 units that would be acceptable at every public campus within California. We were told this legislation was aimed mainly at the UC system and was not as good as arrangements already existing between CSU and the community colleges.

Transfer works reasonably well between community colleges and CSU, which is very dependent upon transfers to fill upper division classes. It works less well between the community colleges and UC. Even where it works well, however, there are problems. The California Postsecondary Education Commission tries to gather data on the successes and failures of transfer through a special section in its annual report, *Student Profiles*. Commission efforts are somewhat inhibited, however, by the absence of a student information system that permits cohort tracking. As a result, CPEC must rely upon institutional reports that, as previously noted, are widely perceived as self-serving.

The results of all these efforts fall significantly short of the ideal. A community college representative told us that despite the amount of attention paid to transfer, very little has been accomplished in terms of true seamless movement. A legislative staff member said, "Transfer and articulation are a mess in California because of turf issues. There are transfer agreements but they are all negotiated and fought out to the extent that they are not always very effective." A state senator told us that he became involved in working on a major bill on transfer primarily because of anecdotal evidence from individuals who were having great difficulty.

There is general agreement that the systems need to work together more closely to be sure that students are prepared to succeed. Currently, however, the intersegmental coordinating council, a voluntary body, provides the only arrangement for working across segmental boundaries. Whatever is not worked out voluntarily is left to the legislature, where contending interests have the opportunity to pursue their special points of view.

CONCLUSION

In California, three public sectors of higher education (one with constitutional autonomy and the other two with various degrees of state oversight), along with a fairly strong and diverse independent sector, have maintained a balance over time that seems to have met both public needs and institutional aspirations. In the early 1990s, market forces in California were weakened due to declines in state support for student aid, particularly for those students attending private colleges and universities. This situation has abated in the past two fiscal years. Recent external pressures on the state budget and expected growth in college enrollments may force a reexamination of the structure and its ability to respond to state priorities.

NOTES

1. Data in this paragraph are drawn from *Chronicle of Higher Education Almanac* 43, no. 1 (September 1996), pp. 42–44.
2. K. Halstead, *State Profiles for Higher Education 1978 to 1996: Trend Data* (Washington, D.C.: Research Associates of Washington, 1996), pp. 9, 12.
3. P. Schrag, "California's Elected Anarchy," *Harper's Magazine* (November 1994), pp. 50–58.
4. J. M. Burns, J. W. Peltason, and T. E. Cronin, *State and Local Politics: Government by the People* (Englewood Cliffs, N.J.: Prentice Hall, 1990), p. 113.
5. G. W. Adams, "How California Can Maintain Its Commitment to Higher Education," prepared for the Rules Committee of the California State Senate, August 23, 1994, pp. 14–19.
6. S. J. Carroll, K. F. McCarthy, and M. Wade, "California's Looming Budget Crisis," in *Rand Research Review* 18, no. 2 (fall 1994), pp. 1–4.
7. Enrollment information compiled from California Postsecondary Education Commission, *Student Profiles 1996* (Sacramento, Calif., 1996); other information compiled from E. G. Hill, *Cal Guide Reprint: Higher Education* (Sacramento, Calif.: Legislative Analyst's Office, 1994), pp. 3–4.

8. Halstead, *State Profiles*, pp. 9, 12; K. Halstead, *Higher Education Report Card 1995* (Washington, D.C.: Research Associates of Washington, 1996), p. 61.

9. CPEC, *The Challenge of the Century* (Sacramento, Calif., 1995).

10. A. C. McGuinness, Jr., R. Epper, and S. Arredondo, *State Postsecondary Structures Handbook* (Denver, Colo.: Education Commission of the States, 1994), p. 165.

11. W. Trombley, "Shared Governance: An Elusive Goal," *CrossTalk* 5, no. 1 (winter 1997).

12. Schrag, "California's Elected Anarchy."

13. L. E. Gladieux and J. E. King, *Trends in Student Aid: California* (San Jose, Calif.: California Higher Education Policy Center, 1995), p. 11.

14. California State University, Office of the Chancellor, *The California State University 1996-97 Support Budget*, "Chancellor's Budget Message."

15. We asked for a copy of a budget change proposal and were told by the staff person we were interviewing that such documents were confidential.

16. C. Kerr, "The California Master Plan: An *Ex Ante* View," in *The OECD, the Master Plan, and the California Dream: A Berkeley Conversation*, ed. S. Rothblatt (Berkeley, Calif.: Regents of University of California, 1992) pp. 47–60.

CHAPTER 4

New York

Like California, New York has a segmented higher education structure that operates in what is predominantly a regulatory state policy environment. The state groups its public institutions into two geographically distinct, heterogeneous subsystems, each managed by a chancellor and a governing board. Baccalaureate- and associate's degree-granting institutions serving New York City constitute one system, the City University of New York (CUNY). The other system, the State University of New York (SUNY), has many small and diverse campuses that are widely dispersed across the state outside New York City, including 30 community college districts that have local governing boards. Independent colleges and universities dominated higher education in New York for more than two centuries and are still an integral part of the system.

A unique state agency, the board of regents of the University of the State of New York, has statutory responsibility for coordination of education at all levels (K–12 and higher education), including quality assurance, long-range planning, and program approval. The regents' actual influence in setting overall policy, however, is limited at best, largely because they lack budget authority. As in California, there is no one group or organization in New York with the ability to establish and implement a statewide policy agenda.

The public and private higher education sectors operate in an intensely competitive and partisan political environment. The governor of New York, who has been granted strong veto and other powers by the state constitution, has historically exercised strong leadership on higher education issues. A full-time legislature divided between upstate Republicans who dominate the senate and downstate (urban) Democrats who control the assembly serves as the "custodian" of higher education, with a fairly significant role in setting the missions for the public campuses. In many ways, the differences between the two chambers of the legislature are now more significant for higher education than the governor's priorities. Most observers we spoke with agreed that no one is truly looking out for the whole picture.

Although the state economy suffered in the early 1990s, it has now leveled off. Changes in the economy have led to significant changes in higher education funding. During the early 1990s, Bundy Aid, which is paid directly to independent colleges and universities, declined from approximately $100 million to about $40 million. Meanwhile, the need-based Tuition Assistance Program (TAP) has grown dramatically, due to its entitlement nature. In 1992-93 for the first time, the amount of TAP funding going to students at public institutions surpassed that going to students at private institutions. The election of Governor George Pataki in 1994 on a platform that promised to cut taxes and shrink government brought significant reductions in state funding to both CUNY and SUNY in 1995 and 1996, and increased competition for funds.

The fragmented political structure overseeing higher education in New York (based on regional biases and political divisions) inhibits the development of coordinated work processes: Information gathering and utilization are weak and fragmented. The budget process is dictated more by projections of tuition revenues than by enrollment demands, and fiscal flexibility is lacking when midyear adjustments are required. Statewide planning for higher education is difficult since it is not linked to the budget process, and since regional and political concerns often dominate the process. System articulation is not a major issue due to the structure of the regional subsystems and the choices provided by private institutions.

Compared to other study states, particularly California and Michigan, institutional autonomy is weak in New York. A highly regulatory policy environment in the state, combined with heavy reliance on market forces such as the provision of aid to private institutions and a significant student financial aid program, create a contentious environment for higher education. The annual state appropriations process provides the only forum to deliberate the roles, responsibilities, and support of public and private higher education. As a result, there are few clear long-term messages sent to higher education from the state policy environment.

STATE CONTEXT

Few states can match the complex environment for higher education offered by New York, the nation's third largest state. Geographically, demographically, economically, and politically, the state is divided between New York City in the south and upstate New York. More than one-fourth of the state's 18.5 million people are minorities and 23 percent of its families speak a language other than English at home.[1] New York City is home to more than 40 percent of the state's population and a majority of the state's ethnic minorities. Of the 25,000 new high school graduates expected between 1994-95 and 2003-04, almost 50 percent will be from the New York City and the mid-Hudson regions. New Yorkers are generally well educated, particularly in terms of the percentage of the population with graduate or professional degrees.

The governor of New York has been granted strong veto and other powers by the state constitution,[2] and the pivotal role the governor plays in higher education policy is evident from past developments associated with specific governors: Governor Dewey with the establishment of SUNY; Governor Rockefeller with SUNY's expansion and with institutional support of independent campuses; Governor Cuomo with declines in that support and with neglecting his role in the planning process; and at present, Governor Pataki with budget cutbacks. The governor has line-item veto authority; oversees negotiation of collective bargaining agreements for SUNY; and names, with senate approval, all appointed SUNY trustees, 10 of the 15 appointed members of the CUNY trustees, and 4 of the 9 members of local SUNY community college boards of trustees.

New York has a full-time legislature whose staff has grown dramatically since the early 1970s. A senior legislative staff member described legislators as "custodians" of higher education with a "fairly significant role" in setting the missions for the public campuses. The senate, as it had for the previous five years, in 1995-96 had a Republican majority elected primarily from upstate districts. In the same year, the assembly remained heavily Democratic with more than two-thirds of its majority elected from New York City. The assembly tends to focus on the key New York City issues of access and CUNY. The senate is more interested in quality, economic development, job creation, and SUNY. Under a Republican governor, the senate appears to have more influence. Staff members of the Senate Higher Education Committee attend governing board meetings and work to assert legislative priorities with trustees and institutional officers.

Although some regulatory measures have been softened (including the elimination of budgetary "line controls" on campus expenditures), campus presidents and former system executives criticized the continuing "excessive regulatory climate of state government." Most public higher education staff are employees of the state, subject to civil service and other state regulations. At SUNY, both staff and faculty are employed under bargaining agreements negotiated by the governor's Office of Employee Relations. Tuition is effectively controlled by the governor and legislature through the establishment of gross revenue targets as well as statutory restrictions on tuition differentials and restraints on when trustees are allowed to set tuition schedules. The state controller and the attorney general retain considerable expenditure and contract authority. The state Division of the Budget can alter downward at any time the approved budget for state-operated campuses.

New York ranks first among study states in per capita income[3] and in potential tax revenues.[4] The state derives more than 50 percent of general tax revenues from a personal income tax. Appropriations to elementary and secondary education encompass one-third of the total state budget, and health and social welfare encompass more than one-fourth. Although New York is considered a high-tax state, it spends a relatively small proportion on public higher education (48th among the 50 states and the District of Columbia in 1994-95). This is due in part to the considerable size of the independent sector. Since the beginning of the decade, higher education's share of state tax dollars has been declining on both a percentage and dollar basis.

In November 1994 Republican George Pataki defeated the three-term Democratic incumbent governor on a platform that promised to cut taxes and shrink government. Governor Pataki submitted his first budget to the legislature in January 1995 proposing a 31.5 percent reduction in appropriations for SUNY and a 27 percent reduction for CUNY. These cuts were to be offset by tuition increases and expenditure reductions. Opposition from the legislature as well as from the higher education community led to a budget compromise that restored some of the proposed cuts, but still reduced state support significantly and prompted steep tuition increases. Each system was also required to produce a plan, due in December 1995, that would address issues of efficiency and cost-effectiveness and that would focus on long-term strategies as opposed to short-term tactics such as deferring maintenance or freezing hiring. Moreover, the long-term plans would not rely on tuition increases or campus closures. Both systems submitted plans as required. The campus closure ban seems attributable to the political clout of SUNY's geographically dispersed campuses; we were told by one respondent that "every senator has a SUNY campus in his district."

The governor's budget for 1996-97 again proposed reductions for SUNY and CUNY, and again the legislature rejected many of these cuts. The governor included several recommendations from SUNY's December 1995 report, *Rethinking SUNY*, in his budget. The major such recommendation proposed by the governor and adopted by the legislature created provisions that allow reserve funds, which would have otherwise reverted to the state, to be carried forward to the next year by the campuses. The legislature rejected recommendations for a single budget line for the system and for differential tuition across SUNY campuses. Legislators also made it clear that the increases to the governor's budget were provided to avoid a tuition increase at SUNY (CUNY had not sought an increase).

The general belief among those in state government during our visits was that CUNY had done more to address issues of productivity and efficiency than SUNY. This more favorable impression of CUNY was attributed by a CUNY administrator to "bad feelings" or "bad experiences" that the governor and senators may have had with SUNY, but not with CUNY. A legislator suggested that CUNY has fared better because its chancellor is more astute than SUNY's in political matters. He added, "The governor knows that CUNY's urban constituency will put up a tougher fight than heavily suburban and rural SUNY." Since our visit, the chancellor of the CUNY system resigned after newly appointed activist trustees raised fundamental questions about the core mission of CUNY and the future of the system.

CHARACTERISTICS AND HISTORY OF HIGHER EDUCATION

Higher education in New York consists of 314 degree-granting institutions. Public two- and four-year degree-granting institutions are organized into two university systems: SUNY and CUNY. Each system has its own board of trustees, established by statute. The private higher education sector is very diverse, with large and prestigious graduate and research centers, prestigious liberal arts colleges and universities, and numerous small colleges struggling with financial and enrollment problems.

In 1996, total head-count enrollment at public and private institutions was approximately 970,000. The distribution and composition of the student population has been changing. The number of high school graduates in New York declined from more than 240,000 in 1979 to about 158,500 in 1993.[5] Between 1990 and 1995, enrollment in baccalaureate-granting SUNY institutions declined by almost 10 percent while enrollment at similar CUNY institutions increased by almost 5 percent. Enrollments in the private sector remained relatively constant. Minority students make up 30 percent of the total enrollment in higher education in New York. By 2000, half of CUNY first-time freshmen will have been born outside the United States. Already, 47 percent speak a native language other than English.

The board of regents of the University of the State of New York—to be distinguished from the State University of New York (SUNY)—was established in 1784 to govern King's College, now Columbia University. The 16 regents are elected by the legislature for five-year terms and serve without pay. The regents' administrative arm is the state Department of Education, whose commissioner they appoint. The regents are responsible for the general supervision, planning, and coordination of education at all levels.

The State University of New York and CUNY are large, complex, multicampus universities with a wide array of institutions. Both have origins as aggregations of older colleges. In 1948, the state placed all public campuses in the state other than those governed by CUNY under a new board and a new chief executive officer. The State University of New York's statutory mission is to provide "educational services of the highest quality, with the broadest possible access, fully representative of all segments of the population in a complete range of academic, professional and vocational programs."[6] In 1996, SUNY included: 4 graduate research universities; 13 comprehensive colleges with selected master's programs; 4 specialized professional schools; 4 colleges of technology; 2 colleges of agriculture and technology; 5 "statutory colleges" located at Cornell University and Alfred University; and 30 community colleges.

The State University of New York is governed by a 16-member board of trustees. The State University of New York's chief executive officer has the title of chancellor. With one exception, each of the two- and four-year, state-operated campuses has a nine-member campus advisory council that reviews annual budgets, recommends candidates for the presidency (who are appointed by the SUNY board), and manages buildings and grounds.

The SUNY trustees act as a coordinating board for the subsystem's 30 community colleges, each of which has "local sponsors" (usually one or more counties) whose financial contribution must not fall below 26.2 percent of the operating budget. Community colleges are governed by their own nine-member boards of trustees. Community college leaders see inclusion of their institutions in SUNY as adding prestige but very little practical help. Articulation with SUNY's four-year campuses is uneven at best, and largely dependent upon local factors.

The State University of New York's board of trustees has responsibility for setting tuition at the state-operated campuses, though the legislature can influence the level of tuition through specific language calling for limited or no tuition increases. Undergraduate tuition at SUNY's four-year institutions averaged $3,400 in 1995-96, a 28 percent increase over the previous year. The State University of New York's community colleges set their own tuition. For 1995-96, community college tuition averaged $2,167, a 10 percent increase over 1994-95. From 1990 to 1995, tuition increased 127 percent at the state-operated campuses and 58 percent at the community colleges.

The faculty and professional staff at SUNY's state-operated colleges bargain collectively with the governor's Office of Employee Relations. The State University of New York's classified staff are part of the state civil service system. Relationships between the faculty union and the SUNY faculty senate, often contentious in the past, were described to us as good. The union, according to a member of the faculty senate, bargains over "terms and conditions of employment for faculty, while the system-wide faculty senate serves as an advisor to the chancellor on education policy issues." Local community college unions bargain directly with their respective boards.

The City University of New York grew out of the 1926 merger of separate boards for City College and Hunter College into the board of higher education. The name of the merged institutions was changed to City University of New York in 1961, when authority to grant doctoral degrees was given. The City University of New York consisted of 19 institutions including a system-wide graduate center, 13 four-year and 6 two-year colleges. The system is governed by a single board of trustees (comprised of 17 members, 5 of whom are appointed by the mayor of New York City, 10 by the governor). Except for a student and a faculty member who serve *ex officio* for one-year terms, all trustees serve seven-year terms and must be confirmed by the senate.

The City University of New York has an explicit mission dating in substance from the founding in 1847 of the Free Academy, the predecessor of City College. The statutory mission, which is broadly accepted within CUNY, calls for "the strongest commitment to the special needs of an urban constituency."[7] A senior CUNY officer told us that CUNY benefits from the views of state residents "about immigrants in the best possible sense of that word. They are not anti-immigrant, and they remain proud of the city's role in providing immigrants with the first step of upward mobility." Central administrators emphasized the trustees' "loyalty and dedication to the university despite six-hour :neetings, the lousy food they serve them, and the tension."

Thirty years ago, the CUNY system consisted of highly selective colleges that, fully supported by the City of New York, did not charge tuition. The City University of New York now has open admissions, charges substantial tuition, and has seen its four-year colleges become state supported. Tuition at CUNY's senior colleges averaged $3,200 in 1995-96, an increase of 31 percent over the previous year. Community college tuition averaged $2,500, an increase of 18.5 percent over 1994-95 levels. The system has, according to a senior administrator, "the poorest students of any place in the country, but also perhaps the most talented; . . . 21,000 students in CUNY [are] on welfare." Even with CUNY's close relationship to the public schools, it is as yet unclear how CUNY will accomplish its difficult urban mission under these challenging circumstances.

Well-known campuses—Hunter, Queens, Brooklyn, and City College of New York—enjoyed substantial autonomy prior to their consolidation into CUNY in 1961. For several years, it was unclear whether the founding chancellor would be able to exercise much central authority, but the present perception as summarized by a legislative aide is that "CUNY tends to be much more of a system than SUNY." This is perhaps because of the geographic proximity and public transportation links to its campuses, its system-wide graduate center, its relatively specific mission, and the absence of the "prestige pyramid" found in SUNY.

The City University of New York faculty are organized through the Congress of Federated Unions. Whereas SUNY faculty negotiate collective bargaining agreements directly with the state, CUNY faculty negotiate with the CUNY central office.

Private institutions dominated higher education in New York for almost two centuries and are still highly influential. There are 138 private colleges and universities in the state, most of which are represented in Albany by the Commission on Independent Colleges and Universities (CICU). As well as enrolling 41 percent of the state's students (by head count), independent colleges and universities produce 58 percent of the bachelor's degrees, 69 percent of the graduate degrees, and 83 percent of first professional degrees.[8]

DESIGN OF THE HIGHER EDUCATION–STATE GOVERNMENT INTERFACE

A unique statewide agency—the board of regents of the University of the State of New York—provides limited coordination of all degree-granting public, independent, and proprietary colleges and universities in New York. Under board oversight, the Office of Higher and Professional Education within the Department of Education coordinates the development of new campuses and academic and degree programs, accredits every curriculum in the state, and periodically reviews academic degree and proprietary school programs to assure quality and compliance with state and federal regulations. A former SUNY chancellor described the regents as "a very strong board with a great deal of authority," but said that they do not play a significant policy role in higher education. A senior CUNY officer agreed, but noted the value of the regents' periodic review of doctoral programs and the link that the regents provide between the public schools and four-year teacher education programs.

The role of the regents as a statewide coordinating agency appears to be declining. The regents' broad responsibilities for elementary and secondary education and the pervasive problems in that area severely limit the time, energy, and interest they can devote to higher education. Their primary authority lies in their ability to approve or terminate programs. The regents' master planning process, widely considered ineffective for some time, has been further diminished by recent legislation. The regents lack budget authority in a time when policy decisions in New York have been dominated by fiscal considerations. Currently, the annual state appropriations process is the only place where the roles, responsibilities, and support of public and private higher education are deliberated. In the appropriations process, the primary problems and priorities are fiscal ones and the focus is on short-term solutions. The state's capacity to develop explicit public policy goals, build consensus around them, and assess progress in meeting them is very limited.

While the regents consider themselves apolitical, the process by which they are selected is not free of party influence. When a vacancy occurs, the chairs of the higher education committees of the two houses are notified, and the legislature, according to a legislative staff member, "basically runs help wanted ads. . . . As many as three dozen [respondents] may be interviewed." Those chosen by the leadership must then be elected by the legislature. Recently, Democrats have controlled the process because they outnumber Republicans.

Governors, according to a former commissioner, "have generally resented the independence of the regents, and have seen them as a legislative adjunct." As one example, the regents' statewide plan languished on Governor Cuomo's desk for two years before he approved it, and he never acted on subsequent ones. Governor Pataki called for the elimination of the regents' planning function, but a compromise resulted in lengthening the planning cycle from four to eight years.

There is a long history of contentiousness between public and private higher education in New York. This conflict has been in part the result of New York's use of market forces, such as aid to private institutions and aid to students. Prior to the mid-1960s, a merit-based student aid program benefited private institutions, as well as covering the full cost of tuition at SUNY. Increasing tuition undermined the competitive position of private institutions. Acting on the recommendations of a commission appointed by Governor Rockefeller, the state authorized essentially unrestricted "Bundy Aid," paid directly to independent colleges and universities, and based on the number of degrees awarded. The need-based Tuition Assistance Program (TAP), administered by the State Higher Education Services Corporation, was initiated in 1974 to help students attend the institutions of their choice.

From 1990 to 1992, state funding for Bundy Aid declined from approximately $100 million to some $40 million. In 1992-93, for the first time, the amount of TAP money going to students at public institutions surpassed that going to students at private institutions. Since 1990, TAP funding has increased from just under $400 million to more than $600 million because of its entitlement nature and because of increases in tuition in the public sector. About 40 percent of the students at SUNY and in the private institutions receive TAP awards; at CUNY about 70 percent do. In the 1995-96 state budget, a cap of 90 percent of tuition at CUNY and SUNY was placed on TAP awards to students in those systems. Many in the private sector believe that TAP awards are now disproportionately used by students in the public sector. Advocates of public higher education argue that state generosity to students has been at the expense of institutional funding of public campuses.

We studied SUNY during a time of major changes. Almost half of the system's governing board had been in place for less than a year; a new chancellor, whose tenure was ultimately very brief, had assumed office just prior to the appointment of the new board; budget cuts had been imposed and further cuts were anticipated. Major issues were very much "in play," including the appropriate roles of campus administrations and the system office, the size and scope of the system staff, the cohesiveness of SUNY as a system, the role of the governing board, and its relationship to system and campus administrators. Many respondents said that the new trustees were appointed to bring the governor's priorities for reduced state expenditures to SUNY. A college president told us: "The governing board is hell-bent on destroying the university." This same respondent criticized the former board as an "absentee board," saying, "They didn't show up or read the materials." Others saw the new trustees as an advantage in providing access to the new governor. A faculty member was impressed with the board's willingness to listen to faculty concerns. And a former chancellor praised the board's selection of his replacement.

The State University of New York campuses seek to acquire greater autonomy and control over functions such as tuition and collective bargaining. Similarly, under a chair who believes that "central planning is counterproductive,"[9] newly appointed board members favor a free-market approach and devolution of authority to the campuses. Many SUNY campuses were designed as small, regional institutions. As such, their costs per student are high, particularly at the six two-year agricultural and technical colleges. In some program areas, these colleges duplicate offerings at the 30 community colleges. Many Republicans in the legislature oppose campus closures because the campuses are of economic benefit to their districts; many Democrats oppose closures because they would reduce student access. In *Rethinking SUNY*, the board of trustees stated that SUNY "is encouraging strategic alliances" to link together some of the smaller campuses and to build partnerships with the private sector. The future of several campuses remains uncertain.

During our study, the CUNY board took several controversial actions to respond to the recent budget cutbacks, actions that have been widely criticized by faculty and employee groups. In the summer of 1995, the CUNY board declared that the system was in a state of "financial exigency," which allowed the board to take some cost-saving actions permitted by state law only in times of fiscal crisis. The board voted to terminate 159 tenured faculty and to "abolish, consolidate, or merge" more than 30 academic programs at its four-year institutions.[10] Several groups, including the professionals' union and the faculty senate, brought a lawsuit against the board for taking these actions. In April 1996, a state court invalidated the trustees' actions, arguing that the state of fiscal emergency identified in February 1995 with the governor's proposed budget had largely disappeared by June 1995 when the board voted on the cost-cutting measures. This ruling was overturned in December 1996 by a state appellate court, which ruled that the trustees had acted "properly and in good faith" in their declaration of a fiscal emergency. This action clears the way for the original board action.[11] Prior to either the lower court or appellate ruling, however, the board declared a second state of fiscal emergency in March 1996, this time just for the four-year colleges, "paving the way for possible layoffs of more than 1,300 faculty and staff members."[12] The court rulings do not affect this most recent declaration.

Despite criticisms and recent contentiousness, most of those we interviewed appeared generally satisfied with the statewide organization of higher education in New York.

WORK PROCESSES

In New York, the political environment of higher education is characterized by the shifting interactions of three major players: the governor and the respective leaders of the two legislative houses. Political party affiliations, regional interests, and personal philosophical preferences overlay the formal roles of these players. For public higher education, less visible but still influential are the state control agencies that regulate other state agencies, as well as colleges and universities.

Higher education maintains and advances New York's policy priorities of access, quality, and equity through planning, budgeting, and program review. All of these processes rely on information, and all are interdependent. At the same time, no single agency within the state has responsibility for maintaining a higher education database or for translating such data into information that can be used in the policy process.

Information Management

The regents monitor graduation rates and require institutions to publish time-to-degree information, including successful completion of licensing examinations by graduates of various programs. A regents' officer noted that there "is a lot of lip service and report cards going on around the country, but . . . the basic information that people should know is still lacking." He added that the regents are now working on performance indicators, ones that would allow the institutions to set their own directions. He noted also that the independent sector "really relies on the data that we collect," and uses it to make their cases to the legislature.

The State University of New York central staff told us that they believe that good information about performance and relative levels of quality and activity at different institutions is available from their information base, but that neither the central office nor the trustees have used it to the extent that they should. The CUNY central office is upgrading its management information system, which, according to a campus head, does not currently provide needed information for the campuses.

It is not at all clear that more information or better information would have altered the decisions that shaped higher education during the period covered by our study.

Budget Process

Typically, SUNY and CUNY submit preliminary budgets to the state Division of the Budget based on division guidelines, including allowed inflation adjustments and estimates of institutional revenues. Formal submissions are made after the respective boards act on the budgets. The governor submits the executive budget request in January and has 30 days thereafter to amend it. Under the state constitution, the legislature is required to pass a budget by March 31; but it often does not do so until May or later. In the public legislative hearings that follow submission of the governor's budget, legislators focus on the total proposed expenditures rather than on special items or special treatment of campuses—with the exception of capital projects.

The budgets for CUNY and SUNY are essentially "noncompeting," because of CUNY's political support in the Democratic assembly and SUNY's support from the governor and the senate. In the budget process the legislature maintains the "facade" that CUNY is the city's university, according to a legislative staff member. The City University of New York's four-year institutions are budgeted as a city institution, then reimbursed by the state for 100 percent of the city's costs.

Until recently the budget requests of both SUNY and CUNY were aggregations of campus requests after internal review. At present, however, both systems appear to be maintaining this aggregation for a core budget request for items such as salary increases and inflation, but consolidating special campus requests and tying them to system-wide initiatives. In SUNY, campus heads sometimes lobby their legislators for a specific project that may show up in the state budget as "higher education miscellaneous," rather than as part of the regular SUNY budget.

Neither SUNY nor CUNY uses explicitly enrollment-driven formulas in developing their budget requests to the state. At SUNY, however, the level of tuition income is an incentive for meeting the enrollment levels stated in the budget request. If a campus is overenrolled, it does not receive additional funds. If it is under-enrolled, it could face trouble in the next budget cycle. After campus leaders argued that campuses should be able to retain tuition income, a device was developed with the state Division of the Budget to permit this to a limited extent. At CUNY, four-year campuses are allowed to keep tuition dollars in excess of projections, but they must also carry forward responsibility for deficits.

The State University of New York and CUNY are given greater flexibility than other state agencies in how appropriations can be spent and distributed. Although there is a schedule of payments to each campus, money can be shifted from one campus to another (but in most cases this would have to be justified to the legislature). After midyear reductions in the state budget are made, both systems are free from the usual control limits on shifting funds across line items. In SUNY, allocations are seen as "essentially across the board," according to one campus head, a perception that may be based on the inability of the allocation process to deal with precipitous enrollment losses at several campuses. In CUNY, although the allocation process seems to be in flux, the central office is perceived to be allocating funds to reflect the chancellor's priorities. For example, the chancellor's office has funded a central institute for English as a Second Language with funds that had been originally requested for campus programs.

The State University of New York places a maximum on the tuition that community colleges can charge, but few are at that limit. A community college president stated that neither "SUNY central nor the SUNY Board of Trustees takes a critical look at our budgets. . . . This is all done locally" by local boards of trustees. The CUNY Board of Trustees is the "local board" for the community colleges in that system.

Both SUNY and CUNY build incentives into the allocation process. The State University of New York has attempted to improve articulation by giving additional funds to four-year colleges based on their enrollment of graduates of two-year campuses. The City University of New York uses its control over new faculty positions to encourage compliance with system-wide objectives.

Program Planning and Review

For many years, the regents have overseen a planning process that required SUNY, CUNY, and the independent institutions to prepare four-year master plans, with interim two-year progress and amendment reports. The plans, however, had little impact on executive or legislative policy or—excepting program review—on state higher education. In 1995, Governor Pataki proposed to eliminate the regents' planning role, but he accepted a compromise that changed their role in three major respects: (1) the planning cycle was lengthened to eight years with amendments every four years; (2) the regents will review only major changes, such as a campus's desire to go from a two-year to a four-year institution or to begin to offer either master's or doctoral degrees; and (3) the regents will review mission changes only for quality implications, and no longer for their appropriateness to the campus.

Statewide planning in New York is weak because it is almost completely isolated from the budgetary process. A CUNY officer characterized the regents as having a "nominal planning role." A SUNY officer stated that the regents' "planning process and the document produced has long been considered as an ineffectual chore." Yet the regents remain the only agency with responsibility for all of higher education in New York. Their long-range plans—essentially, their commentary and actions on SUNY and CUNY plans—provide, as a regents' officer stated, "an opportunity to lay out goals and aspirations and ways to measure progress for higher education." As a practical matter, however, the statewide planning process is useful only as a context for the regents' program review responsibilities.

The formal requirements of the regents' planning process have largely determined planning at SUNY and CUNY in the past. Yet except as a rationale for changes in programs or institutional missions that ultimately required the regents' approval, past SUNY and CUNY four-year master plans have had little impact on system operations. Aside from the formal planning required by the regents, the SUNY central office has developed plans (*SUNY 2000* and *SUNY 2000, Phase II*) focused on the availability, demand, and centrality of academic programs at the campuses. According to a senior SUNY officer, however, opposition by some campus presidents and interested legislators prevented adoption of a comprehensive plan that might have led to campus closures or mergers.

In 1995, the legislature requested multiyear plans from both SUNY and CUNY that would improve the efficiency of system and campus operations. The legislature, recognizing that CUNY had already initiated on-going program review in 1991, qualified the request to CUNY, specifying that it outline "its progress on and proposals for . . . efforts to improve program quality and efficiency."[13]

A senior SUNY administrator doubted that the legislature expected much from its request for a plan but said that the "trustees decided to dig into the requirement." The plan that was submitted, *Rethinking SUNY*, was written, according to most respondents, under the direct guidance of the trustees, who established four committees for that purpose.[14] *Rethinking SUNY* calls for giving additional authority to the campuses, reducing central office staff by 30 percent, allowing differential tuition at the campuses, increasing faculty productivity, promoting "strategic alliances" among campuses, and shifting two of the three SUNY hospitals to local nonprofit organizations. Although most of these proposals have been under discussion in the state for some time and some would require legislative approval, the plan is significant as an aggregation of a range of proposals by those—the trustees—who are primarily responsible for implementing them. Several of these proposals were included in the governor's budget, but, according to a senior SUNY administrator, they were not high priorities when the governor negotiated the budget and therefore were not adopted by the legislature.

The plan does not go as far in terms of campus closure and the statutory colleges as some people had either feared or hoped. It is generally believed that SUNY is "overbuilt" but that political reality has prevented simple closure of selected campuses. One strategy in *Rethinking SUNY* is to give the campuses greater autonomy and let the market force mergers or closures. The five statutory colleges (four at Cornell University and one at Alfred University) have not been subject to the same budget constraints as the rest of SUNY. From 1988 to 1995, SUNY's core operating budget was reduced by almost 25 percent, while state funds "passed through" by SUNY to the statutory colleges increased by almost 9 percent.[15] In *Rethinking SUNY*, the board advised the governor and legislature that it was working toward fiscal solutions with Cornell and Alfred, but more fundamental questions about the value of the statutory college model were not raised.

The City University of New York's December 1 report outlined several actions undertaken to improve quality and efficiency, including: (1) attempts to restructure areas such as freshmen assessment, remediation, basic skills, and English as a Second Language; (2) encouragement of strong campus-based planning and distinct campus missions; (3) periodic review of all degree programs, including guidelines for determining when program suspension, closure, and consolidation should occur; and (4) efforts to improve instructional productivity and to find efficiencies in campus operations.

Academic program review in New York takes place at three levels: at the state level, by the regents; at the multicampus system level, by the CUNY and SUNY central offices; and at the campus level, by campus personnel. In all three instances, outside specialists often assist in the reviews. At the state level, the regents' major point of contact with institutions is in the quality-review area. Programs offered in-state by institutions that are from outside the state are subject to regents' approval, and the regents' insistence on quality is said to have avoided having "degree mills" in the state. Program review is periodic and usually takes place at an institution once every 10 years. In the 1970s, the regents terminated several doctoral programs in SUNY, and when challenged by the state university, the regents' authority to do so was upheld in court.

There are differing views on the value of having regents approve new programs. A former SUNY chancellor said such reviews "duplicate what the system already does, and that program approval would be better handled by the SUNY central administration." A SUNY campus president agreed, noting that the regents back down under pressure of the private sector when competing programs are an issue. In contrast, a senior administrator at CUNY said the regents' periodic reviews of doctoral programs are valuable, noting that outside experts are brought in to review all doctoral programs in a given area for the entire state. Such reviews provide leverage for accomplishing goals that might otherwise be difficult to achieve.

The City University of New York's academic program planning includes review of existing programs as well as approval of new ones. This planning process was initiated to guide reallocation of support and has not been perceived as simply a way to give money back to the state. In the three years following its initiation in 1992, 128 programs at CUNY colleges were suspended, consolidated, or phased out. During the same period, 38 new programs were approved by the board. The City University of New York requires periodic program reviews at its campuses and is drafting guidelines for ad hoc reviews of particularly weak programs that fail to sustain adequate levels of activity and resources.

System Articulation

The articulation of two- and four-year institutions has not been a contested issue in New York. This may be the case, we were told, because articulation works well in the two regional subsystems, each of which encompasses both two- and four-year institutions. Both CUNY and SUNY have focused attention on improving transfer. The State University of New York has given additional funds to four-year colleges based on their enrollment of graduates of two-year campuses. And the politics of race and ethnicity at CUNY ensure continuing vigilance to make certain that successful CUNY students who are required to matriculate in a community college find appropriate upper division opportunities in baccalaureate-granting institutions.

The absence of concern about articulation at the state level may also be related to the market competition among the less visible independent institutions and the under-enrolled SUNY campuses for a declining number of high school graduates. Or it may in part be a function of the absence at the state level of any agency with specific authority or responsibility for articulation. Each subsystem gives whatever attention it considers necessary to articulation among its member institutions. The results appear acceptable to state policy officials.

CONCLUSION

New York's extensive use of market forces to support the independent sector, combined with a public higher education system that is structured to respond to political concerns, has provided state political and educational leaders with a fair amount of satisfaction over the years. This combination of forces appears to have met past challenges for the state regarding higher education. Recent efforts to increase political influence (board appointments, the governor's tax-cutting agenda) suggest that the New York structure is moving toward a system that will tilt the balance increasingly in favor of pressure for regulation and oversight. The tuition increases in the public sector have created a situation where the state is forced to provide additional aid for students, due to the entitlement nature of the student aid program. This means a shift from support for institutions toward support for students. The result for students is likely to be increased tuition. The result for public institutions is a focus on efficiency and productivity. For private institutions, the result is a growing dependence on their own institutional resources, as their "market share" of the Tuition Assistance Program is lost to the public institutions.

NOTES

1. *Chronicle of Higher Education Almanac* 43, no. 1 (September 1996), pp. 79, 81.
2. J. M. Burns, J. W. Peltason, and T. E. Cronin, *State and Local Politics: Government by the People* (Englewood Cliffs, N.J.: Prentice Hall, 1990), p. 13.
3. *Chronicle of Higher Education Almanac*, p. 79.
4. K. Halstead, *State Profiles for Higher Education 1978 to 1996: Trend Data* (Washington, D.C.: Research Associates of Washington, 1996), p. 65.
5. SUNY Office of University Relations, *Overview: State University of New York 1995* (Albany, N.Y., 1995), p. 34.
6. SUNY Board of Trustees, *Rethinking SUNY* (Albany, N.Y., 1995), Appendix C.
7. New York State Education Law, Article 125, Section 6201.
8. CICU, *The Commitment and Capacity to Serve New York State* (Albany, N.Y., 1995), p. 24.
9. E. Bernstein, "SUNY Grand Vision and Pragmatism Collide," *New York Times* (March 4, 1996), pp. A1+.
10. P. Schmidt, "State Court Overturns Cuts Ordered by City U. of New York," *Chronicle of Higher Education* (May 10, 1996), p. A41.

CHAPTER

Florida

Florida's policy framework for higher education can best be described as a mix of regulation and consumer advocacy, with legislative oversight and leadership establishing higher education priorities for the state. The state uses regulation to manage and organize its system of higher education, and to ensure that consumer priorities such as access and affordability are maintained. A strong system chancellor's office balances state forces with institutional priorities. Program planning and the use of slots in private colleges and universities help the state to maintain some market forces in its system of higher education.

Elected officials set the policy agenda for higher education through a political process that some campus actors perceive as micromanagement. The Appropriations Committees of the house and senate make the most important decisions about higher education spending. Under single-party domination, past governors have provided significant leadership on higher education issues, but with the emergence of a more competitive political system, gubernatorial influence has weakened.

Priorities for higher education in Florida must be inferred from legislative actions as well as from the statements of public officials. The high priority placed on efficiency and improved productivity is apparent from a recent legislative initiative to limit the number of state-funded credit hours for the associate's degree and baccalaureate, as well as from the governor's emphasis on performance-based budgeting and accountability. The legislature remains committed to maintaining access through low tuition.

The single governing board for all public four-year institutions in the state, the board of regents of the State University System (SUS), reacts to legislative priorities and attempts to dampen the effects of legislative actions on SUS institutions. The community colleges are organized separately from the university system, and local community college boards have similar responsibilities to the SUS Board of Regents. A statewide coordinating board for community colleges has only limited authority and no capacity for data collection or setting priorities. The Postsecondary Education Planning Commission (PEPC) has advisory responsibilities to the legislature. The state board of education (composed of the state's elected cabinet) is widely regarded as a "rubber stamp" for higher education policy decisions.

The design of Florida's higher education system represents a segmented model—though of the segmented systems we studied, Florida's is closest to a unified model. Florida's weak information system depends upon the cooperation of system and institutional leaders, which undermines its usefulness in the policy making process. The budget process relies heavily upon negotiation between legislative leaders and system leaders or local boards (in the case of the community colleges), rather than on solid information about needs and priorities. Information gathered through special legislative studies, however, provides needed data to legislators on their priorities. There is no single agency in Florida other than the legislature with responsibility for articulation and collaboration.

Florida experienced a severe recession in the early 1990s, when state revenues were stagnant for three years. The absence of a sales tax and the passage of citizen-led initiatives setting revenue and spending limits will make state funding of higher education increasingly problematic and competitive. At the same time, both the younger and older segments of the population are growing, which is placing increased pressures on social services. These conditions could pose formidable challenges for higher education in Florida in the future.

STATE CONTEXT

From 1980 to 1990, a population growth rate of 33 percent moved Florida from the seventh to the fourth largest state, with a total population of nearly 14 million. While more homogeneous than most other states in this study, Florida has a rapidly growing Hispanic population (12 percent) and a significant African-American population (14 percent).[1] The state is experiencing rapid growth in younger and older populations and ranks first in the percentage of people over age 65.[2] Florida ranks lowest among the study states in the number of new high school graduates per 1,000 population,[3] and it has the highest high school dropout rate. Florida also ranks low in the percentage of the population that has baccalaureate, graduate, or professional degrees.[4]

For many years a staunchly Democratic state, Florida has changed in recent years. In the 1994 election, Republicans won a majority in the senate and were only three votes shy of a majority in the house. Most observers believe that changes in the composition of the legislature have provided more voice to the urban areas of the state. An initiative process that allows voters to propose new laws directly through public referendum, as well as the introduction of eight-year term limits for the governor and state legislators, contributes to the sense of changing times. Florida also boasts the nation's first "sunshine" law, which requires that all meetings where the public's business is conducted be open and publicly announced. Observers suggested to us that Florida might be headed down the same path as California in terms of citizen-led initiatives focusing on fiscal restraint.

Florida's governor has been described as "weak" in terms of the powers conferred by the state constitution.[5] Although the governor can propose budgets and can veto single line items, many of those we interviewed described his budget as "unrecognizable" at the end of the legislative process, or "ignored" by the legislature altogether. The governor appoints the SUS Board of Regents and the boards of trustees for the local community colleges, as well as the members of the PEPC and the State Board of Community Colleges (SBCC). The governor's cabinet, including the commissioner of education, is elected, and comprises the state board of education. The previous governor, Bob Graham, was an influential leader on higher education issues; he made higher education a top priority and had the good fortune of working with a legislature from the same party. Since the emergence of a more competitive political environment, the governor's influence over major policy issues has weakened.

About 70 percent of the state's general fund revenues comes from sales taxes. Florida's constitution prohibits the enactment of a state income tax. The property tax is the most important revenue source for local governments, along with fees and charges. While a large temporary population comprised of tourists, visitors, and part-time residents accounts for a large portion of the state's economic activity, it also places demands on transportation, the health care system, and law enforcement. The share of the state budget devoted to higher education in Florida declined 13.6 percent from 1990 to 1995 (from 13.2 to 11.4 percent).[6] Total state appropriations to higher education over this period increased from $3.4 billion in 1990 to $4.1 billion in 1995.

Florida experienced a major recession in late 1990 that began receding slowly in early 1993. The three largest spending areas of Florida's state government are education, transportation, and health and welfare. Deep cuts came in all three areas during the recession. A "hodge-podge" of revenue enhancement strategies—including tuition increases at the state universities and community colleges, along with spending cuts—helped the state make it through the recession.[7] Public sentiment during the recession favored reduced spending rather than increased taxes, and this sentiment has not abated. Florida voters passed a property tax limitation in 1992 during the depths of the recession. Voter animosity toward property taxes has carried over into other areas, particularly user fees, making it more difficult for state leaders to find alternative revenue-generating strategies. In 1997 a constitutional amendment limited growth in all state revenues to the average growth rate in Florida personal income over the preceding five years.[8]

The legislative process drives higher education policy in Florida. Most of the important decisions about state priorities and spending are made by the House Appropriations Committee and the Senate Ways and Means Committee. Because committee chairs change frequently, higher education leaders confront a confusing and constantly changing array of priorities. The senate, which historically has had a contentious relationship with SUS, has in recent years focused on performance-based budgeting, student credit hours, tuition, and the "deregulation" of higher education. The house has been more concerned with how to accommodate the growing demand for higher education in the state, especially in relation to the number of freshmen permitted to enroll at the University of Florida (UF) and Florida State University (FSU), the two most "oversubscribed" institutions in the state.[9]

Legislative staff often conduct independent studies that result in legislation. Following a recent study, the legislature capped the state-funded credit hours a student could take. Although the state appropriation to SUS is provided as a lump sum, many provisos about expenditures are attached. Most higher education professionals do not see legislative involvement in matters of higher education policy in a positive light. Campus respondents complained bitterly to us about "micromanagement."

Independent colleges and universities have a strong influence in the state legislature, and the legislature does not hesitate to utilize the capacity of independent institutions to help meet state needs. The present staff director for the Independent Colleges and Universities of Florida, to which most of the independents belong, is also chairman of the Senate Higher Education Committee. His recent appointment caused some concerns about conflict of interest among higher education leaders.

CHARACTERISTICS AND HISTORY OF HIGHER EDUCATION

Florida's system of higher education consists of 111 institutions, including 10 campuses of the State University System (SUS), 28 public community colleges, and many privately controlled institutions (ranging from the University of Miami to three historically black colleges and a small liberal arts institution with less than 500 students). In 1994, more than 83 percent of all students were in public institutions. The state operates a relatively low-cost system of higher education with primary access through community colleges.[10] Approximately 83 percent of the state's first-time-in-college students begin their careers in the community colleges. Florida's "two-plus-two" policy and the statewide articulation agreement guarantees entry to SUS for transfers with associate of arts degrees.[11] Historically, SUS has had fairly high admission standards for first-time students. It enrolls about twice as many upper division as lower division students, and roughly two-thirds of them are community college transfers.[12]

The first university system in the state was created in 1905 when the legislature consolidated existing institutions for whites into a university for men in Gainesville (UF) and a university for women in Tallahassee (FSU). Concurrently, the State Normal School for Colored Students was designated as a postsecondary education institution, Florida Agricultural and Mechanical University (Florida A & M). The board of control, which reported to the state board of education, was also created to oversee these three institutions. The legislature maintained control over campus location and the size of buildings, the number of positions, and the expansion of academic programs. In 1956, a statewide study called for by Governor Leroy Collins led to legislative authorization for significant expansion, including the creation of a state community college system. The report also identified issues of quality, concentration, and research at upper division universities, and emphasized the need for access and equity in the new community college system.[13] In the following two decades, six new universities were established, four of them initially designated as upper division institutions. A 10th campus, Florida Gulf Coast University, opened in fall 1997.

In 1965, the legislature abolished the board of control, established a nine-member board of regents, and gave the new board specific powers to govern, regulate, coordinate, and oversee the institutions. In 1968, the executive branch of state government was reorganized and the board of regents became a unit of the Department of Education. This centralization diminished the autonomy of older institutions and led to the consolidation of university operating and building budgets. The chancellor and his staff became the chief advisors to the regents in these areas. In 1969 the regents approved a "comprehensive development plan" for SUS that provided a framework for system development. In the late 1970s the legislature strengthened the autonomy of individual campuses, focusing the regents' authority on: adopting system-wide rules and procedures; planning for the future; reviewing and evaluating campus institutional, research, and service programs; selecting presidents; and monitoring fiscal performance. The number of board members was increased from nine to 13 by the 1981 legislature in an attempt to end the perception of allegiance of each regent to a single university. Currently, members of the SUS Board of Regents are appointed by the governor and confirmed by the senate to six-year rotating terms.

A continuing debate about sharing authority among the campuses, the regents, and the legislature contributed to the establishment of the Postsecondary Education Planning Commission (PEPC), which was created through an executive order signed by Governor Bob Graham in 1980. The Postsecondary Education Planning Commission was housed in the office of the commissioner of education and was charged with preparing a master plan for postsecondary education for the state board of education. The same executive order further reduced the authority of the SUS regents by focusing their responsibilities on policy development rather than on the details of daily campus life.

The first public community college in Florida was established in 1933 as part of a local county school system approved by the state board of education. A committee of local citizens advised the county board on junior college operations. In 1955, the legislature established the Community College Council. In its 1957 master plan, the council recommended a comprehensive system of public community colleges to provide open-door, post-high school education at reasonable costs within commuting distance of 99 percent of the state's population. The last of the planned 28 community colleges was established in 1972. All of these colleges offer the first two years of a baccalaureate, vocational education, and adult continuing education. No local taxes are involved in their support.

Independent local boards of trustees with legal responsibility for maintaining and operating each community college district were established in 1968. Trustees are appointed by the governor, after consultation with local representatives. The 1979 legislature established a State Community College Coordinating Board and reorganized it in 1983 as the 13-member State Board of Community Colleges (SBCC). The State Board of Community Colleges has the delicate task of ensuring effective coordination while supporting local control by boards of trustees. Its members are appointed by the governor.

Florida's private colleges and universities enroll more than 100,000 students, about 65 percent of whom are Florida residents. While Florida's private colleges and universities enroll fewer than 17 percent of all higher education students, they account for about 36 percent of those enrolled in baccalaureate-granting institutions. Independent institutions in Florida receive state funds through students (via the state student aid programs) and through direct institutional grants designed to improve access and choice and to provide specialized educational services. State funding for private colleges and universities now exceeds $53 million annually.

The Florida system of higher education faces major growth in the next decade. By 2005, the number of high school graduates in Florida is expected to increase by 38 percent. From 1986 to 1994, participation rates increased from about 47 percent to 50 percent.[14] Increasing numbers of eligible students and rising participation rates are expected to increase the number of high school graduates in SUS by 33 percent (40,000 FTE students) and in the community colleges by 32 percent (66,000 FTE students) over the next 10 years.[15] Much of the growth will be in the southern part of the state.

Legislation passed in 1995 reduced the importance of the state's College Level Academic Skills Test (CLAST), which is a rising junior exam that a student must take prior to moving to upper division status, for sophomore students. Students are now allowed to demonstrate readiness for upper division work by scoring well on SATs or earning good grades in specified high school or college courses. The change has helped to reduce tensions between community college and legislative leaders over the use of this exam as a "gatekeeper."

Beyond maintaining or expanding access, higher education faces legislative concerns about productivity and accountability. A new law limits the number of credit hours students can take to receive an associate's degree or the baccalaureate. The law also imposes a limit of 36 credit hours for general education. Tenure is under fire, and the legislature has introduced cash incentives for good teaching. Community college presidents and university presidents have been required to meet to address issues of transfer and course requirements. And SUS and community college system leaders have been requested to submit accountability plans as a first step toward implementing performance-based budgeting.

DESIGN OF THE HIGHER EDUCATION–STATE GOVERNMENT INTERFACE

In Florida, no one group or organization is charged with the responsibility and authority to set a statewide policy agenda and cooperate with other entities to implement it. The board of education, which is composed of the elected cabinet, is the chief policy and coordinating body for public education. The board must approve all rules adopted by the SUS regents. The board also adopts and transmits the SUS legislative budget request. However, because board of education members focus primarily on their own agencies or on K–12 education, higher education policy receives little attention.

The Postsecondary Education Planning Commission, created by executive order in 1980 and given statutory authority in 1981, is the advisory body to the board of education. The commission is responsible for developing the master plan for Florida postsecondary education; it also has responsibility for reviewing and commenting on program proposals, as well as conducting research and policy analysis when requested by the legislature or the governor's office. The Postsecondary Education Planning Commission plays an important role in drawing private colleges and universities into the master plan for higher education. The commission also reviews all contracts, including the purchase of student slots in private colleges and universities. Twenty-three of the largest and most prestigious private institutions in Florida belong to the Independent Colleges and Universities of Florida, which[16] represents their interests in Tallahassee.

The Postsecondary Education Planning Commission's 12-member board, including one student, is appointed by the governor. The first board, acting as a blue ribbon commission, provided statewide direction for higher education. Since then, observers told us, the general quality of members has declined and its opportunities to influence higher education policy have weakened. The widespread perception that commission members favor community colleges contributes to reduced influence on issues that involve SUS. Because PEPC does not have a central information system, it must rely on the cooperation of the segments to provide needed information. The commission has a small staff and periodically relies on consultants to assist with special projects.

By default, the legislature is the chief policy-making body for higher education. Many observers told us they have concerns about this because the legislature tends to focus on immediate issues, not long-term problems and solutions. Many also said they believe this places too much power in the hands of legislative staff, whom university officials consider unprepared for the responsibility.

Legislative concern about access is evident from the number (29) and dollar value (about $114 million in 1995-96) of financial aid programs administered by the Office of Student Financial Assistance, whose executive director reports directly to the elected commissioner of education. Four of these aid programs have a major impact on public and private institutions. Undergraduate Scholars Grants for students attending either public or private colleges and universities in Florida are the nation's second largest merit-based program, behind Georgia's Hope Scholarships. Public Assistance Grants provide need-based awards to full-time students attending state universities or community colleges in Florida. Private Assistance Grants offer similar support for students attending in-state private colleges or universities. Resident Access Grants provide tuition assistance to full-time undergraduate students registered at accredited, independent nonprofit colleges or universities. In addition, SUS and the community colleges are authorized to reserve 5 percent of matriculation and tuition fees as student aid to be distributed by institutions. In 1994-95, tuition dollars generated about $16 million in student assistance for SUS and $11 million for community colleges.[16] Most of the aid from tuition dollars is awarded on a need basis. Florida also offers a Prepaid College Program that allows families to lock in tuition costs at a fixed rate. If the beneficiary of a plan attends a community college instead of an SUS institution, the difference in tuition is refunded. Local community colleges also have authority to grant tuition waivers.

The SUS Board of Regents was described by some as analogous to a corporate board of directors, with the chancellor as its chief executive officer. Each state university is delegated responsibility for its own organization. The chancellor has a direct line of communication to the governor and the commissioner of education.

The division of authority between the chancellor's office and the legislature appears to be fairly well understood. According to one university official, the legislature may legitimately tell the system to limit student enrollment, or conversely, take more entering freshmen than has normally been state policy. On the other hand, the legislature is not welcome to tell the board of regents that a new educational program may or may not be approved or where it should be located. It is difficult to discuss SUS in isolation from the influence of its current chancellor, whose powerful leadership was acknowledged by all. The chancellor's office gives university presidents a fair amount of latitude in establishing the missions of their institutions. The chancellor deals "head on" with the legislature, while presidents run their campuses.

Observers said they see strengths and liabilities in this arrangement. Campus administrators praised: shared resources in times of crisis (for instance, Hurricane Andrew); the effective management of competition (reducing program duplication); institutional flexibility in pursuing institutional missions; the advantage of having a national flagship institution within the system; and cost effectiveness in various services (legal staff, costs of individual governing boards). Many outside SUS criticized the bureaucracy of SUS and the costs of centralization. Some also said they are concerned that the strength of the chancellor had diminished the role of presidential leadership to "cheerleading and fund-raising." Several state officials saw the SUS central office as an impediment to addressing statewide priorities and solving problems, describing it as "reactive" to state priorities instead of helping to develop an agenda for higher education.

Strengths and weaknesses of the interface design for SUS are evident in the chain of events that followed a proposal for deregulation that was drafted by a university president and shared with legislative leaders, their staff, and the media before it was discussed with the full board of regents and with other SUS officials. The board chair chastised the president in a handwritten letter, later made public, suggesting that this type of behavior was inappropriate and, if continued, might result in the president's need to look elsewhere for employment. Editorial writers came to the president's defense, portraying the system as an entrenched bureaucracy. Legislative leaders who had been discussing the ideas with the president for several months said they believe that SUS was trying to silence him and that regents were threatened by his ideas of change and deregulation. A bill was introduced to significantly weaken the authority of the system office and change the chancellor's title to executive director. The bill was not enacted.

The system clearly operates through carefully negotiated, but often unwritten, rules of conduct. Some presidents may complain directly to the board of regents about such issues as lack of funds, but the rule is that most complaints go through the chancellor's office prior to involving the regents. The expectation is that all contact with the legislature will follow this route. Violation of this basic rule in the case of the deregulation proposal helped to produce the exceptionally strong reaction from the regents.

Florida has weak collective bargaining legislation. State University System faculty are unionized and the chancellor meets with their representatives several times during the year. If the board of regents is unable to negotiate an agreement, the legislature imposes a settlement. An SUS executive, speaking about faculty work rules and other conditions of employment, told us, "From the perspective of system control, it is better to have a weak union than no union at all."

Many people who expressed frustration over the centralization of the university system said they have similar concerns about the decentralized nature of the community colleges. Some believe that the trustee appointment process allows for little accountability to local communities. Others talked about the lack of a system-wide database that could provide better information on which to base policy decisions. Many described the State Board for Community Colleges as a weak effort to coordinate the system. Problems exist not only in the transfer of credit from two- to four-year institutions, but also within the program requirements of different community colleges. Some members of the legislature and their staff are currently trying to convene community college faculty to work through the confusion about various degree requirements.

WORK PROCESSES

The Florida system of higher education has a slightly greater capacity to engage in statewide planning than the states we have discussed in earlier chapters, in part because of the active role taken by the legislature. Data collected by the state planning agency are somewhat suspect because the information is provided by the two subsystems: the state university and community college systems. The legislature responds by conducting studies of its own. Because institutions do not have constitutional autonomy, the legislature exercises direct statutory control over some operations.

Information Management

Since PEPC does not currently manage an information database on higher education, it must rely on the willingness and cooperation of the segments to provide needed information. Enrollment projections for SUS and the community colleges are reached through an enrollment estimating conference made up of representatives from the sectors. The Postsecondary Education Planning Commission plans to develop an enrollment model to provide better projections. While the Office of Student Financial Assistance occasionally undertakes reports for the legislature, most of the policy reports on financial aid are completed by PEPC or the legislature. The Department of Education provides summary totals for state-funded financial aid to the private sector and public community colleges.

The SUS chancellor's office develops and manages its own statewide database for higher education. Most of the information on four-year institutions needed by the legislature comes from this source. Some state officials expressed general satisfaction with the quality of data and the response time generated by the system office. Others lamented the lack of a system-wide database that could provide better information on which to base policy decisions. One legislator asserted that the most significant argument for adopting performance-based budgeting for the university system is the inadequate data. And legislative staff reported frustration with the need to rely on the university system to produce the data.

Currently, most community college data are collected at the local level; no statewide database on community college students exists. To learn more about specific issues, like the number of excess credit hours students take to earn degrees, the legislature and other agencies must rely on special studies and the cooperation of the various sectors. Legislative staff complained to us about the lack of good data on the community colleges.

In addition to the data collection efforts of SUS, the individual community colleges and PEPC, the legislature produces annual statistical reports and profiles on higher education.

Budget Process

Prior to the development of the state budget, the governor, lieutenant governor, cabinet, and legislative leaders agree on revenue estimates (called "consensus estimates") for the state. All parties then work from the same estimates in developing the budget. Although the governor submits his budget to the legislature, the legislature develops its own budget. After the leaders of the house and senate agree on lump-sum levels to be provided to different areas of state government, each of the committees is responsible for setting its priorities for spending within those levels. The conference process resolves disagreement over spending priorities between the house and senate. Once the conference committees reach agreement, the two chambers usually support the outcome and the budget goes to the governor for approval.

Each campus in SUS is responsible for submitting a budget to the central office. Budgets are based on historical allocations, changes in enrollment, institutional mission, and system priorities. The State University System submits a consolidated budget through the board of education to the governor and the legislature. Because the legislature works from a different formula than the regents, the budget process can conceal differences in priorities. Several years ago the university system was given the increased flexibility of a single lump-sum budget for the system, to which the legislature typically attaches expenditure provisos. The central office allocates funds to the institutions based on a series of formulas. The institutions then have the flexibility to move dollars among program areas and among types of expenditures.

Formulas notwithstanding, higher education officials are not always clear about how each year's budget is determined. "In the final analysis," said one, "the budget amount for SUS is negotiated with the legislature." Currently, the board of regents cannot act unilaterally on setting tuition for the system. Legislative approval for appropriating tuition dollars requires compromises to be reached on tuition levels each year.

Community colleges in Florida do not receive local funds unless a referendum has passed that allows the district to institute a tax to support community colleges. The success rates for such referenda are quite low. Full-time-equivalent enrollment figures for each community college are established every funding session and are instrumental in determining general revenue funds. The state provides a lump sum to each community college and expects each local board of trustees to develop priorities for programs that meet local needs. The legislature also provides the local boards of trustees with the flexibility and responsibility to set policy on pay and salary increases. In addition, each year the legislature establishes an average student fee charge; local boards have the flexibility to set their fees anywhere within 10 percent above or below this average amount. The legislature also provides categorical funding for special projects or state priorities.

While enrollment is the primary driver of the funding formula for the community colleges, the formula takes into account the base budget from the previous year, the costs to continue operation, and the enrollment workload. Additionally, the formula accounts for the need for new facilities and new programs. The legislature has decided to hold the community colleges harmless with regard to enrollment losses, especially if the declines are due to an improving economy or a decline in the number of high school graduates. This has introduced some inequity in funding among the colleges, with some rural community colleges spending as much as $800 more per student than most urban districts.

All state agencies in Florida are in the process of moving toward performance-based budgeting, a product of Governor Lawton Chiles's efforts to "reinvent" government. According to the governor's office, each state agency will be required to identify goals that they intend to reach over a defined period of time. Specific measures will be developed to determine if the agency is meeting its goals, and the achievement of these goals will be linked to the budgeting process. In exchange for specifically identifying goals and establishing measures to assess progress toward those goals, agencies will be given a lump sum of money with increased management flexibility.

Both SUS and the community college system have been requested to submit accountability plans, the first step in implementing performance-based budgeting. The community colleges, the first to use the performance-based budgeting system, will be the "guinea pigs," as described by legislative staff. The first performance-based budget was submitted to the legislature by the community colleges in FY98. Three major areas driving the performance-based budget for the community colleges are measures of effectiveness related to the A.A. degree, the A.S. degree, and remedial and college preparatory coursework. The university system will be required by the legislature to produce a performance-based budget in the next few years.

To ease community colleges into the performance-based budgeting plan, the legislature challenged community colleges and area technical centers to place 5 percent of their budgets in an incentive program that the legislature would support with an additional $12 million. The 5 percent, plus more, could be earned back by demonstrating success on outcome standards related to completion and graduation rates and placement. Eventually, 20 of the 28 community colleges signed up for this program.

Program Planning and Review

The Postsecondary Education Planning Commission develops the master plan for Florida postsecondary education and has responsibility for reviewing and commenting on program proposals. The 1993 master plan calls for Florida to: (1) increase the utilization of independent schools, colleges, and universities to improve access to a degree; (2) include the independent sector in attaining one coordinated system of education in the state and in improving the number of minority teachers; and (3) improve the use of non-state resources and expand access in areas of unmet state need.[17] In the past, little has been asked of independent colleges and universities in return for state funds. This, however, will change in the near future. Under new legislation that directs

PEPC to develop a statewide master plan for higher education, the private colleges and universities will also be asked to submit a strategic plan to be coordinated with the other sectors of higher education.

How to manage the expected growth in enrollment while maintaining access is the number one planning issue. One strategy proposed by the board of regents and supported by the governor's office, the commissioner of education, and key leaders in the house is to "expand to allow 20 percent of Florida high school graduates to enroll as first-time-in-college (FTIC) students at state universities." From 1994, when the issue was first studied, to 1996, the SUS share of FTIC students has grown steadily from about 15 to 16.9 percent. Representatives of the community colleges have argued that the university system should not increase the number of first-time freshmen that it admits and PEPC has supported them on this point, leading to SUS charges of bias within PEPC.

During 1995, PEPC recommended that the legislative funding formula for SUS include a new allocation process designed to fund FTIC students for the costs of only lower level instruction. The Postsecondary Education Planning Commission stated:

> The commission recognizes and supports the importance of public service and research in the state universities but believes that these functions should not be components of undergraduate enrollment funding. If it continues to be necessary to fund these functions as a part of undergraduate enrollment, they should be funded only as a component of upper level enrollment growth.[18]

The Postsecondary Education Planning Commission has also raised questions about the number of Florida high school students eligible for SUS and the need for better data before changing the current policy, which allows 16.9 percent of first-time freshmen to enroll at SUS.

Largely as a result of this disagreement over FTIC freshmen, the legislature passed language that required PEPC to complete its master planning process before the university system, community college system, and private and independent colleges completed their strategic plans. The legislation also encouraged these subsystems of higher education to explain how their institutions fit into the statewide master plan.

Traditionally, the master plan provided limitations on the number of research universities in Florida. State officials told us that the master plan no longer effectively serves this purpose and that the only constraints on changing institutional mission are system-wide program approval mechanisms and the amount of money appropriated by the legislature. Competition among various programs tends to occur where two institutions are in proximity (such as FSU and Florida A & M, which are both in Tallahassee).

Virtually no statewide planning occurs that unifies the various institutions responsible for vocational and occupational education in the state. As a result, there is some duplication between the vocational programs offered by community colleges and those offered by technical centers under school district supervision.

System Articulation

Florida's two-plus-two policy promotes the recognition and utilization of the community colleges as the primary point of entry for postsecondary education. A statewide articulation agreement guarantees community college transfers (who have associate of arts degrees) admission to the upper division of one of the state universities. They are not guaranteed admission, however, to a specific program or institution. The transition of students through the education system is supported by the Articulation Coordinating Committee, the statewide course numbering system, discipline-specific articulation agreements among institutions, a network of institutional articulation officers, and acceleration mechanisms, such as dual enrollment, early admission, and credit by examination.[19] In spite of the two-plus-two policy, serious articulation problems remain.

The Postsecondary Education Planning Commission has documented in a recent report that "a bottleneck currently exists for both university native students and community college transfer students as they enter [the] upper division of the university."[20] The commission cites resource constraints and the growth in lower division enrollment in both sectors as the primary culprits for the shortfall in the number of courses offered, the number of faculty utilized, and the space available for more classes. Many students transfer to four-year institutions prior to completing the associate's degree. Some students transfer with 60 credits, but do not complete the general education course credits. Many transfer students may get credit for their coursework, but that credit does not meet the specific requirements of individual institutions. Problems exist not only in the transfer of credit from two- to four-year institutions, but also within the program requirements of different community colleges, particularly in areas such as nursing.

Legislators learned as a result of their credit-hour study that many of the excess credits that students accumulate are taken by those who begin their higher education in community colleges. This has heightened interest in better articulation and has led them to convene community college and university presidents to address the issues of transfer and course requirements for various fields.

In response to anticipated student growth, two alternatives are under consideration that would place additional pressures on articulation. In the first, community college campuses would be authorized to offer coursework for the baccalaureate that would be conferred by four-year institutions. A second proposal, recommended in a recent report from the Business Higher Education Partnership, would make better use of private colleges and universities by having the state purchase student spaces in those institutions.[21] Already, the State Board of Community Colleges has been working with private institutions to develop a comprehensive articulation agreement.

CONCLUSION

Many observers of Florida higher education have concerns about the structure of their higher education system, including: (1) the limited capacity to address issues that the various sectors of higher education have in common (for example, vocational education and general education for students seeking the baccalaureate); (2) lack of a statewide database for effective policy decision making; (3) legislative interference in higher education operational issues; (4) lack of a statewide agenda for higher education; and (5) excessive centralization in SUS and excessive decentralization in the community college system. At the same time, there is little sentiment for change. In a recent report, the influential Florida Business/Higher Education Partnership stated:

> Florida has an excellent structure for higher education. In our judgment, the form of governance and organization for Florida's 10 state universities, 28 community colleges, and 23 accredited private universities and colleges has provided Florida with a superb system.[22]

The combination of state regulation and consumer advocacy inherent in the Florida model appears to have protected public needs regarding higher education in the state, particularly in the early 1990s. The state's system of higher education faces contextual transformations, however, including term limits, revenue restrictions, fiscal changes, and demographic shifts, all of which will challenge legislators and higher education leaders to continue to find appropriate balances between institutional and market forces.

NOTES

1. *Chronicle of Higher Education Almanac* 43, no. 1 (September 1996), pp. 49–50.
2. S. MacManus, "Florida: Reinvention Derailed," in *The Fiscal Crisis of the States: Lessons for the Future*, ed. S. D. Gold (Washington, D.C.: Georgetown University Press, 1995), p. 205.
3. K. Halstead, *State Profiles for Higher Education 1978 to 1996: Trend Data* (Washington, D.C.: Research Associates of Washington, 1996), p. 17.
4. *Chronicle of Higher Education Almanac* 43, pp. 49–50.
5. J. M. Burns, J. W. Peltason, and T. E. Cronin, *State and Local Politics: Government by the People* (Englewood Cliffs, N.J.: Prentice Hall 1990), p. 113.

6. S. D. Gold, *State Spending Patterns in the 1990s* (Albany, N.Y.: Center for the Study of the States, 1995).

7. S. MacManus, "Florida: Reinvention Derailed," p. 214.

8. State of Florida, "Constitutional Limitation on State Revenues," brochure, Tallahassee, Fla., 1995.

9. "Oversubscribed" describes those institutions where more eligible students apply than can be accommodated.

10. K. Halstead, "Quantitative Analysis of the Environment, Performance and Operation Actions of Eight State Public Higher Education Systems," commissioned by the California Higher Education Policy Center, San Jose, Calif., 1995.

11. PEPC, *Access to the Baccalaureate Degree in Florida: Report and Recommendations*, Report 4 (Tallahassee, Fla., 1994).

12. Florida State Senate, Ways and Means Committee, *Education in Florida, 1995-96 Edition* (Tallahassee, Fla., 1996).

13. PEPC, *The Structure of Public Postsecondary Education in Florida: Report and Recommendations of the Florida Postsecondary Education Planning Commission*, Report 9 (Tallahassee, Fla., 1990).

14. *Postsecondary Education Opportunity*, no. 49 (Iowa City, Iowa: Mortenson Research Seminar on Public Policy Analysis of Opportunity for Postsecondary Education, July 1996).

15. Ibid.

16. Florida State Department of Education, Office of Student Financial Aid, *State Student Aid Expenditures Report* (Tallahassee, Fla., 1991-92 to 1994-95 editions).

17. PEPC, *Access to the Baccalaureate Degree in Florida*.

18. Ibid., p. 15.

19. Ibid.

20. Ibid., p. 9.

21. Business/Higher Education Partnership. *The Emerging Catastrophe and How to Prevent It* (Tallahassee, Fla., 1996).

22. Ibid, p. 3.

CHAPTER 6

Georgia

Of the seven states in our study, Georgia provides the most simply designed system of higher education: a unified system with constitutional autonomy. In 1931, all degree-granting public institutions of higher education were placed under the supervision of a single governing board, the board of regents of the University System of Georgia (USG). Following a 1941 attempt by the governor to intervene in the hiring and firing of administrators, the state ratified an amendment that gave the board constitutional status to govern, control, and manage the system. In 1996, USG included 15 two-year and 19 four-year institutions. Even though private institutions account for about 20 percent of the higher education enrollments in Georgia, they have not been actively involved in discussions of state policy issues.

The unified structure of Georgia's system of higher education is closely overseen by the governor, who exercises his influence through the budget process and through appointment of the board of regents. The governor can set priorities for higher education, but because of constitutional autonomy, these priorities must often be addressed through nontraditional mechanisms. To address relatively poor college-going rates in the state, the governor instituted a scholarship program in 1993 that is funded by the state lottery. This program, Helping Outstanding Pupils Educationally (HOPE), provides full tuition and fees to students who maintain at least a B average in high school and enroll in a public institution in Georgia. Those who maintain at least a B average in college continue to receive the award. The HOPE scholarships provide an example of how the Georgia system exhibits characteristics of a consumer advocacy policy environment.

While elected leaders actively identify and support priorities for higher education, as evidenced by the focus on access through the HOPE scholarships, many of the priorities arise from within the constitutionally autonomous public system. At the same time, the current chancellor, who is highly regarded by elected leaders, spends much of his time communicating with the governor and legislators to ensure support for priorities that, if not announced by elected leaders, are cleared with them in advance.

The USG Board of Regents has the power to define institutional missions, to determine the array and size of institutions in the system, to allocate funds to institutions, and to determine how much higher education will cost. Upon recommendation of the chancellor, the board acts upon all institutional proposals regarding appointments (faculty, research, administrative, and other employees, including institutional presidents). Through its chancellor, the board can also set admission standards and limit enrollments. Because USG enjoys constitutional status, the only real power reserved to state government is determining how much state money the system will receive.

The effectiveness of board management of the four work processes depends to a large extent upon executive leadership. The system makes strong use of strategic planning, but provides less information to the state on performance than federal systems generally provide, partly to limit the capacity of external actors to insert themselves into system decisions. Despite providing less information, the system's communication with state government is quite good because the system maintains a single point of contact for the governor and legislators. With strong executive leadership, the system's program review processes enable it to prevent mission creep, ensure program quality, and avoid unnecessary program duplication. The board uses the budgeting process to support strategic objectives. The inclusion of two- and four-year institutions in the same system promotes effective articulation and transfer. The board of regents does not generally consider the inclusion of private institutions to be part of its planning responsibility. When elected leaders have confidence in system leadership, the unified system requires little oversight from state government.

STATE CONTEXT

With a population of 7.1 million people, Georgia is the 10th most populous state in the country. The state has grown significantly over the last two decades. The Atlanta metropolitan area—which hosted the Olympic games in 1996 and is experiencing substantial in-migration—has helped Georgia become one of the most economically vibrant of the 50 states. Georgia has a relatively low per capita income ($21,300), but it also has a lower-than-average percentage of its population in poverty.[1] Georgia is about average relative to other study states in the percentage of its population that has a baccalaureate or professional degree, as well as in the number of new high school graduates per 1,000 population.[2]

The powers conferred upon the governor by the state constitution have been described as "moderate," largely due to the governor's line-item veto authority (which is exercised regularly) and his appointment powers.[3] Democrat Zell Miller served 16 years as lieutenant governor prior to his election to governor in 1990. In his first gubernatorial campaign, the governor called for the establishment of a lottery whose proceeds would support education. This was a tough sell to many Georgians who consider gambling to conflict with their religious beliefs, but in November 1992, voters approved a constitutional amendment allowing the lottery to operate. Miller was reelected in 1994 for a second four-year term (and his last under Georgia law) by a very slim margin—largely, most believe, because of his education initiatives. The governor is perceived as "middle of the road," "pragmatic," and able to work successfully with legislators from both political parties.[4]

Governor Miller has been able to take such political issues as privatization and tax cuts away from his Republican opponents. In early 1995, he formed a commission to examine privatization of a wide range of state services, including computer services, medical facilities, and prisons.[5] The commission's discussions have included higher education as well, with consideration given to privatizing the state's student aid agency. The governor vetoed a tax cut proposal passed by the 1995 assembly at the last hour on the grounds that it was unconstitutional. The following year he proposed his own tax reduction package that passed swiftly.

Despite being granted modest powers by the state constitution, Governor Miller has exercised a good deal of influence over higher education through appointments to the USG Board of Regents and through his authority over the budget process. Governor Miller was described to us as an "education governor" who has made improvements in higher education. We were told frequently that Miller's experience as a college professor before entering politics is one reason for his support. His second inaugural speech focused exclusively on education issues. A legislator told us, "He has a commitment to education that is not just political rhetoric." This commitment is most evident in his designation of lottery funds to education. The governor was said to "jealously guard" the use of lottery money for three specific initiatives: a focus on pre-kindergarten at-risk children; an emphasis on technology; and HOPE scholarships, which have become a model for creating a national scholarship program. Through these scholarships, the governor has attempted to increase participation in postsecondary education and to improve student performance.

All seats in Georgia's general assembly, which meets 40 days each year, are up for reelection every two years. In 1995-96, both houses had a Democratic majority, though the Republicans gained a significant number of seats in the 1994 elections.[6] While the Senate Higher Education Committee and the House Committee on the University System of Georgia technically have responsibility for policy issues, the appropriations committees in both houses in fact have the most direct impact on higher education. The chair of the higher education committee in each chamber, however, typically chairs the Appropriations Subcommittee for USG, which provides these members with more influence than in other states, where higher education committees typically are not connected to the appropriations process.

During our visits there was a good level of communications among the USG chancellor and key legislators. The central office handles relationships with the assembly, although institutional presidents talk to their own representatives, presumably in the interests of the system. Because USG has constitutional autonomy, the only real levers for change are provided by new money or new initiatives. Legislators and university administrators agree that the assembly has "kept its meddling in higher education to a minimum" and that it respects the authority and responsibilities of the board of regents. While the assembly has been supportive of higher education, the high turnover of legislators over the last four to six years has left no towering figures responsible for higher education in the assembly.

Some legislators told us that the assembly needs to do a better job of holding institutions accountable, even though they have constitutional autonomy. According to one legislator, "We don't have the oversight we should have from a policy perspective. We could be stronger within our existing system." Another legislator suggested that while there has not been much scrutiny of the money spent in previous years, questions will soon be asked by legislators who want to see results. The chancellor has tried to anticipate these developments by presenting a voluntary annual accountability report.

Higher education has been the beneficiary of a strong economy and a supportive governor. After a decline in state appropriations in the early 1990s, USG enjoyed increases in state appropriations of 6, 13, and 20 percent for fiscal years 1993, 1994, and 1995, respectively.[7] State finances, which rely on income, sales, and property taxes, are in "excellent shape," according to a recent national publication on state policy.[8] Employment growth in the state during the early 1990s was more than 12 percent, compared to a national average increase of 3 percent for the same period.[9] Most people we spoke with believe that the state's economy will continue its growth for several years, but some have predicted a downturn. State revenue increases are projected to slow over the next four to five years, and the state passed a tax reduction package that will essentially eliminate the sales tax on food over a three-year period.

To address potential revenue declines, the governor called on all state agencies in the 1996 budget process to find 5 percent of their previous year's budget that could be eliminated, and then propose how they would reinvest it in their highest priority areas. In their overall budget request, agencies were directed to ask for no more than a 6.5 percent increase (the estimated rate of economic growth) over their budgets for the previous fiscal year. Salaries and capital projects were not included as part of this limit. Depending on how the governor and general assembly assessed their redirection of funds, agencies were told to expect from 95 to 106.5 percent of the previous year's budget.

CHARACTERISTICS AND HISTORY OF HIGHER EDUCATION

In the fall of 1995, the 34 institutions comprising USG enrolled more than 206,000 students, making it the fourth largest public system of higher education in the country. This number represents an increase of 50 percent from the 136,000 students enrolled in 1985. Enrollment increased 156 percent in two-year colleges; 14 percent in research institutions, which still award the largest proportion of degrees; 73 percent in regional universities; and 49 percent in senior colleges. Ninety percent of all students were Georgia residents. About 37 percent attended part-time, and 20 percent were African Americans.[10] The number of new high school graduates in the state is expected to grow from 70,930 in 1996-97 to 91,930 in 2006-07, an increase of 30 percent.[11] The chancellor's office projects that higher education enrollment will increase by approximately 11 percent during this time. Part of the enrollment growth is projected to be caused by the state's concerted efforts to increase aspirations for college among all high school graduates.

Today's USG grew out of a 1931 consolidation of 26 diverse institutions—including universities, senior colleges, historically black colleges, junior colleges, A & M schools, and agricultural experiment stations—under an 11-member board of regents appointed by the governor. In 1941, 10 institutions were disaccredited by the Southern Association of Schools and Colleges because of "unprecedented and unjustifiable political interference," particularly on the part of Governor Gene Talmadge. In the election that followed, Talmadge was defeated by Ellis Arnall, who, soon after taking office, submitted an amendment to grant constitutional authority to the board.[12] The amendment, passed in 1943, created a board of 15 members (10 from congressional districts, five from the state at large) that no longer included the governor as an *ex officio* member. Board members were appointed by the governor for seven-year terms, subject to what has generally amounted to *pro forma* approval by the senate. Slight modifications were made when Georgia revised its constitution in 1982. Vacancies on the board can no longer be filled temporarily by appointment by the regents. In addition, the general assembly must approve the establishment of new public colleges or universities and any changes in the missions of institutions established after 1982.[13]

The 34 institutions in USG are divided into four categories: research universities, regional universities, state universities and senior colleges, and two-year colleges. The research universities include the University of Georgia, the Georgia Institute of Technology, the Medical College of Georgia, and Georgia State University. The two regional universities include Georgia Southern University and Valdosta State University. There are 13 state universities and senior colleges and 15 two-year colleges. The two largest institutions, the University of Georgia and Georgia State University, enroll 29,000 and 24,000 students, respectively. Of the senior colleges, only one institution (Kennesaw State University) enrolls more than 10,000 students; most have enrollments of less than 5,000. DeKalb College, with more than 16,000 students, is the largest of the two-year institutions; all other two-year colleges have enrollments under 5,000.

In fiscal year 1995, the total budget for USG was $2.2 billion, with $1.1 billion coming from state appropriations. This accounted for approximately 12.5 percent of the state budget. In fiscal year 1995, the system's four major research universities accounted for over 47 percent of the system's budget, compared with 19 percent for the senior colleges and 11 percent for the two-year colleges.[14] State policy calls for tuition to be set at 25 percent of the cost of instruction. In fiscal year 1995, tuition averaged $1,995 at the research universities, $1,494 at the senior colleges, and $1,020 at the two-year colleges. There were double-digit increases in tuition in the mid-1980s, but annual tuition increases have averaged about 4 percent for the past seven years. Students and their families contribute on average 24 percent of the total cost of higher education (which is measured by state appropriations plus tuition)— compared to a national average of 32 percent.[15] Out-of-state students will be asked to pay the full cost of their education by 1998.

Comprehensive research universities are responsible for graduate education, professional education, research, and public service. Regional universities can establish doctoral programs in specialized areas that are responsive to the demands of their communities and compatible with institutional missions. Senior colleges offer baccalaureate programs that are not as comprehensive as those of universities; their faculty research is oriented toward instructional effectiveness. Graduate programs at senior colleges are confined to the master's level in high-demand areas. Two-year colleges offer the first two years of academic coursework and are the primary provider of developmental studies.[16]

The category of "regional university" was established in 1990 to respond to the requests by those in the southern part of the state for a full university.[17]

The new designation established Georgia Southern as a regional university with two additional colleges, Armstrong State and Savannah State, designated as "affiliates." Each affiliated institution was to remain independent but participate in the graduate and research activities of the new regional university. Presidents of the two colleges would also be "provosts" of Georgia Southern. In 1994, the chancellor's office suggested that the state remove the designation of "affiliate" and authorize Armstrong State and Savannah State to offer graduate programs and confer graduate degrees. According to the regents, the change will retain a "regional approach to graduate programming" while "vesting" program authority more clearly.[18]

Most of those we interviewed told us that the distinction between senior colleges and regional universities has very little meaning. Senior colleges have argued that they should be accorded the "increase in status" that comes with being a regional university. The board of regents, concerned by what some perceive as continuing tendencies toward mission creep, has in the past threatened to change the system structure, possibly by breaking it up and moving to more of a regional organization. Strengthened by new appointments and a new chancellor, however, the board, with the assistance of powerful legislators, has turned its attention to stopping change-in-status efforts, with the hope of getting away from the terminology of status altogether.

Two-year colleges in USG are similar to traditional "junior colleges," providing the first two years of the baccalaureate curriculum. The colleges also offer vocational programs, but they have never been called community colleges and not every community has access to a two-year institution. Their inclusion in USG has been a source of controversy almost since the establishment of the consolidated system in the 1930s. The Strayer Report, written in 1949, recommended changing the two-year colleges to local institutions under the supervision of the state board of education.[19] Opponents to including two-year colleges in USG told us that the absence of a community college subsystem is a weakness. They said that two-year institutions "hold the university system back" on many issues, level the system downward, and require an inordinate amount of time to handle issues regarding transfer and the core curriculum. In contrast, the chancellor and regents described two-year colleges as the "cornerstone of access." Others who shared this perspective pointed to the greater cooperation permitted by the consolidated system and noted the advantages of addressing transfer and articulation within a single statewide system. They praised system leadership as a key ingredient in such collaborative initiatives as transfer, the establishment of a rising junior test, and mandated developmental studies. To encourage more students to begin at two-year colleges, USG reduced tuition at these institutions by 5 percent at the same time that tuition rose at the four-year institutions by the same percentage.

Georgia's 44 private colleges and universities accommodate approximately 21 percent of the state's higher education enrollment.[20] There is a great variety of institutions, including small religious colleges and women's colleges, military institutions, major research universities such as Emory and Mercer Universities, and some of the nation's most prestigious colleges and universities that have historically served African-American students. According to one state official, "Private institutions provide an education that is not available in the public institutions," particularly through the religious and military institutions.

The Department of Technical and Adult Education (DTAE) administers 34 technical institutes that provide adult literacy training, continuing education, customized training for business and industry, and technical education to the associate's degree level. In fiscal year 1995, DTAE enrolled 223,450 students, including 69,327 in credit courses and 154,123 in noncredit courses. The Department of Technical and Adult Education is governed by a 16-member board that is appointed by the governor. In fiscal year 1996, DTAE received $205 million from state funds, less than 2 percent of the state budget.[21]

The Georgia Student Finance Commission oversees HOPE scholarships, tuition equalization grants, and a number of smaller grant programs such as military scholarships, law enforcement grants, and other legislative initiatives. The USG chancellor describes HOPE scholarships as "Georgia's GI Bill." About 50 percent of high school graduates are eligible for HOPE scholarships under these guidelines. Students who maintain at least a 3.0 GPA in college continue to receive the scholarship for four years. The class entering in 2000 will be required to have at least a 3.0 GPA in the core disciplines in high school, a change that is expected to significantly reduce the percentage of eligible graduates.[22] Helping Outstanding Pupils Educationally scholarships of $1,500 per year are available to Georgia residents who attend private institutions. Low-income students who are eligible for the HOPE program but who are receiving federal grants have their HOPE awards decreased by the amount of federal aid they receive. Critics of the HOPE program charge that since it provides no additional money to the state's poorest students, it assists only those in the middle and upper income brackets. Nonetheless, the program is generally seen as a model that uses a market strategy to encourage access in a state that has not historically placed a high priority on higher education.

Since the inception of the HOPE scholarships in 1993, more than 191,000 students have received them. Total state funding for student financial aid has grown by more than 700 percent. In 1995-96, 43,150 students at USG institutions, 43,840 students at technical institutes, and 29,640 students at independent institutions were beneficiaries of the HOPE program.[23] In the same year, more than 90 percent of the Georgia resident freshmen at the University of Georgia and the Georgia Institute of Technology received these awards.[24] Additional HOPE funding is given to students who plan to go into teaching (and maintain at least a 3.6 GPA), as well as to graduate students who participate in a small number of high-demand teacher education areas. The goal of these programs is to attract the best students as teachers in Georgia.

DESIGN OF THE HIGHER EDUCATION–STATE GOVERNMENT INTERFACE

The legislative intent in creating USG was to unify and coordinate the work of member institutions, to integrate the educational program, and to free the state from wasteful duplication while still providing maximum educational opportunity.[25] After the creation of USG, institutions no longer were to function as separate, competitive entities. To insulate USG from undue political interference, the board of regents was given authority to govern, control, and manage the system; including program approval or discontinuation, allocation of the budget, facilities construction, and decisions on adding, closing, or merging institutions.

The regents operate through six standing committees: executive; education, research, and extension; real estate and facilities; financial and business; audit; organization and law; and strategic planning. Observers told us that the regents do not micromanage, nor are they a rubber stamp for the chancellor's office. Focusing primarily on statewide concerns, the board leaves day-to-day details to the central office and the chancellor. Most significant decisions are made after consultation with the governor. The assembly rarely considers legislation that has not previously been reviewed by the board of regents.

A chancellor appointed by the board serves as its executive officer and as the chief administrative officer for USG. The chancellor participates in all board meetings and committee activities but does not have the authority to vote. The position has very broad powers and responsibilities for the system, including approval of "all institutional recommendations regarding faculty, research, administrative, and other employee appointments," before they are submitted to the board.[26] He is also responsible for presenting to the board the suggested allocation of state appropriations to the institutions.[27] He recommends the appointment of institutional presidents, who report directly to him, as well as all employees of the central office.

A new chancellor took office shortly before our study began, marking the first time in more than 30 years that the board of regents had selected someone from outside the state for this position. The new chancellor arrived with a very aggressive agenda for change that the regents welcomed. After two years on the job, he was well respected by the governor and assembly, and had been able to "get what he wanted" from them, according to a legislative staff member. Part of the secret of his success is good communication. He walks the halls during legislative sessions, staying in touch with the leadership and developing their trust in him. In addition, he has regular conversations with the governor.

The principal role of the system office is to provide leadership, especially in the area of strategic planning; to advocate for resources for the system; and to make sure that money for higher education in Georgia is well spent. One of the chancellor's first actions was to assess the organization of the system office. Every process was reviewed to assess the value that it added. As a result of the study, some processes were discontinued and several vice chancellor positions eliminated. Through this reorganization, the chancellor tried to send two messages: the importance of setting priorities for academic programs, human resources, and capital development; and the importance of collaborating across organizational boundaries.

Institutional presidents in Georgia are a step or two removed from the political process. They serve on an advisory council that meets at least quarterly and makes educational and administrative recommendations through the chancellor to the board of regents. The chancellor expects campus presidents to establish a consensus opinion for each major issue, speaking "with one voice" for the system. Presidents are asked to lobby individual legislators "in the name of the system" rather than for their own institutions. One campus president told us, "We are all a part of a single vision and we understand our individual role and mission within that vision." The chancellor meets in a retreat format with presidents, both in large groups and by institutional type. Agendas at these meetings, said one president, are "very tangible and real," dealing with issues like budgets, planning, and how to talk with elected officials about past and future state investments in higher education.

Campus presidents do not always attend board meetings unless called in by the chancellor for a specific purpose. In periods when chancellors have been weak, institutional presidents have had more authority. We were told, for example, about a weak chancellor in the early 1990s who tolerated a great deal of mission creep among institutions as presidents sought to improve the "status" of their institutions. While there are some tensions and difficulties in working with a consolidated board, most said the system has "worked reasonably well" in Georgia. One president said that he would like to be able to act in a more entrepreneurial way at times, but that "we've been able to work that out pretty effectively."

Opinions differ on relationships between public and private institutions. One representative from the private sector said, "Georgia does not have much history of animosity." A USG counterpart suggested, however, that there is "a fair amount of tension" between the two because of competition for state dollars. About 25 private institutions belong to a lobbying organization called the Association of Independent Colleges and Universities in Georgia. This group focuses primarily on maintaining information about and supporting the tuition equalization grants, keeping the general assembly informed about private institutions, and fine-tuning the HOPE scholarship program.

Most collaboration between public and private institutions occurs locally. Perhaps the best example is the University Centers of Georgia, an organization composed of about 18 public and private institutions in the Atlanta area, as well as the University of Georgia at Athens. Presidents of the member institutions rotate the responsibility for serving as chair annually. Activities include a cross-registration program, a speaker series, and an inter-library loan program. Representatives of the private sector, predicting that there would be more cooperation over the next decade in preventing duplication of programs, pointed to the state's purchase of medical school slots in private institutions. The absence of uniform data encompassing independent colleges and universities, however, makes it difficult for anyone to know how effectively such institutions are being used.

There is no direct state aid to independent colleges in Georgia, but students attending the independent institutions receive state grants in two ways. Tuition equalization grants provide Georgia residents who attend an independent college or university with $1,000 from the state. Such students may also receive an additional $1,500 per year from the HOPE scholarship fund. With the creation of the HOPE program, argued one state official, the use of aid to encourage students to attend private institutions has been somewhat "revitalized." And in fiscal year 1996-97, the HOPE grant for students at private institutions increased to $3,000. However, many told us that HOPE scholarships make public institutions so attractive (because tuition is free to those who qualify for the scholarships) that students are less likely to enroll in independent institutions.

WORK PROCESSES

The board of regents coordinates all of the key work processes in Georgia. The board and the chancellor's office have sought to make institutions more responsive to system-wide priorities through a strategic planning process that is linked to the budget. At the time of our study, additional budget dollars above base amounts were tied to those priorities, and as a result the system was considered by policy makers to be responsive to state needs.

Information Management

The University System of Georgia has attached relatively little importance to collecting data and making information about the system and its performance available to the public and the policy community. A president told us that information is collected, and, while not used to a significant extent in decision-making processes, is available if anyone wants it. We were also told that there are few reporting requirements within the system, and that faculty and presidents like this arrangement because they do not have to produce many reports. A legislator said that as far as he knows there is not a great deal of information coming from the system to the assembly. A state official pointed out that the central office of the board of regents is a bureaucracy and that it is often difficult to get information from them. "Even though Georgia has a consolidated system," said one official, "differences in institutions and the way they gather information make cross-institutional comparisons difficult."

All of this may change. While there is currently no accountability legislation in the state, many of those we interviewed said that legislators are interested in accountability and assurances about the use of state money. According to one USG official, "The issue of accountability is one that we . . . feel strongly about and have tried to address before the legislature comes to us with specific mandates." Advances in technology may also lead to improvements. No one we spoke with said that withholding information is a conscious USG strategy. Rather, the lack of good information seems to be simply an oversight—one that can be tolerated particularly easily within a system protected by constitutional status.

Budget Process

Georgia funds higher education through three appropriations: one for USG, one for the Georgia Student Finance Commission, and one for DTAE. Appropriations for the Student Finance Commission include money from the Lottery for Education account (specifically for the HOPE scholarships) as well as general fund dollars for other state scholarship programs.

The regents submit a unified budget to the governor that is divided into two main components: formula and non-formula budgets. The formula budget, which accounts for 90 to 95 percent of state appropriations to USG, includes costs of instruction and special initiatives for improvement. A salary request is inserted into the formula budget after agreement has been reached with the assembly and governor on the rate increase. The non-formula budget provides funding directly to the institutions for special initiatives. General obligation bond requests include regular priority projects, payback projects, and minor capital outlay projects.

The governor's Office of Planning and Budget receives the regents' request and develops the governor's budget. As staff members consider the regents' request, they communicate primarily with policy and budget officials from the USG central office rather than with individual institutions. After the governor's budget is submitted to the assembly, there is typically not much negotiation or argument over the formula request; most legislative battles are over special requests in the non-formula budget. Although the governor can veto special initiatives, he must veto entire items and cannot simply reduce funding amounts.

Once the assembly and governor have approved a budget, the USG Board of Regents makes lump-sum allocations to individual institutions. These allocations, according to most individuals we spoke with, are based primarily on the previous year's budget. The regents do, however, take into account possible changes in institutional income. For example, when tuition at two-year colleges was lowered by 5 percent in fiscal year 1996, the system made sure that the institutions' overall budgets were not hurt by the reduction in tuition income. While the governor and assembly can state their priorities for appropriations, the regents are free to allocate as they see fit. The regents' budget allocation process is very political in its own right, said one legislative staff member, but the politics occur between institutions and the board rather than with the governor or assembly. This arrangement makes it difficult for the governor or assembly to institute real policy changes without the support of the regents. For the past several years, faculty salaries have been a top priority for all three. The goal is to increase average faculty salaries so that they are the highest of the Southern Regional Education Board (SREB) states. In fiscal year 1996, the governor committed to increase faculty salaries 6 percent per year for four consecutive years; by the time of our study, two 6 percent increases had been granted.

To address the governor's requirement (in the 1995-96 budget) that all state agencies redirect budget savings to meet agency priorities, the board of regents said that it would use a 1.7 percent increase in new formula funding for incentive purposes. The regents asked institutions for proposals for collaborative activities or programs that would establish patterns of national excellence. Approximately 21 collaborative activities and three "patterns of national excellence" were funded.

Also in the 1995-96 budget session, the governor recommended funding for eight special student-centered and technology-driven initiatives amounting to $43.8 million. These initiatives included connecting teachers and technology, purchasing advanced technological equipment for classrooms and laboratories at two-year institutions, and establishing a statewide electronic library. The emphasis on special funding initiatives continued with the 1997 request, which called for preschool-to-college (P–16) reform, master planning, renovation and rehabilitation of facilities, and model classrooms for the regional universities and the two- and four-year colleges.[28]

According to the chancellor, the adoption of special funding initiatives signifies an important change in the budget process. Instead of distributing increases based on enrollment growth, USG's new budget uses incentives to reflect state priorities. The intent is to develop a culture of collaboration among the institutions. A state official told us that the system is "trying to get away from an enrollment-driven formula and focus more on quality." Another suggested that it is "somewhat unprecedented" for the system to get such large amounts of money for special initiatives, and that the state is "grappling" with what to do about the continuation of funding for special programs. One state official said, "The chances for funding for this year's [fiscal year 1997] new initiatives are going to be slim," because of the tight budget year and the call for a major redirection of funds.

Despite this prediction, the initiatives were all funded—though not nearly at the $65 million level requested by the regents. The governor's budget request was for $19 million in special initiatives and the final budget provided $16.5 million. A significant part of the difference between the regents' request and final funding was in renovation and rehabilitation of facilities, where policy makers saw the increase as too much too fast and appropriated $6 million rather than the $30 million requested.

Not all USG administrators are delighted with the new approach to funding. A number of presidents who supported the "party line" on the surface told us they are concerned, as one president said, about "the extent to which special-targeted, earmarked initiatives were beginning to dominate flexible formula funding." While all agree that earmarked funding supports valuable projects, one administrator argued that they end up costing resources because the funding never quite provides for all of the program. "And then what happens," he said, "is you're short on formula money" and you have difficulty meeting some of your core objectives. But state officials like the arrangement. "With the new strategic planning initiatives from the board of regents," said one state official, "every budget request refers back to a set of strategic planning goals. This is appreciated in the political process because it clarifies how everything ties into the overall strategic plan."

Program Planning and Review

Strategic planning has been the cornerstone of the new chancellor's attempt to take advantage of the "window of opportunity" represented by a strong economy, a supportive governor and general assembly, and institutions "refreshingly ready for change." Moving quickly to inaugurate his agenda, the chancellor in the fall of 1994 organized the development of a mission/vision statement and a strategic planning process. We were told that the initiatives developed through this process reflect the goals and priorities of the state for higher education as articulated by the chancellor and the governor. The priorities emphasized three themes: addressing the needs of the state and distinguishing between the needs and the wants of institutions; placing greater emphasis on working and acting as a system; and emphasizing excellence and quality.

The University System of Georgia established a three-phase process for implementing the "change agenda," with each phase lasting about a year. The first phase involved the development of the vision and guiding principles, as well as specific policy initiatives. The second phase included a charge to the campuses to develop implementation plans for the different initiatives identified by the board. Task forces on the campuses, composed of students, faculty, and community representatives, were responsible for implementation. In the second phase, the board established major directions, and the institutions developed plans in response to those directions. The third phase involved institutionalizing new initiatives to make them part of USG culture.

The vision statement, entitled "Access to Academic Excellence for the New Millennium," was developed by consulting the board and the presidents. In separate groups, board members and presidents were asked to identify system issues and priorities, and to provide a vision for the direction for the system in the next century. The resulting vision statement suggests that USG be characterized by: "a whole that is greater than the sum of its parts"; "active partnerships with business and industry, cultural and social organizations, and government"; "leadership in establishing higher state standards for postsecondary education"; and "the continuing improvement of every unit and of the System as a coordinated whole" through a constitutional board that "requires full accountability from all and that insures responsible stewardship."[29]

Accompanying the vision statement is a set of "guiding principles for strategic action," broken down into such areas as academic excellence and recognition, development of human resources, efficient use of resources, system strength through governance, and effective external partnerships. From the principles, the chancellor and regents developed a set of policy initiatives that included: a mission development and review process featuring a coordinated reform of missions for all institutions; an admissions initiative calling for stronger coordinated admissions requirements throughout the system; the creation of active partnerships between USG and K–12 schools, businesses, and other organizations; a partnership with DTAE; a P–16 initiative that aims for a systemic collaboration among all sectors of education; movement toward a semester calendar; faculty and staff development, including a post-tenure review system; a new tuition policy; and several other processes.

The initiatives were presented by USG as concise statements listing goals, linking those goals to the strategic planning directives, and suggesting some general courses of action for the system and its institutions. The University System of Georgia left the implementation design to the institutions. Although campus presidents were consulted in the development of these initiatives, most communications took place quickly through the exchange of facsimiles; presidents had about a week to offer comments before the initiatives were brought to the regents.

The initiative calling for a partnership between USG and DTAE has resulted in an agreement between the USG chancellor and the DTAE commissioner. The agreement addresses animosity and competition between the two-year colleges and technical institutes by suggesting that students be able to move between systems, with USG concentrating on general education and DTAE focusing on job-entry occupational instruction. As part of the agreement, local recommendations on articulation are reported to a central council where decisions are made that bind both systems. The main objective, however, is to have students start in the right system. Those we talked with described the agreement as pragmatic and good for the state, particularly since some technical institutions are located across the street from two- or four-year institutions. If USG had not addressed this problem, the assembly might have intervened because of legislative concerns about excessive program duplication.

The P–16 initiative, which has been strongly supported by the governor, attempts to coordinate the entire educational system in working toward a set of common goals. The USG chancellor has set up several local P–16 councils charged with raising the level of educational achievement. The councils are developing plans for collaboration among elementary, secondary, and higher education institutions to address local educational needs. In addition, a statewide P–16 council was appointed by the governor to provide policy recommendations and leadership on two goals: reforming teacher education and raising curricular standards at all levels, with specific emphasis on students who are considered to be "at-risk" in academic situations.[30]

A third initiative is aimed at raising admission standards on the grounds that the dual set of minimum standards USG had been operating under since 1988 were little different than open admissions. While high school students, to be admitted to an institution within USG, were "required" to complete a college preparatory curriculum approved by the board of regents and endorsed by the state board of education, institutions were allowed to maintain a second, "provisional" admissions category, and most did.[31] In fall 1994, some 19 percent of freshmen in USG had not met the appropriate college preparatory requirements in at least one area. While the percentage of freshmen without the requirements was very small in the research institutions (less than

1 percent), it was progressively higher in the regional universities, senior colleges, and two-year colleges.

Under the new initiative, all institutions, including the two-year institutions, are expected to decrease the percentage of students who enter without meeting the requirements of the precollege curriculum. The initiative also calls for different standards by institutional type, "rather than the lowest common denominator." Under the initiative, admission requirements would be most flexible at the two-year colleges and become progressively more stringent at the senior colleges and research universities. The technical and adult institutions would become the only "open door" institutions. The language of the initiative also stresses the initiative's status as a "companion piece" to the P–16 efforts aimed at improving student preparation.

In yet another initiative, an external committee is studying the mission of the entire system and trying to establish specific identities or missions for each institution. The program review process has already been changed to add a probationary period for new programs. Programs approved on a probationary basis are allowed to develop over four or five years before receiving final approval. The mission review process may trigger additional changes in program review.

All proposals for new degree programs must come to the board of regents through its education committee after preliminary screening by the chancellor. If approved by the board, a proposal is developed into its final form, which also must be approved by the board. At any time in the process, another institution can raise questions about whether a program would be duplicative or whether it is educationally sound. This process, described to us as "fairly rigorous," causes some tension, but it has worked reasonably well.

While most policy leaders we spoke with were highly positive about the initiatives of the "change agenda," the pace of change has provoked conflicting reactions from long-term system incumbents. A president told us that the initiatives had been well received on campuses because of the many tangible benefits produced by the previous year's budget. In contrast, an institutional administrator described most people as "numb" from all the activity, and added, "Faculty have been stunned by the speed with which changes are taking place," particularly since they have been involved primarily in implementation rather than policy.

System Articulation

The University System of Georgia requires that students demonstrate competence in the areas of reading and writing to receive an associate's degree or the baccalaureate. A two-part test including a reading and essay section is administered to all students. Those who have earned 75 quarter hours of college credit and have not passed both parts of the exam must take remedial reading and/or writing courses until they have passed both tests. In 1993-94, approximately 72 percent of the students passed the regents' test on their first attempt; almost 50 percent of those who repeated the test eventually passed it.

Those we interviewed agreed that the transfer process works fairly well among USG institutions, which share a core curriculum. Approximately 5,000 students transferred from two- to four-year institutions in fiscal year 1994. More than one-quarter of these students came from DeKalb College, which is more than three times the size of the next largest two-year institution. Forty-four percent of all transfers from two-year institutions enrolled in one of the four research universities, with the majority attending either Georgia State or the University of Georgia.[32] Transfer between DTAE and USG institutions has not worked as well, partly because the two systems do not share a core curriculum. The partnership agreement between USG and DTAE was designed to address this problem area. The P–16 initiative was designed to address the need for better articulation across the educational spectrum.

CONCLUSION

A unified board in Georgia attempts to balance public and professional interests in a system with constitutional autonomy. Because of its unified nature, the system is very dependent upon executive leadership, probably more so than any of the state structures in this study. With strong executive leadership, a supportive governor and assembly, and a strong state economy, the system is able to establish and work toward state priorities. Changes in the state economy or upsets in gubernatorial or higher education leadership, however, could inhibit the system's ability to continue to meet those priorities.

NOTES

1. *Chronicle of Higher Education Almanac* 43, no. 1 (September 1996), pp. 51–52.
2. K. Halstead, *State Profiles for Higher Education 1978 to 1996: Trend Data* (Washington, D.C.: Research Associates of Washington, 1996), pp. 21, 24.
3. J. M. Burns, J. W. Peltason, and T. E. Cronin, *State and Local Politics: Government by the People* (Englewood Cliffs, N.J.: Prentice Hall, 1990), p. 113.
4. *State Policy Reports* 14, no. 6 (March 1996), p. 3.
5. Multistate Associates, Inc., *Legislative Outlook 1996* (Alexandria, Va., 1996), p. 14.
6. Ibid.
7. USG, *Information Digest, 1994-95* (Atlanta, Ga., 1995), p. 71.
8. *State Policy Reports* 13, no. 24 (December 1995), p. 16.
9. Southern Regional Education Board, *SREB Fact Book 1994-95* (Atlanta, Ga., 1995), p. 26.
10. USG, *Information Digest*, p. 21.
11. *Chronicle of Higher Education Almanac*, p. 51.

12. C. Fincher, *The Historical Development of the University System of Georgia: 1932–1990* (Athens, Ga.: Institute of Higher Education, 1991), pp. 24–25.
13. Ibid., p. 32.
14. USG, *Information Digest*, p. 69.
15. Halstead, *State Profiles: Trend Data*, pp. 23, 104.
16. Drawn from Fincher, *Historical Development*, p. 110.
17. Ibid., p. 107.
18. USG Board of Regents, *Institutional Relationships, Mission and Academic Programming: Armstrong State College, Savannah State College and Georgia Southern University* (Atlanta, Ga., 1994), p. 7.
19. Ibid., p. 39.
20. *Chronicle of Higher Education Almanac*, pp. 51–52.
21. Drawn from Georgia Department of Technical and Adult Education, *Responding to Georgia's Workforce Development Needs* (Atlanta, Ga., 1996), not paginated.

CHAPTER

Texas

T exas's state role with regard to higher education may best be described as regulating. The state uses regulatory mechanisms to address priorities such as access and affordability. The legislature has maintained a long-standing policy of low tuition in all of its public institutions to keep the system affordable for its residents. The state has also funneled significant funding into some regions of the state to address inequities in funding and to enhance opportunity for disadvantaged populations.

The higher education structure in Texas, described by many observers in the state as "ever-changing" and "unplanned," can be characterized as a federal model. The Texas Higher Education Coordinating Board (THECB), created in 1965, serves as the interface between higher education and state government. The higher education system includes: 35 public four-year institutions organized in six multi-institution subsystems and four free-standing campuses; 50 community college districts; three public technical colleges; and 40 private institutions. The state's strong emphasis on local control and local decision making creates a constant, dynamic tension among the institutions, the legislature, and the coordinating board. It is this tension that allows the state to continually renegotiate its balance between market forces and institutional autonomy.

In Texas, leadership on higher education issues has come from the legislature and the lieutenant governor rather than from the governor, who is granted weak powers by the state constitution. Legislative actions revising the governance arrangement and allowing colleges to change missions have been based primarily on growth and political influence rather than planning. Depending upon whom one asks, THECB was created either as "an attempt by the legislature to limit its own discretion," as an attempt "to coordinate the disorganization," or as a referee or scapegoat to keep subsystems from having to make unpopular decisions. Regardless of how its role is characterized, the coordinating board must carry out its responsibilities in an environment that often involves antagonism from the legislature and from some of the subsystems.

Because of the state's emphasis on local control and due to the influence of shifting political forces, priorities for higher education in Texas must be inferred more from legislative action than drawn from official statements. In general, the legislature has supported access through a policy of low tuition at all public institutions. Legislators have also been interested in quality and accountability, as is evident from legislative support of the rising junior exam, legislative backing for the remediation embodied in the Texas Academic Skills Program, and two unsuccessful legislative attempts to implement performance funding. Through competitive programs for funding faculty research and advanced technology applications, the legislature has spent more than $650 million each biennium since 1987 to support economic development.

There is little competition between public and private institutions in Texas due to the fairly small size of the private sector and to the political dominance of the public institutions. Private higher education is not actively involved in discussions of state policy issues. A need-based tuition equalization grant is the primary means for including independent institutions in state plans for meeting student demand for higher education.

The work processes in Texas maintain a balance between institutional and state priorities. The statewide information system, which is managed by THECB, is linked to the budget process. The formula elements of the budget, combined with THECB's ability to revise them, create a budget process that minimizes budget battles and that system participants describe as "fair." Processes of program review—based on criteria involving cost, need, and quality—help the state in its relatively weak planning efforts. At the time of our study, THECB did not have specific initiatives to improve transfer and articulation.

The most important impending challenge in Texas involves a projected growth of 100,000 students (12.5 percent) from 1994 to 2000, with disproportionate increases among minority populations. If Texas is successful in increasing participation rates among minorities so that they equal those for whites, the projected increase in enrollments would more than double.[1] Although the state economy has recovered from a severe recession in the late 1980s, higher education will continue to face increasing competition for state resources. In the absence of significant change in Texas's system of higher education, growth in enrollment and student diversity will most likely outstrip the current capabilities of the system.

STATE CONTEXT

With more than 18 million residents, Texas is the second most populous state in the country. It is a very diverse state (25 percent Hispanic, 12 percent African American, 2 percent Asian American), with a rapidly growing Hispanic population. The population in Texas grew by more than 2.76 million people in the 1980s, a 19.4 percent increase, compared to a 9.8 percent increase nationally. Only California and Florida experienced greater growth in that decade. Texas's population is projected to increase by an additional 8 percent between 1995 and 2000, with the greatest growth expected in urban areas.[2]

Compared to the other study states, Texas residents are relatively young and poor. Texas has the highest percentage of its population (39 percent) under the age of 24, and ranks at the bottom of case study states in per capita income. In addition, when measured by the percentage of families receiving Aid to Families with Dependent Children (AFDC), poverty in Texas is higher than in any of the 50 states.[3] While Texas is second among states in this study in the percentage of its population with a baccalaureate and is about average in the percentage of its population with a graduate degree, it has the highest dropout rate (tied with Florida) of the study states and one of the nation's highest illiteracy rates (33 percent).[4] Texas is first among states in this study in the percentage of its population who do not speak English at home.[5]

Although Democrats controlled state elected offices in Texas for many years, this balance of power has shifted somewhat. In 1995-96, the governor was a Republican and the lieutenant governor a Democrat. While the house and senate remained under the control of Democrats, their majorities shrank significantly after the 1994 elections. Even though the composition of the legislature is changing, most of those we talked with suggested that changes in the philosophy of legislators have been minor.

The governor's influence comes primarily through a line-item veto and control over numerous statewide appointments. The lieutenant governor, who serves as the head of the state senate and appoints senate committees, including all fiscal committee chairs, is regarded as the most powerful elected official in the state. Along with the legislative leadership, the lieutenant governor sets higher education policy (as well as policy for other state services). The state legislature meets from January to June in alternate years. The senate has only 31 members; a university administrator described it as "a nice little club," very "collegial." Senators may introduce what are known as "local bills," which in theory affect only the geographical area of the individual who introduced it. Senatorial courtesy guarantees passage of these bills, and re-flects Texas's strong resistance to centralized decision making over local issues.

According to the *Texas Charter for Higher Education*, adopted in 1987, the role of the legislature is to set "broad policy while delegating implementation to appropriate officials."[7] In relation to public higher education, the legislature exercises its influence primarily through the funding process. The key actors are the members of the Legislative Budget Board, a nonpartisan agency charged with developing the first budget bill in each legislative session. Its members include the lieutenant governor, the speaker of the house, the chairs of the Senate Finance and State Affairs Committees, the chairs of the House Appropriations and Ways and Means Committees, two additional senators appointed by the lieutenant governor, and two additional representatives appointed by the speaker.

The power of the legislature relative to the governor is evidenced by an attempt by the legislature to avoid line-item vetoes in the higher education budget. When a previous governor threatened to use the line-item veto for certain areas of the higher education budget, the legislature began combining all items into one lump-sum appropriation and then providing detailed direc-tions in supplemental language about how the appropriation was to be used. This tied the hands of the governor, whose only choice was to veto the entire higher education appropriation or let it stand.

In the mid-1980s, Texas experienced a widespread recession as a result of a depression in the oil and gas industry. The economy began recovering in the 1990s, while the rest of the country was in a recession. In the 1990s, the state has been able to diversify its economy, particularly by attracting many compa-nies moving from California.[8] Diversification and growth in the mid-1990s contribute to what many have described as a generally healthy economy in the state. Growth, however, is much slower than it has been, and with increasing demands on state services, the competition for state resources is intensifying.[9]

There is no state personal or corporate income tax in Texas, and most of the state's revenue comes from sales and property taxes. In the past, a great deal of revenue was generated from a tax on natural resources; as this has decreased, property taxes have increased. The lack of an income tax, some Texans argue, makes it very difficult for the state to support its public services. "Texas is a state that is allergic to taxes," a university administrator told us, and the citizens, he said, make many demands that they are unwilling to pay for.

State general revenue appropriations in 1996-97 were $44.5 billion, repre-senting an increase of 11.1 percent over 1994-95. A rising prison population; increased federal mandates; and court-ordered reforms in public schools, prisons, and mental health facilities have prompted increased spending in these areas and have inhibited legislative flexibility in setting priorities and shifting resources. While higher education in Texas did not experience the decreases in actual dollars that many systems in other states experienced, it did see its total share of the state budget decrease. From 1984-85 to 1994-95, the state's allocation to public higher education as a percentage of total tax revenues fell from 18.4 to 12.2 percent.[10] Per student general revenue appropriations over this decade increased from $4,043 to $4,690, a 16 percent rise. When inflation is taken into account, however, per student appropriations in constant 1984 dollars decreased by 16 percent from 1984-85 to 1994-95.[11] General revenue funding for higher education in the 1996-97 biennium was $6,288.8 million, an increase of $428.9 million (or 7.3 percent) over the previous biennium.[12]

A recent report notes that the state's revenue system is not keeping pace with the expansion of the state economy.[13] Services such as corrections, K–12 education, and welfare programs will most likely continue to shrink higher education's share of the budget, since higher education is one of the few areas of the budget in which the legislature has discretion on how much to spend. Additional concerns are raised by impending changes resulting from the "devolution" of federal programs, which will place increasing pressure on the state to meet social service needs for health and welfare.

Texas has historically adopted a low-tuition policy to improve access to higher education. The state ranks in the bottom 10 nationally in terms of tuition charges. In 1995-96, average tuition and fees averaged $1,624 at the four-year institutions, $864 at community colleges, and $1,168 at the technical colleges. Texas students and families pay a much smaller proportion of the total cost of education (measured by state appropriations and tuition) than in the majority of the states.[14]

Tuition is set by the legislature for all four-year institutions. Every student pays the same tuition, regardless of the institution attended. Tuition has been increasing at an incremental rate of $2 per credit hour per year since 1985, and will continue to increase at that rate until 2000-01. Until 1995-96, institutions were not allowed to keep the funds generated by the tuition increase. Institutions do have the ability to charge higher tuition at the graduate and professional levels and can propose general use fees at their campuses. These fees have increased significantly faster than tuition over the past few years. A new law submitted by the University of Texas (UT) and passed by the legislature in 1995 allows governing boards to raise general use fees to the same level as tuition ($32 per unit for fall 1996). Because general use fees can be used at the discretion of the institution, some critics have argued that this fee increase really represents a tuition increase. The legislature also sets minimum tuition rates for community colleges and the Texas State Technical College System, but individual governing boards set the actual tuition rates for these students.

Texans disagree about the role tuition increases should play in paying for enrollment growth. A former politician told us, "Low tuition is good public policy." He added that any increase in tuition would be part of the problem, not part of a solution. A university board member agreed that tuition increases should be modest because the major influx of new students would be from minority and low-income backgrounds and would be unable to pay if the price were too high. In contrast, a legislative staff member suggested that tuition could play an important role in accommodating future demands, and that tuition must increase significantly. A former THECB member, arguing that low tuition is a subsidy for the rich, said that increased tuition is necessary.

CHARACTERISTICS AND HISTORY OF HIGHER EDUCATION

There are more than 150 institutions of higher education in Texas, including a combination of two- and four-year, public and independent, upper and lower division, and technical and professional institutions. Texas ranks fourth nationally and third among the study states in the number of colleges and universities. Almost 90 percent of the enrollment in Texas higher education is in public institutions, the greatest percentage of any of the study states. Yet the state is about average in enrollment per 1,000 population.[15] Currently, there are approximately 800,000 students enrolled in public higher education in the state, with about 50 percent enrolled in community colleges. Projections of enrollment growth over the next decade reveal that if minority participation in higher education remains at the same level that it is today, the state can expect an increase of 100,000 to 250,000 students. If minority participation rates were to increase to the same level as participation rates for whites, the growth would be about 400,000 students.[16] Currently, nearly 23 percent of the state's Hispanic students and 20 percent of African-American students fail to finish high school.[17] Texas has a fairly low-cost system of higher education, ranking 29th in terms of state per-student appropriations, and 45th in total support (when appropriations, tuition, and fees are taken into account).[18]

Public higher education in Texas includes a mix of large subsystems, smaller regional subsystems, free-standing campuses with individual boards, individual colleges and universities, and community colleges, all of which fall under the purview of THECB. At the time of our study, four primary university systems with separate central offices headed by chancellors—UT, Texas A & M University (A & M), the University of Houston, and Texas State University (TSU)—had oversight of 28 universities, 6 health science centers, 1 upper division center, and 3 two-year campuses. Three of these subsystems (all but the TSU system) consisted of a flagship university and a variety of other institutions with differing missions and capacities. Two smaller subsystems, Texas Tech University and the University of North Texas, each oversaw one university and a health science center. The Texas State Technical College System consisted of three two-year campuses. Four institutions remained free-standing. Each university or college system and free-standing institution was governed by a nine-member board of regents with members appointed by the governor to staggered six-year terms.

There are 50 community college districts (with more than 70 campuses) in Texas, each with its own locally elected board of trustees. One board staff member described the historical relationship between THECB and these institutions as "benign neglect," but added, "It is much improved now." The increase in the amount of federal money coming to the state through the Perkins Act, combined with a greater emphasis throughout the state on technical education and workforce preparation, has created a more integral relationship between THECB and community colleges. Moreover, the authority of THECB in relation to the community colleges has expanded. Previously, federal and state funds for vocational and technical education were administered by the Texas Education Agency, while THECB was responsible for academic programs. Now, THECB has responsibility for vocational, technical, and academic programs, a change that has brought about much greater involvement by THECB in issues relating to the community colleges.

The Texas higher education system includes 40 independent colleges and universities and one independent medical school. Although these institutions must obtain certificates of authority from THECB to grant degrees in the state, their programs are not subject to review or approval by the coordinating board. The state supports students enrolled at least half-time at independent institutions through need-based tuition equalization grants. The maximum award is $2,500, which is half of the amount the state pays in general revenues for each student at a public institution. In addition, the state provides a direct appropriation of $33.8 million annually to the Baylor College of Medicine. In 1995, the legislature appropriated $2.5 million to establish centers for teacher education at predominately minority, private, general academic institutions.

Public senior institutions in Texas developed in a variety of ways. Some were created as general purpose, state-supported institutions. Others began as teachers' colleges and gradually developed into comprehensive institutions. A few began as private or public junior colleges, and then developed into four-year institutions under state control. Still others began as upper division institutions, though at least four of these have expanded to offer lower division opportunities as well. Several higher education officials suggested to us that most of the development of higher education in the state has derived from decisions based more on growth than rational planning.

The governance structure in Texas has evolved substantially over the past century. The first subsystem of institutions was the State Board of Normal Schools, established in 1911, which eventually became the TSU subsystem.

The composition of some subsystems, most notably UT and A & M, is continually changing as increasing numbers of campuses are being incorporated into one of the two systems. Respondents told us that the free-standing campus is becoming a "dinosaur" and is "disappearing fast."

The most significant changes to the structure of the higher education subsystems in Texas came as a result of the South Texas initiative, seen by most as a response to a lawsuit filed in 1987 by the Mexican American Legal Defense and Education Fund (MALDEF) on behalf of the League of United Latin American Citizens (LULAC). The lawsuit, which claimed that there were inequities of opportunity for higher education in South Texas, accused the state of discriminating against Mexican Americans, citing low spending on higher education and the limited number of graduate programs (less than 1 percent of the state's doctoral programs) in the southern region of the state.[19] While the trial court found in favor of MALDEF, the decision was overturned by the state supreme court, which found that the state's discrimination had not been intentional. Following this decision, the legislature called upon the UT and A & M systems to bring some of the South Texas institutions into their systems to build up those campuses. As a result, two southern institutions were incorporated into UT, and three into A & M.

Incorporating these institutions into the two largest subsystems was intended to give them more political clout. In addition, the legislature appropriated additional funds to South Texas/Border Initiative schools to provide new buildings, additional faculty, and new programs. In 1993 alone, the legislature approved $460 million for nine colleges and universities, which resulted in the introduction of nearly 100 new academic programs, the hiring of hundreds of additional faculty members, and the construction and renovation of buildings.[20] The total included $96.4 million to improve and expand undergraduate, graduate, and doctoral programs, compared to $35.2 million for the same purposes in 1991-93[21] and $13 million in 1989-91.[22] The infusion of money and expansion of program offerings has been accompanied by enrollment surges at many of the South Texas institutions. From fall 1993 to fall 1996, enrollment increased 57 percent at Texas A & M International University, 37 percent at UT Brownsville, and 26 percent at Texas A & M Corpus Christi.[23]

The governance structure continues to evolve. The Lamar University system was created by a powerful state senator who felt his district would be best served with a system that included its own board of regents. In the years prior to our study, enrollment at the university had declined, and the president was involved in a contentious relationship with the Lamar board over what some saw as the board's micromanaging tendencies. When the senator who created the system was voted out of office in 1994, the state representative from the area stepped in. This representative believed that it was in the district's best interest to include Lamar University within a larger system, and came to the conclusion that TSU offered the best opportunities. This shift appeared beneficial for both parties: the system would gain an institution located in an area with a great deal of political clout, while the institution would get rid of a board that was at cross-purposes with its president. Those we spoke with suggested that despite these benefits, this shift—which took place in 1995—would not have occurred without political involvement.

During the same legislative session, the senator from Laredo attempted to move Texas A & M International to the UT system. The legislation, which according to one university president came as a surprise to the institution, was introduced by the senator as a "local bill," virtually guaranteeing its passage in the senate. The representative from Laredo, however, disagreed with the change and made certain that the legislation did not get out of committee in the house. Attempts by the senator to attach the provision to other higher education bills failed, and the institution remains in the A & M system. As a result of the political battle that developed in this proposed shift, one university administrator predicted, correctly it turned out, that THECB would be strengthened, giving it more say about which systems should absorb which institutions.

The higher education system in Texas was generally described to us as "not neat," "not rational," "ever-changing," and "unplanned." "We have an amoebic system," said one legislative staff member. The fact that the composition of the individual subsystems changes regularly contributes to this impression. Texans believe subsystem changes are the result of political influence and the political process. "It's a crazy way to do it, but it's grown up over time and it's hard to change," said one higher education official. The fact that Texas is such a local-control, weak-central-government kind of state, said one political staff member, means that chaos in the system will continue. The result, one respondent told us, is a system that has needless duplication and overlap. Others believe that the two main subsystems (UT and A & M) have become too large and unwieldy.

While Texans like to laugh at the somewhat chaotic way in which their system of higher education is organized, they are not for the most part eager to change it. In 1989, THECB established a special committee on statewide governance of higher education to examine possible changes to the organization of higher education. Citing problems such as an inability to conduct statewide planning, insufficient regional coordination, insufficient buffering of institutions from the legislative process, and continuing compromises in the quality of the flagship institutions, the committee recommended a new structure that would have included only four subsystems: a smaller UT, a smaller A & M, a subsystem focused on undergraduate education, and a multipurpose subsystem.[24] Those who criticized the proposal focused on its adverse impact on the current balance of power. One source told us that the people in

Houston and Lubbock did not agree with the proposal because they saw it as limiting their ability to develop a university of high prestige. He added that any recommendations identifying some subsystems as more prestigious than others or grouping institutions in ways that distinguish high versus low status would be unacceptable. Another argued that the plan to regionalize some of the subsystems would have pitted one part of the state against another, and this was not desirable. The report's recommendations were never adopted.

Although the state system of higher education may not appear rational, most Texans we talked with believe it works pretty well. A political staff member told us that while the system would be easier to understand if all institutions were to fit into nice organizational boxes, he said that institutions have done a good job of trying to address statewide issues and needs. A former president said that the lack of logic to the structure could be problematic if there were a great deal of political competition among institutions as they vied for funds, but he said that this has not been a problem in Texas because its funding process is based on formulas.

DESIGN OF THE HIGHER EDUCATION–STATE GOVERNMENT INTERFACE

In 1965, the Texas legislature created THECB and granted it responsibility for achieving "excellence" in college education through unified development of the system, efficient and effective use of resources, elimination of duplication in program offerings and facilities, and advocacy for adequate resources for higher education institutions. The board was initially established under Governor John Connally to determine where new campuses were needed, to contain growth, and to help the legislature police itself. One former politician suggested that the board was "an attempt by the legislature to limit its own discretion." According to another elected official, the board "coordinates the disorganization."

The Texas Higher Education Coordinating Board, comprised of 18 members appointed by the governor to six-year terms, advises the legislature on higher education issues. The governor also appoints the chair and the vice chair. Typically, when a new governor is elected, chairs step aside. The Texas Higher Education Coordinating Board is responsible for preparing a master plan for higher education, preparing funding formulas for use by the legislature, and approving new degree programs and some construction processes. According to one staff member, the coordinating board should be seen as an impartial and objective source of information. The board also oversees the student loan program, which is self-supporting.

The commissioner is appointed by and serves at the pleasure of the board. There have been some attempts to give this power of appointment to the governor, but these have not been successful. The commissioner at the time of our study had been in this position for 20 years. During that time, every governor with the exception of Ann Richards and George W. Bush has come into office with the intention of firing the commissioner, but to no avail. One staff member attributed this in part to the way that board appointments are managed, and to the independence of the board. Another respondent said that the commissioner has done a marvelous job of balancing institutional aspirations against the overall needs of the state, and the board has been smart enough to realize that. A former university president suggested that the commissioner is "brilliant" and able to win "through logic and argument" rather than relying on personal relationships or lobbying.

According to one former board member, THECB limits the proliferation of graduate degrees and plays an integral role in the design and execution of the formula-funding process. A former regent of UT said that the primary role of the board is to prevent unnecessary duplication in the state, and he said that they do quite well in this regard. Coordinating board members, he argued, are strong advocates of the public purposes and functions of higher education in the state, and they encourage greater public commitment to the enterprise. Not everyone, however, viewed the board in such a positive light. A political staff member described a "love-hate" relationship between the coordinating board and the institutions, and between the board and the legislature. He said that institutions and the legislature appreciate THECB for some activities but are quick to criticize the board for others.

There are disagreements among legislators about THECB's role. A former politician, who argued against centralized planning by the coordinating board, said that the legislature should be responsible for planning, since they are responsible for the distribution of state funding. In contrast, the Senate Education Committee recently proposed that the coordinating board take on a stronger and more centralized approach to planning. A faculty member noted that allowing the legislature to handle planning often results in chaos, creating a situation where an institution's future depends almost entirely on the political skills of its president.

Citing what he described as the "fiasco" of the South Texas initiative (where the legislature mandated specific degree programs at specific campuses), a political staff member argued that the enabling legislation of THECB does not guarantee limits to legislative intrusion on responsibilities assigned to the coordinating board. A former board member agreed, saying that THECB loses when political leaders will not let the system work. In contrast, a faculty member argued that occasional preemption of the coordinating board by the legislature is a small price to pay for desirable limitations on the board's authority.

Adversarial relationships have been aggravated by the tendency of sub-system central offices to pass tough decisions (especially campus requests for new programs) along to the coordinating board. In carrying out its role as guardian of the public interest, THECB has found itself in conflict frequently with the wishes of the subsystems and associated institutions. "This is the best show in town," said one THECB staff member. "We have terrible shoot-outs here and an incredible amount of political pressure over such things as programs and budgets." A legislator suggested that the board serves as the "scapegoat" when the subsystem central offices need someone to blame. A former president said that conflict is "inevitable" since the subsystem board advocates for member institutions, while the coordinating board referees among competing interests. The legislature contributes to the conflict that THECB experiences by assigning issues to the board that require legislative resolution but that are "too hot to handle politically."

Both THECB and the legislature have made attempts to improve their relationship. The coordinating board, most agree, has always been weak in its legislative relations, but it is now recognizing the need to do more in the political arena. In June 1995, the governor, lieutenant governor, and speaker of the house issued a statement saying that in the future no changes in system structure could be made without some approval or review by the coordinating board. There was not a great deal of optimism, however, about the extent to which that directive would hold.

WORK PROCESSES

The coordinating board exercises statutory authority for the four major work processes identified in this study. The work processes are also the greatest source of tension among the board, the institutions, and the legislature.

Information Management

The coordinating board is the primary agency responsible for the collection of statewide higher education data on faculty assignments, enrollment by class, and individual student records. Historically, the collection of information regarding higher education was designed from a regulatory perspective and as a basis for formula funding, providing data regarding faculty workloads, performance on the Texas Academic Skills Program (TASP), and federal funding criteria. In the past eight years, the board has moved toward an information management system approach. The coordinating board is now able to track students across two- and four-year sectors and provide cohort data for each institution.

The legislature requests both technical and policy information from the coordinating board. The Legislative Budget Board requests fiscal notes on all bills related to higher education, a requirement that generates 300 to 500 requests each legislative session. Beyond fiscal notes, THECB receives more than 200 requests from the legislature annually for information related to higher education.

Budget Process

Most funding for higher education in Texas is distributed to the various institutions on the basis of formulas. Six formula advisory committees—comprised of institutional administrators, faculty, students, and laypersons—develop recommendations to the THECB commissioner regarding different cost elements. The commissioner, whose advice is seldom contested, recommends adjusted formulas to the coordinating board. In recent years the commissioner's recommendations have been based on his estimate of the amount necessary to bring per-student funding up to the average of the 10 most populous states. The legislature decides the level at which each formula will be funded. Each institution is designated exactly the same amount for each hour it teaches of a particular course, but not all formulas are funded fully or equally. In 1996, approximately 87 percent of the amounts generated by the formulas were funded. During the same year, faculty salaries, traditionally the highest priority for the legislature, were funded at a higher percentage than the other formulas.

After the appropriation is made by the legislature and approved by the governor's office, institutional governing boards decide how funds will be used, but there is a general expectation that presidents will not deviate much from the formula allocations outlined in the budget. The instruction formula provides nearly one-half of formula-generated funding based on the mix of courses taught by an institution and the number of students enrolled. Formula funding, according to some respondents, has the disadvantage of not allowing the state to target priorities such as access for minority students or workforce preparation.

Formula appropriations are supplemented by non-formula special-item funding, which involves appropriations to individual institutions for specific activities and can range from 7 to 20 percent of an institution's annual budget. Some people told us that special item funding is a way for the legislature to address priorities. Others disagreed, saying that special-item funding is soft money that might or might not appear in the next budget cycle and that such funding is, in reality, "pork," a way for legislators to fund pet projects rather than address priorities. One community college president said that special-item funding leads to a breakdown of the equitable system that formulas try to preserve.

In 1991, the appropriations bill called on THECB to develop and implement a new system of funding distribution based on performance. The bill did not specify how much funding should be allocated by performance criteria, but left that up to the board. The coordinating board first proposed to institutions that 5 to 10 percent of each institution's appropriations, as calculated by the regular formulas, be set aside to be earned back based on a set of performance criteria.[25] According to this proposal, performance would be measured against a set of 10 standards, some of which would be recommended by the coordinating board as measures of statewide concern, with others selected by the institutions.

Institutions objected to this proposal, saying that the amount to be earned back was too high. They argued that it should be no more than 2 or 3 percent of their budgets and that it should be added to the formula amounts, not taken from institutional appropriations. Beyond differences about amounts and sources, there was concern about the complexity of negotiating with 35 institutions, developing standards of performance, and collecting data to determine accomplishment on the 10 different measures. As a result, a second plan was developed calling for the legislature to decide how much of the total higher education appropriations should be applied to performance, either as an addition or a set-aside. The coordinating board also recommended a number of possible performance measures, from which the legislature would choose those it would reward. Institutions would compete for the funds allocated for each goal.

This second approach also faced strong institutional resistance. Ultimately, neither approach was implemented because legislative advocates of performance funding lost their influential positions in the 1993 session, and institutions were able to convince the new power structure that the existing funding process should be maintained. In the 1995 legislative session, Texas tried again to implement performance funding for all state agencies. The process worked well in most state agencies, but not for higher education—in part because of difficulties in assessing quality in a system where UT Austin is the standard, and in part because of the history in Texas of treating all institutions of higher education the same. Legislators wanted to protect their local institutions and were not interested in developing performance measures that might make a local institution look less effective. In the process, the Legislative Budget Board and others who were asked to propose criteria for performance funding got "brutalized" by the legislature.[26]

Among college and university administrators, formulas are widely regarded as the great equalizer in Texas. Most said that the process, though not perfect, keeps the institutions from getting into political battles over state resources. "Prior to the formulas," said one political staff member, "Texas had funding based on clout, and legislators do not want to move back to that inequitable system."

While some institutions come out slightly ahead in the budget process due to the awarding of special-item funding, the real difference in support of institutions involves income from the Permanent University Fund (PUF), which is treated as an endowment with two-thirds going to UT and one-third to A & M. Permanent University Fund monies are not available to all institutions in these subsystems—only to those that were members in 1985 when the PUF criteria were last changed. Subject to approval of the respective subsystem's boards, income can be used for construction bonds, renovation, major library acquisitions, and major instructional and research equipment. After bond obligations are met, the remainder of funds goes either to UT Austin or to Texas A & M for "excellence" projects, which over time have become fairly broadly defined. At one time, as much as $90 million was available to UT Austin for this purpose; that number is now down to about $70 million. A constitutional amendment would be required to increase the number of institutions eligible for PUF monies, an action most regard as highly unlikely.

Institutions not eligible for PUF funding, including those outside of UT and A & M, receive construction money under the Higher Education Assistance Fund (HEAF). The fund money is distributed primarily through a formula that is based on student population, complexity of programs, current physical facilities, and predicted growth. The funds can be used only for construction, remodeling, equipment, and library resources. The legislature appropriated $450 million to HEAF for the 1996-97 biennium. Of that, $350 million will be available to the HEAF institutions and $100 million will be set aside to establish an endowment fund similar to PUF.

Program Planning and Review

In 1987, the legislature authorized THECB to develop and regularly update a master plan. At the same time, the legislature rejected a proposal by the Select Committee on Higher Education to enact specific missions for each public university. This was interpreted by many to mean that the development of a highly specific master plan was not politically viable. This impression was reinforced when the board's first draft of a master plan was successfully resisted by institutional presidents as both too specific and too prescriptive. The master plan format that was eventually adopted was characterized to us as "very general" and "never implemented," with no one paying "any attention to the results." During our site visits, the chair of the Senate Education Committee proposed the need for a master plan "similar to California's," although most sources questioned whether the powerful subsystems would support a stronger master planning role for THECB or the development of highly specific missions for each institution.

While master planning may not be in vogue in Texas, the coordinating board has carried out a range of strategic planning activities, the most important of which is the maintenance of a table of the academic programs that each public institution is authorized to offer. The board has the authority to review and approve all new program proposals. Each institution must submit a mission statement to the board every five years. Proposed programs must fit the institution's mission, must not result in unnecessary duplication, and must meet criteria related to cost, need, and potential quality. Approval for master's degree programs is more difficult to obtain and is given somewhat more rigorous review than new programs offering bachelor's degrees. Doctoral program review is the most demanding, and the board utilizes out-of-state consultants to examine these proposals. Institutional or subsystem plans for new programs often do not take statewide needs or capacities into consideration. During 1995-96, three doctoral programs in nursing were proposed by UT institutions, and all three were approved by the subsystem office, leaving the coordinating board with the difficult responsibility of choosing among them.

The coordinating board also reviews existing doctoral programs through a two-stage process described to us as no more burdensome than the internal review process conducted by most universities. In the first stage, institutions conduct a self-study of the program, with the results forwarded to THECB. A committee of outside peer reviewers evaluates the self-study results. If the reviewers find them satisfactory, the review process ends. If the committee raises questions, the process enters a second stage that involves site visits by committee members. The process has resulted in the termination of some programs. At UT and A & M, the eliminated programs were described as those the subsystems wanted to discontinue anyway.

The coordinating board also develops enrollment projections that are used to stimulate institutional planning. Because the board is authorized to set enrollment limits, institutions may be required to present their enrollment management plans for board consideration. As in the case of program development, institutions are often unaware of the enrollment plans of other institutions, so they overestimate enrollment growth by planning to recruit the same students. The coordinating board attempts to influence institutional planning from a statewide perspective. The board also influences institutional planning through its facilities approval authority.

In an effort to address concerns about quality of education and performance of students coming into and leaving higher education in Texas, THECB's Committee on Testing issued a report in 1986 entitled, *A Generation of Failure: The Case for Testing and Remediation in Texas Higher Education.* This report called for the implementation of mandatory statewide testing of students entering higher education—to assess basic reading, writing, and mathematics skills. The report also recommended that institutions provide academic advising and remediation for those students who fail one or more sections of the test. These recommendations led to legislation that made testing and remediation mandatory statewide, through the establishment of the Texas Academic Skills Program (TASP).

The TASP test measures skills in reading, writing, and mathematics. All incoming students at public institutions (two- and four-year) are required to take the exam before completing the first nine semester hours at the college or university. The TASP requirements do not apply to students at private institutions unless they transfer to a public institution on a permanent basis. Students in certificate programs of less than 42 semester credit hours are not liable for TASP requirements. Students who have not taken the TASP test prior to the end of the term in which they accumulate nine or more semester hours or the equivalent cannot enroll for subsequent collegiate hours until the test is taken. Students cannot move on to upper division courses without passing the exam. The purpose of the exam is to identify students with difficulties in the three major skills areas, and then to provide them with assistance to address those deficiencies. All institutions are required to provide remedial assistance to their students.

System Articulation

The Texas Academic Skills Program requirements complicate transfer and articulation relationships between two- and four-year institutions, relationships that most observers told us do not work as well as they should. In 1990, approximately 35,800 students transferred from public community colleges to state universities in Texas, compared with 32,600 in 1994.[27] Texas Higher Education Coordinating Board staff told us that the decrease in the number of transfers could be traced to a lack of emphasis on the associate degree by many community colleges, and to colleges having missions that are much broader than preparing students for transfer (such as workforce and career preparation).

Historically, THECB has maintained a neutral stance on initial enrollment in community colleges, in part because universities (several of which are essentially open-admissions) have had financial incentives to recruit freshmen. Under TASP requirements, however, that picture is beginning to change as universities show increased interest in community colleges as sites for students in need of remediation. While there is no common general education transfer core, community colleges and universities have voluntarily developed a common course-numbering system, by which similar courses at all colleges can be identified. The coordinating board issues a guide to transfer of credit, including approved transfer curricula for individual majors. In addition, the board makes final determinations in any disputes concerning transfer of course credit from one institution to another. Local transfer initiatives are under way that affect those universities and community colleges situated in the same communities.

CONCLUSION

A healthy tension exists between THECB and the legislature, and between the coordinating board and institutions, making the Texas system appear somewhat contentious. This friction is exacerbated due to state-local differences that exist in the overall policy environment. These tensions, however, serve to balance institutional and market interests. It remains to be seen whether the state will need to increase its use of market forces as it faces upcoming demographic and fiscal challenges.

While the coordination function of THECB is sometimes viewed as a form of excessive bureaucratic intrusion, it is generally believed to be effectively performed. For instance, the coordinating board helps to minimize duplication of programs and provides a statewide perspective in a state that is heavily dominated by local interests. While the organizational structure appears "messy" to many within the system, the federal structure does provide some flexibility to promote change.

NOTES

1. THECB, *Enrollment Forecasts, 1995–2010*, Study Paper 27 (Austin, Tx., 1995), p. 44.
2. THECB, *Master Plan for Texas Higher Education, 1995* (Austin, Tx., 1995), p. 3.
3. Ibid., p. 6.
4. Ibid.
5. Unless otherwise noted, data in this paragraph are drawn from *Chronicle of Higher Education Almanac* 43, no. 1 (September 1996), pp. 98–99.
6. J. M. Burns, J. W. Peltason, and T. E. Cronin, *State and Local Politics: Government by the People* (Englewood Cliffs, N.J.: Prentice Hall, 1990), p. 113.
7. Texas State Legislature, *Texas Charter for Higher Education*, 1987, p. 6.
8. S. McCartney and K. Blumenthal, "Lone Star Rising: Texas Strives to Avoid California's Mistakes, and It Is Prospering," *Wall Street Journal*, September 13, 1995.
9. THECB, *Master Plan*, p. 2.
10. J. Sharp, *Disturbing the Peace: The Challenge of Change in Texas Government* (Austin, Tx., State Comptroller's Office), p. 5.
11. Ibid.
12. Legislative Budget Board, *Fiscal Size-Up, 1996-97 Biennium, Texas State Services* (Austin, Tx., 1996), pp. 6–13.
13. J. Sharp, *Disturbing the Peace*, Appendix I, Part 2.
14. K. Halstead, *State Profiles for Higher Education 1978 to 1996: Trend Data* (Washington, D.C.: Research Associates of Washington, 1996), p. 88.
15. Ibid., p. 85.
16. THECB, *Enrollment Forecasts*, p. 44.
17. THECB, *Master Plan*, p. 6.
18. THECB, *Facts on Higher Education in Texas* (Austin, Tx., 1995), not paginated.
19. K. Mangan, "Universities in South Texas Sprout New Programs and Campuses," *Chronicle of Higher Education* (October 4, 1996), p. A29.

20. Ibid.
21. Ibid. "More Money for South Texas Colleges," *Chronicle of Higher Education* (June 23, 1993), p. A23.
22. "Lawsuit Brings Two New Doctoral Programs to S. Texas," *Chronicle of Higher Education* (February 19, 1992), p. A21.
23. Mangan, "Universities in South Texas Sprout New Programs."
24. THECB, *Texas Public Higher Education Governance for the 21st Century: Final Report* (Austin, Tx., 1991), pp. 12, 13.
25. Most of this discussion of performance funding is drawn from K. H. Ashworth, "Performance-Based Funding in Higher Education, The Texas Case Study," *Change* (November-December 1994), pp. 8–14.
26. P. Healy, "Texas Lawmakers Take Activist Role on Higher Education Issues," *Chronicle of Higher Education* (June 13, 1997), p. A29. During the 1997 legislative session, after our study was completed, legislators created a new appropriations process for higher education, collapsing 16 formulas into four that were based on instruction and operations, the teaching loads of tenured and tenure-track faculty members, enrollment growth, and infrastructure. They also attached riders to the appropriations bill that would require THECB to establish minimum average "teaching goals" and minimum class-size standards for each institution, and threatened to withhold funding from universities that do not develop plans for reviewing faculty with tenure.
27. THECB, unpublished data, April 1995.

CHAPTER 8

Illinois

Of the seven case study states, Illinois has achieved the greatest balance between market influence and institutional autonomy and professional values. Illinois provides the best example of a state that steers its higher education system toward meeting public priorities, and this steering function is well aligned with its federal structure.

The governor of Illinois, who has strong veto and other powers under the state constitution, historically has exercised leadership on higher education issues. In 1961, the state established what has become known as the "system of systems" for higher education, though it is more accurately described as a system of subsystems. This system of systems was created partly to bring together and thereby improve the capacity of several smaller four-year institutions to compete with the University of Illinois (UI) and Southern Illinois University (SIU), which remained as separate subsystems. The overall system was coordinated by the Illinois Board of Higher Education (IBHE), which was given relatively weak statutory authority. One of the first actions of this new board was to create a network of locally governed community colleges, coordinated by a state community college board that was subordinate to IBHE. The state also instituted policies to increase the use of market forces in higher education. First, private nonprofit institutions, historically strong in the state's urban areas, were defined as an integral part of the Illinois system in the late 1960s, thereby limiting the growth of public four-year institutions. Concurrently, Illinois created a need-based Monetary Award Program to assist undergraduates at public and private institutions. By 1994, this program was the third largest in the nation. In 1995, the legislature ended the system of systems by abolishing two subsystem boards and replacing them with individual governing boards for seven of the eight affected institutions.

At the time of our study, Illinois boasted a healthy economy and high per capita income. Forecasts predicted stable enrollment growth for higher education. The major challenge for elected leaders involved finding ways to respond to growing demands from public safety and health care in the face of declining federal dollars. Republican domination of both houses of the legislature and of major elected state offices has provided a supportive environment for system changes in governance structures, with the avowed purpose of making regional universities more responsive both to state government and to their constituents. None of the contextual changes seemed of sufficient magnitude to require significant structural or performance changes in Illinois higher education.

The work processes in Illinois serve to maintain the careful balance of forces influencing Illinois higher education. Of all the study states, Illinois has the most sophisticated information system, which state and institutional leaders rely on for policy decisions related to the budget process and program planning. The Priorities, Quality and Productivity (PQP) process is the best current example among the study states of an effort to achieve state priorities. The information system allows state officials to connect one work process with another to achieve desired goals. Existing strong relationships between some two- and four-year colleges and between some higher education institutions and their K–12 counterparts are more the product of individual leadership than statewide articulation efforts.

STATE CONTEXT

Illinois, with nearly 12 million residents, ranks fifth among study states and sixth in the United States in the size of its population. It is the 14th most diverse state in the United States, with a population that is 15 percent African American, 8 percent Hispanic, and 3 percent Asian American.[1] Although its African-American population is relatively stable, its populations of Hispanics and Asian Americans are growing rapidly. The state is about average among study states in potential tax revenues.[2] Illinois residents are relatively affluent, young, and well educated. Illinois ranks at or near the top of the study states in terms of per capita income and the proportion of high school graduates in the population. It has a relatively low proportion of its population in poverty. It is also about average in its high school dropout rate and the percentage of families who report that English is not spoken in the home.[3]

The governor of Illinois enjoys strong veto and other powers granted by the state constitution.[4] The general assembly operates full-time. The 1994 elections in Illinois produced significant changes in state administrative and legislative offices: Republican majorities were elected to both chambers of the general assembly, and Republicans were elected to every major state office. The predecessor to the current governor was in office for 16 years. During most of this period, the same individuals served respectively as president of UI and executive director of IBHE, the state coordinating board. Also during this time, the Democratic House of Representatives successfully resisted a number of initiatives aimed at modifying the higher education system.

The governor provides active leadership on key legislative measures. He also sends subtle messages to the higher education community by his actions and appointments. A senator told us that the current governor, Jim Edgar, during his first years in office did not increase the budget for higher education in some years and provided less than appropriated for K–12 in other years. According to this senator, this was the governor's way of getting word to higher education that it should become more accountable. The governor instituted higher education reforms by appointing a strong chair of IBHE. During our study, the chair was delivering a message that both the governor and lieutenant governor endorsed: "Emphasize quality, do what you do best, prioritize, and focus."

In some respects, the lieutenant governor is more visible to the higher education community than the governor. He talks about decentralizing all forms of education and linking institutions more directly to accountability by getting rid of unnecessary layers. While the lieutenant governor meets periodically with a variety of education groups, he particularly likes to meet with faculty and may spend up to three hours in such meetings. His message to them, as reported by an assistant, is, "I'm not your biggest critic but the public out there is. I'm just telling you what they are saying." Apart from concerns about the quality of undergraduate education and the desire to eliminate bureaucracy, his top priority may well be to invest in technology to provide a different kind of access to college in the future.

Most legislators approach higher education from the perspective of individual loyalties; having a campus in their district influences their point of view. A former legislative aide described every decision as "project related." During the past decade, IBHE has formally pursued a number of initiatives, including opportunities for underrepresented groups, workforce preparation, productivity improvements, and undergraduate education.[5] Nonetheless, a former legislative aide suggested that IBHE priorities may not be widely understood among members of the legislature. Part of the lack of understanding can be attributed to the realities of political life. Priorities for higher education are most commonly addressed in the appropriations process, where many conflicting interests compete. A legislator told us, "The higher education committee really does not do very much."

Major lobbying groups for higher education with a strong presence in Springfield include representatives of the individual universities and/or systems, the Student Aid Commission, the community colleges (including an influential community college trustee association), the major private institutions, and the Federation of Private Colleges and Universities. Faculty members have representation through their unions, but they are not as visible as institutional lobbyists. Relationships and alliances, which have generally been "quite harmonious," are very important to Illinois higher education. Lobbying representatives for institutions meet as a legislative liaison group to review bills. Because of this strong network, higher education representatives are often better informed than members of the legislature about pending legislation affecting higher education. While some unforeseen events do occasionally occur in legislative budget hearings, this is not usual.

While the University of Illinois clearly dominates public higher education, small campuses such as Chicago State with its African-American caucus can also influence important legislators. With Republicans taking control in both houses, the suburbs have gained influence at the expense of Chicago. A reporter noted, "the anti-city feeling in the legislature has always been strong and seems to be growing stronger." Combined with the anti-city sentiment is an interest in smaller government. Everyone assumes that the legislature will continue to support private institutions, "because they are so influential with key legislators." The University of Illinois enjoys a similar commitment from legislators because it is seen as "the premier state university."

In Illinois, the key to success for higher education is getting the governor to approve a favorable executive budget. Both higher education and K–12 submit their budgets directly to the legislature; the governor's wishes are conveyed to the legislature through the Bureau of the Budget, which one official characterized as the "institutional no." The major concern of the bureau is the "bottom line," although tuition costs and faculty salaries become important policy issues when they place pressures on total costs. While the budget is a political document, the job of the bureau is to provide essentially nonpartisan analysis.

During our site visits, political leaders were preoccupied by issues arising from the prospect of reduced federal dollars as well as changes in the ways that federal dollars can be used. As in other states, higher education in Illinois will continue to be in direct competition for fewer resources with health care, public assistance, and public safety. A legislative staff member observed, "The landscape is changing. It's hand-to-hand combat." A senior senator delivered a similar message: "This year's budget was very fragile. Higher education and K–12 are getting all of the money that they asked for and there is considerable resentment on the part of other state agencies."

Higher education under Republican leadership will be a "leaner, meaner system" that will push efficiency, said a former legislative staff member. Higher education appropriations increased by 14 percent from fiscal year 1990 to fiscal year 1996, an amount just below the inflation rate (14.8 percent). Over the same period, appropriations to higher education declined from 13.3 percent of total general fund expenditures to 11.1 percent, a 16 percent decrease in share.[6] Key legislators believe that money pressures will remain a problem. Several years ago the governor converted a temporary income tax increase into a permanent surcharge for education. The surcharge, which now accounts for 36 percent of the state budget, was identified as one reason for the governor's acceptance of the proposals and budget requests for higher education during the two years of our study.

CHARACTERISTICS AND HISTORY OF HIGHER EDUCATION

The Illinois system of higher education includes 185 degree-granting institutions, 62 of which are publicly controlled, including 49 community college campuses. Total enrollment in higher education (public and private) in Illinois in fiscal year 1996 was 721,575, an increase of just 1 percent since fiscal year 1990.[7] Enrollment growth is expected to be moderate over the next decade, with a projected 17 percent increase in the number of high school graduates.[8] Among study states, Illinois trails only California in the proportion of its population enrolled in two-year institutions. The state also has a relatively large number of private four-year institutions. While the number of public four-year universities is slightly below average, the proportion of students they enroll is similar to other study states. The proportion who enroll in undergraduate, graduate, and professional study is high.[9]

The structure of higher education in Illinois became a federal system with the creation of the system of systems and the establishment of IBHE in 1961. The board's initial focus was on improving access; its first master plan published in 1964 led to establishing the Illinois community college system as well as providing the foundation for the state's overall structure for higher education. The community colleges were placed under the governance of locally elected boards that were coordinated by the Illinois Community College Board (ICCB), which was subordinate to IBHE. Until 1995, the system of systems included four public university governing boards with responsibility for 12 public universities. The subsystems included the board of regents, the board of governors, UI, and SIU.

In Illinois, public institutions were started in rural areas, while private institutions dominated the urban settings. The system of systems was established primarily as a structure of checks and balances to improve the capacity of smaller, four-year, regional institutions to compete with UI and SIU. While the system of systems never achieved the balance of enrollment and resources that was originally intended, it was successful in creating a politically responsive environment (although not one necessarily focused on educational priorities).

The community college system dates to the 1960s. Forty-nine community college campuses are governed by 40 locally elected boards that are coordinated by ICCB. The Illinois Community College Board was described by a member as "a coordinating board that acts as a governing board in certain respects." The board has statutory authority on tuition and can discontinue programs, the two most important powers that IBHE sought in 1995 in unsuccessful legislation to expand its powers.

The Illinois Community College Board sets academic standards to ensure basic levels of quality, and prescribes vision, directions, and policy. Local governing boards determine how these overall directions should be applied within their institutions. The ICCB chair described the board as supportive of local control but with authority to intervene if necessary. The ICCB executive director emphasized the board's role as "coordinating not regulatory." The board exercises this role by implementing massive leadership projects and through emphasizing quality with the legislature. While ICCB staff are responsible for interacting with the legislature, they lack the capacity to quickly provide comparative information for community colleges and other sectors. As a result, most legislative requests for information go to IBHE.

The organization of the public sector and its subsequent growth raised concerns among private institutions. Armed with the results of an independent study completed in the late 1960s, private institutions asked the legislature for need-based financial aid programs and capitation grants to subsidize Illinois students attending private institutions. They also asked that the state use capacity in the private sector instead of starting new programs in public institutions. In return, they agreed to be involved in IBHE master planning. As a result, Illinois is today one of seven states where private institutions are considered integral to the state higher education system.[10] Private institutions are involved extensively in statewide planning. In addition to special purpose grants and contracts in health services education and engineering, Illinois provides direct funding to private nonprofit colleges and universities. The state has the third largest need-based aid program in the country, the Monetary Award Program (MAP). The program was established to assist undergraduates who otherwise would not have the resources to attend colleges, and to enhance student choice for those interested in attending independent institutions. Although private institutions have been losing ground recently to the publics, the student aid program, which is focused on choice, access, and retention, still provides the second largest state allocation in the nation ($256 million in fiscal year 1996).

Because of the close integration of the private sector, some of the private institutions have become involved in the reporting and accountability procedures IBHE has devised for the public institutions. Despite occasional differences of opinion between public and private institutions, the adversarial relationships that are common in many states have never developed in Illinois. The state's extensive student aid program and the significant role of private institutions provide examples of Illinois' use of market forces in directing its higher education system.

The decisions made in the 1960s to use the capacity of private colleges and universities rather than building new four-year institutions—and to create a statewide system of community colleges to accommodate most of the increases in new students at the lower division level—are important legacies that contribute to the shape of contemporary Illinois higher education. From the perspective of current leaders, both decisions have produced substantial benefits for the state.

In spring 1995, the passage of Senate Bill 614 ended the system of systems by abolishing two subsystems, the board of regents and the board of governors, and replacing them with individual boards for seven of the eight institutions that they had governed. The eighth institution, Sangamon State, was redesignated as the third campus of UI. The law also changed the composition of IBHE to remove most of the institutional representatives. The new structure calls for one representative on the board from the public institutions and one from the privates. Principal opposition to the legislation came from representatives of systems not perceived as politically influential and from unions who under the restructuring would have to negotiate with each institutional board rather than at the system level. The last time the proposal for a similar reorganization had been advanced, it was defeated by a single vote in a Democrat-controlled house, due largely to union opposition.

Soon after passage of Senate Bill 614, three additional bills were introduced in the legislature. The first would have increased IBHE's power by giving it authority to set tuition, eliminate programs, supervise construction (including the use of nonpublic funds), and perform an audit function for college and university nonprofit foundations. The bill received little support from the legislature for two reasons. First, it was opposed by UI on the grounds that it was unnecessary and would create a super-board; second, IBHE was divided internally on the measure, with system representatives generally in opposition. A representative from the governor's Bureau of the Budget expressed the view of elected officials when he noted there is no need for anyone to take control over tuition increases since tuition funds are placed in a segregated fund by universities, and require legislative appropriation for use. A second bill aimed at removing ICCB from the jurisdiction of IBHE passed both legislative chambers by huge margins, but was vetoed by the governor. A third bill designed to restore seats on IBHE for institutional representatives of UI and SIU did not make it out of committee.

Many long-term observers of Illinois higher education were shocked by the swiftness with which a highly regarded system was changed by the passage of Senate Bill 614. A reporter said he was "shaking his head that a system that appeared to be working was now being completely shaken up." He added that the recent proposals for governance changes, particularly the move for in-creased power by IBHE, "took people by surprise." While people knew that changes might be proposed, he said, no one expected such quick action and no one really thought through all of the consequences. In marked contrast, a legislative staff member concluded that the shakeout might do some good, adding, "every institution needs a lot of action and drama to get one ounce of good."

Illinois Board of Higher Education leaders reacted to the changes in a number of ways. The Illinois Board of Higher Education fought and appears to have survived the challenge by community colleges to be taken from their jurisdiction. In turn, the board promised increased responsiveness to commu-nity college concerns. The executive director has convened presidents from the public and private four-year and community colleges, whereas previously it was the system heads, not the presidents, who were brought together. And IBHE leaders have not given up the search for a buffer that will either strengthen IBHE or develop some new form of system to keep campuses at arm's length from the legislature.

DESIGN OF THE HIGHER EDUCATION–STATE GOVERNMENT INTERFACE

The executive director of IBHE described the board as "the neck of the bottle. We aren't just higher education. We aren't just government. We take posi-tions that are not as predictable as segmental boards. We try to be advocates of higher education, but they don't always perceive us as such." He continued by comparing the board to a consulting firm with little statutory authority. Authority comes from the way the governor and the legislature have used the board. A former IBHE staff member made a similar observation when he said, "The board of higher education's power is not in statutes but in gathering groups together, achieving consensus, and presenting with one voice."

The president of a comprehensive public university described IBHE as a "steward" and evaluated IBHE performance on three aspects of this role: "defining the important policy issues facing education (the board still has a ways to go on this one); causing universities to think seriously about what they are doing and why they are doing it (getting the system to act like a system . . .); [and being] at the same time both advocates and critics of higher education in the policy arena." A community college president described the board as "controlling," primarily focused on funding, capital matters, and policy development, but with more power over universities than community colleges.

A university president suggested that the board derives its power from a strong governor who always turns to IBHE to allocate resources. He said that the board enhances its authority by focusing on rational, responsible budget recommendations and reducing conflicts among institutions and sectors. A representative of independent colleges described the board as the focal point of political power in Illinois for higher education. The degree to which problems are thrashed out at the IBHE level allows the governor and legislature to be free from hands-on operations of the colleges and universities. The work of IBHE was said by another to be "first-rate and respected across the state."

The board's authority also derives from "quality board members" and a reputation for hiring people on merit, which has prevented it from becoming a political dumping ground. The executive director was characterized as "a creature of the board of higher education who works at nothing but its benefit" and "a seismograph, anticipating issues before they arise." He was also described as "very slow to anger," "very unflappable." According to one observer, his ability to keep the focus on issues rather than personalities has "a calming effect on the staff."

The Illinois Board of Higher Education keeps a low profile. The IBHE offices are modest, to say the least, and cannot be seen from the street. Unlike other state offices, there are no signs on the exterior of the building. The IBHE offices and main conference room are small and contain standard, state-issued furniture. In addition to very ordinary offices, the board has maintained an office car known as "the beast." This ancient Ford reached 125,000 miles before collapsing. The executive director took delight in driving this relic to IBHE sessions and to meetings with campus presidents to contrast their living styles with that of IBHE.

Over the past 15 years, IBHE authority has grown not so much through statute as through its success in promoting a united front among higher education leaders. Board stature has also been enhanced through acceptance of its recommendations by the legislature and governors. A board staff member described this evolutionary development:

> The legislature probably doesn't want an IBHE that is too strong. The first time IBHE tried to exercise influence by recommending a higher level of admission requirements, they were reversed, partly because of resistance from the K–12 sector concerned about cost. Maitland [a senior state senator] put the board's requirements into statute with a delayed implementation date. The statute also added more flexibility

in meeting the requirements than IBHE wanted. This led to sort of a rule of thumb, if you can get there by building consensus, IBHE will do it; if the issue produces conflict, the legislature will probably provide resolution.

A representative from the community college sector made the same point somewhat differently: "In Illinois there has been a great emphasis on harmony and unanimity among the higher education community. IBHE is the big daddy of this process."

A senior staff member for IBHE described the difference between consensus building and negotiation. From his perspective, negotiation means "the compromise of opposing points of view," while consensus building involves "finding areas of agreement about which ends are worth achieving and how to go about achieving them." Other respondents suggested that consensus building involves discussions and papers and perhaps not a great deal of change. A staff member for the lieutenant governor said, "IBHE basically studied the issues it dealt with for a god-awful number of years." A representative from the private sector suggested that conventional governance structures "militate against raising issues that get people upset with you. The incentives for staff at IBHE are on the side of keeping things the way they are and following the status quo. This approach creates a comfort zone for the staff." We were told that ordinarily there is consensus among the segments before issues reach the board.

Within IBHE's consultative, consensus-building processes, some sectors are apparently perceived as "more equal than others." A community college representative suggested that IBHE is "directive to community colleges and universities of lesser status but much more conciliatory with the U of I and private institutions." A university president told us the leadership styles of the president of UI and the executive director of IBHE are highly compatible. The executive director of IBHE, we were told, works hard to keep recommendations consistent with the agenda of UI, knowing that once "U of I was in the barn," other segments are manageable. While IBHE has not articulated its own "vision" for higher education, it has embraced a "vision" promoted by the president of UI that is broad enough and well enough informed to encompass the entire higher education community.

The Illinois Board of Higher Education is sensitive to the political culture. The board chair at the time of our visit had high credibility with the governor and was particularly effective in articulating the public policy agenda. The executive director was perceived as sensitive to issues and forward-looking. The Illinois Board of Higher Education is a source of high-quality information; the board provides quick responses with a small staff that has a reputation for being useful to the legislators. While remaining visible and available, the board is cautious about taking positions on new legislation. In its informational role, IBHE provides a note on each bill that is introduced, which includes a synthesis and relevant information. These notes go to house and senate staff, to Appropriations Committee members, and to the higher education community.

A house staff member told us that the committee he staffs works "with IBHE in particular because IBHE is really the institutional memory of higher education." A senator said he appreciates the comprehensive data provided by the board, including assessments of Illinois higher education affordability, the progress of minority students in higher education, the implementation of workforce preparation policies, and analyses of the Priorities, Quality and Productivity (PQP) initiative in higher education institutions. A community college representative provided a somewhat backhanded compliment when he noted, "IBHE is so inundated with paper, it turns out more information than anyone else. They're good at collecting information and putting it together. However, it is their format and their interpretation." The president of a comprehensive university described IBHE as very good at keeping political representatives happy by targeting resources on favored institutions.

The Illinois Board of Higher Education's basic mode of operation involves working through the administrative structure, particularly the presidents. While the board receives input from four advisory committees, including ones representing faculty, students, and independent institutions, the real action takes place in consultations between IBHE and institutional governing boards and presidents. An official in state government went so far as to state, "The president of the University of Illinois and the executive director of the board of higher education make deals behind closed doors because the director is aware that the president can go around the board of higher education." A senior UI official described the process somewhat differently: "The board [executive director] informs the president of what the board is planning to do. This does not necessarily mean they will always agree but it is a courtesy that each affords to the other." When the bill to increase IBHE powers was introduced in the legislature, it was clearly the absence of such consultation that provoked a very strong reaction from UI.

The absence of standing committees both allows and compels the chair and the executive director to develop and articulate board positions and priorities. The board does not, for example, have standing committees on areas such as legislation. Nor do lobbyists generally try to influence individual members of the board. Moreover, board members disagree as to the extent of their involvement in real policy discussions. During an IBHE meeting, for instance, one member said, "We as a board spend very little time talking about policy. We react only to papers that are generated by . . . staff who pile minutes upon minutes." Another board member contradicted him, noting, "We discuss a lot of policy here and in committee meetings." Later in the same meeting, board members clarified the primary roles of the chair and executive director concerning the legislative initiative to increase board powers.

The board does appoint topical committees in such areas as technology, affordability, PQP, and undergraduate education. A representative of the private sector cited the work of the Committee on Affordability as an example of "balanced incrementalism." The committee, we were told, had a very difficult time getting the right issues on the table and did not go as far as they should have in raising issues regarding students' ability to pay. A second interviewee also criticized this committee, suggesting it had only a small number of people who tried to focus on what the public needed, and came up with soft recommendations that did not amount to much.

At the time of our visit, IBHE was beginning to play a much more visible, activist role. A university president told us IBHE is dominated by the chair, with other members simply falling into line. He continued by noting that the staff is directed as much by the chair as by the executive director. Institutional budgets and IBHE use of information have been the incentives that have driven past board decisions, although the budgets and use of information have seldom been perceived as tools for strategic planning or governance. That situation may also be changing.

The emerging strategy of IBHE has been to focus attention on how well base funding is spent rather than on competition for whatever incremental increases may be available. Through this strategy IBHE has attempted to emphasize the accountability of governing boards rather than focusing on incremental increases. Supporting IBHE's fiscal strategies is the previous experience of the executive director, who worked for the Bureau of the Budget and was fiscal director for IBHE. The executive director has retained primary responsibility for the budget process.

The board chair at the time of our visits said that the fundamental role of IBHE is to push change onto governing board agendas by identifying priorities of a statewide nature. He told us:

> Priorities emerge from political factors, discussions with constituencies, and a host of other sources. It is the entire mix of activities and discussions occurring within a state at a given time that contributes to such priorities. Within the directions suggested by these priorities it is the board's objective to get individual institutions to set their own priorities. If a board can be trusted in terms of its credibility, identifying priorities makes these issues bigger than life. If you have priorities, you have to make decisions in connection with them and this is why IBHE has emphasized the importance of getting institutions to develop priorities. Once institutions have developed priorities, these can be used to evaluate mission. Are priorities in line with mission? Bad

programs must be thrown out. Among good programs, institutions must make decisions about which are most important. Requiring that institutions do this has been a basic board strategy in the PQP program.

This activist approach generates concerns as well as endorsements. A university president, after acknowledging that it is reasonable for IBHE to raise questions about productivity and quality and to reward institutions that change, was apprehensive that the board might subsequently focus on such things as faculty workload, faculty roles, and faculty responsibilities. The possibility that the board might attempt to regulate these issues provoked the advice that IBHE should be careful about the battles it chooses to fight.

WORK PROCESSES

The Illinois Board of Higher Education coordinates public and private higher education in the state through processes that have evolved from the board's statutory authority. By law, IBHE has responsibility to: analyze needs and develop a master plan; recommend budgetary needs for operations and for capital improvements to the governor and general assembly; administer state and federal grant programs; approve new and review existing programs of instruction, research, or public service for the public sector in relation to educational and economic justification; and approve or disapprove operating and degree-granting authority for nonpublic colleges and universities.

Information Management

In many ways, IBHE is, as one person told us, the institutional memory of higher education in Illinois. The list of reports attributed by a senator to IBHE reads like an inventory of state priorities for higher education. The board's cost studies provide a rationale for budget recommendations; its budget preparation encourages exchanges of information between the political and higher education communities. The synthesis that IBHE provides for each higher education bill introduced in the state legislature informs house and senate staff, Appropriations Committee members, and the broader higher education community. The quantity and quality of available information, as well as IBHE's convening authority, does much to build a united front that contributes to the effectiveness of advocacy efforts. Information helps to prevent surprises in the legislative process, making the system more predictable and manageable than might otherwise be the case. Illinois is information-rich because IBHE responds quickly to requests and does a masterful job of getting legislators and others to use their services.

Institutional leaders do not necessarily see this rich information environment as advantageous to their best interests. Community college advocates described the ICCB initiative to create a uniform cost accounting system as "repressive." We were told that university leaders were "livid" when IBHE released its proposals for program elimination in advance of the completion of campus efforts to identify their lists. And IBHE's failure to follow the unwritten rules of advance consultation before legislation was introduced to increase the board's powers provoked an especially intensive reaction from UI.

Accustomed to the give and take of the political process, the political leaders we spoke with seem to view occasional departures from the consultation and consensus-building procedures generally followed by IBHE as healthy, and a reasonable price to pay for speeding up the pace of system response.

Budget Process

Governing boards and ICCB submit their budget requests to IBHE by November. There follows a series of "big picture meetings" in which IBHE staff and the presidents of the 12 public universities discuss the needs of each campus. During these meetings, general rules are established dealing with such issues as salary increases, utility costs, and tuition and fee increases. Institutions disregard these "rules" at their own peril. During 1995, the board of Southern Illinois University (SIU) tried to increase tuition by 13 percent instead of by 3.5 percent as recommended by IBHE. After a variety of pressures were brought through the legislature, SIU changed its mind and went back to the 3.5 percent that everyone else was adopting.

The Illinois Board of Higher Education next drafts a "shadow budget" as an indicator of what it might recommend to the governor. Copies of the shadow budget are given to the presidents and to the governor's Bureau of the Budget. This design encourages presidents to buy into IBHE's requests and concurrently seeks input from the bureau. Even before developing the shadow budget, IBHE tries to get a sense from the legislature and the governor of the resources available for higher education. The strategy used at the time of our study was to try to present a reasonable budget that would be given serious consideration in the legislature and the governor's office. While this process of consultation was cynically described by one president as "asking for what they know they can get," IBHE staff believe they push the limit on what the state can provide. During the time of our study, IBHE cut $90 million from the requests of system boards while recommending a budget that was more than $92 million higher than the previous year in general funds support.

The presidents have the opportunity to comment on the shadow budget, but by January, discussions end; IBHE adopts a budget and sends it to the governor and the legislature. A budget bill is introduced in the legislature; the first act is to amend it to conform to the recommendations of the governor's Bureau of the Budget. At budget hearings, testimony is first taken from IBHE staff, then from the system chancellors or presidents. Typically, the governor and majority and minority heads of each of the Illinois houses meet to negotiate and decide on the final budget. In fiscal years 1995, 1996, and 1997, the governor agreed to the budget advanced by IBHE.

The board conducts several analyses of cost data. Reported costs for an institution are compared with projected costs if the institution were to provide all instruction at the average state cost per student. Institutions whose costs exceed the state average by more than 5 percent are encouraged to reduce costs. Those with reported costs below the state average by more than 5 percent may be encouraged to reduce enrollment. Cost studies helped IBHE to quantify the results of the Priorities, Quality and Productivity (PQP) process, a process developed to prompt institutions to establish priorities, enhance quality, and reduce costs. Since the procedure for creating university cost studies, format tables, and charts have been in use for more than 15 years, there is considerable constancy, stability, and longevity in the financial data.

A representative of the Bureau of the Budget told us that enrollment expectations or projections are not considered at the state level. The chair of the Senate Appropriations Committee said there do not appear to be any formulas or other procedures for relating enrollment to budgets, then added, "After the fact, IBHE looks at costs per student and then tries to adjust requests." An IBHE staff member suggested that while budgets in Illinois are not enrollment-driven, a sizable jump in enrollment at an institution might be considered a justification for an increase.

Chicago State University is a case in point. During the early 1990s, the institution increased its enrollment by 68 percent while receiving only a 19 percent increase in funding. In the 1995 budget cycle, the institution requested a 29 percent increase that was whittled down to an 11 percent increase by the board of governors and finally to 4.5 percent by IBHE. An IBHE staff member justified the small increase by noting that Chicago State had taken a dive in enrollments in the late 1980s while their funding remained relatively stable. The validity of this explanation notwithstanding, Chicago State was able to obtain $1.7 million beyond the amount recommended by IBHE in one of the few exceptions that occurred in the 1995 budget process. We were told this happened because Democratic members of the legislature wanted to challenge the governor's claim that he had an "education budget." Through a series of compromises that year, each of the legislative caucuses received funds they could provide to higher education. The senate minority leader, who was from Chicago, was instrumental in arranging the additional funds for Chicago State.

The budget process does not always seem as rational and well organized to institutional participants as it does to IBHE staff members. The president of a comprehensive university talked about the process as "bizarre." He said, "Institutions are forced to begin planning now for what they will need in the next fiscal year; they work through their own campuses and through their governing boards and then give something to IBHE. At this point, categories of incentive funding miraculously appear, but institutions have not previously been told there is extra money in the budget if they do an especially good job on x or y." The president said that if the process were used correctly it might really drive the way an institution establishes and meets policy objectives. This same president praised the board for providing PQP bonuses in the budgets of those institutions that IBHE felt had done a good job of addressing this initiative. He described the bonuses as a powerful statement about what is important and should be taken seriously.

In the final analysis, we were told that the entire system functions not because its processes are in the statutes, but because they are not. The board has no statutory right to mandate budgets. It can review them, but it does not have final authority over them. The system works because institutions have thought it is in their general interest to cooperate, to present a united front, and not to try to submit individual budgets to the legislature. There have been times when individual institutions, usually UI, have threatened to submit their own budgets because they were displeased by some of the decisions of IBHE, but in the end they have gone along.

Program Planning and Review

The Illinois Board of Higher Education has been successful in exercising a reasonable degree of control over the proliferation of new programs. A board staff member told us that the approval process has been aided by focus statements. The board had previously asked campuses to create mission statements, but found that "campus attempts to write mission statements turned out to be sort of a hundred-year project. They weren't getting any-where." So IBHE decided to write its own focus statements. These statements have more sharply defined the role of each campus and in so doing have confined some of the campuses' more ambitious aspirations.

We were told that the most important steps of the program-approval process happen on campus. When an application is received by IBHE, it is compared with criteria that have been developed for each sector. The review process operates at both the formal level (through advisory committees and other communications) and the informal level (through continuous consulta-tion and collaboration). The process moves very slowly, a source of comfort to people within and outside IBHE. The process is more formal with private than with public institutions and it is better documented. For community colleges, program approval takes place primarily at ICCB with review by IBHE mostly a formality, unless the program is contested by another institution.

Program challenges most commonly involve duplication. Formal criteria address this issue for public institutions (including community colleges), but not for private institutions.[11] The statute authorizing board authority for the private sector was essentially a consumer protection bill, as evidenced by its title in the 1960s as the "diploma mill bill." On the issue of whether IBHE should approve private sector programs that reduce the productivity of public institutions, an IBHE member suggested the board could not stop private institutions from spending their money. The differences in IBHE statutory authority for public and private institutions probably account for some of the feelings that privates are favored in IBHE processes.

A senior administrator from Chicago State who believes his institution should offer a master's degree in social work and an MBA program was critical of the IBHE process for approving new programs. He said, "The process does not allow for the needs of a particular area such as Chicago." To serve the needs of the population in a segregated city, the administrator continued, "We need to have such programs even if they already exist elsewhere."

In 1989, in response to gubernatorial concerns and mixed public perceptions about higher education accountability and productivity, IBHE established a committee on scope, structure, and productivity. In 1991 a new IBHE chair called for institutions to set priorities and to improve quality and productivity. As the initiative evolved into the Priorities, Quality and Productivity (PQP) project, each college and university was directed to focus its mission, to set priorities among programs and services consistent with that mission, and to consolidate or eliminate lower priority and lower quality programs and services. The aim was to free resources for reinvestment that would strengthen the quality of higher priority programs and services.[12]

At a board meeting held in October 1992, IBHE staff recommended, as part of the PQP process, the elimination, consolidation, or reduction of 190 programs at public universities, including 7 percent of all undergraduate programs. In addition to reductions in instructional programs, staff recommendations called for phasing out state support for intercollegiate athletics, redirecting 6 to 9 percent of the expenditures for research and public service to undergraduate education, and paying particular attention to faculty workload assignments for undergraduate education.

In 1993, the initial 190 programs were increased by another 33 identified by IBHE staff as economically and educationally unjustified. Out of this total of more than 220 programs, a staff member told us that about half were either eliminated or reconstituted in a more cost-efficient format. There are different estimates of the savings produced by the process. One IBHE staff member estimated cost savings for the two-year period from 1991 to 1993 at around $90 million, although he conceded this was a difficult number to calculate because of the flexibility campuses have in shifting funds. A former staff member suggested that even if all of the programs on the so-called hit list in the first and second years were eliminated, the savings still would be "nickel and dime stuff." Supporting this latter perspective were the comments of a faculty union representative who told us that most of the faculty in the 125 programs actually eliminated were absorbed into new programs or moved to other existing programs. He called the savings "fictitious," arguing that they came as the result of the attrition of faculty members and their replacement with non-tenured faculty. He also said that some of the resources freed were used to increase faculty salaries.

A university president told us that the common view that institutions retained the funds saved through PQP is not correct. The PQP process was preceded by a state action that rescinded from institutions one-fourth to one-half of the funds they were likely to be able to free. In spite of this rescission, the president said that the results had been positive and that the real reinvestment would provide for a stronger system in the future. Even the former board staff member who described the savings as "nickel and dime stuff" said that about half of the effort was real reform, so that programs make more sense now than they did before.

In the 1995 fiscal year, IBHE gave bonuses ranging from $200,000 to $500,000 to seven of the 12 public universities they judged particularly meritorious in implementing the PQP process. The five institutions that did not get bonuses complained to their local legislators and the heat grew sufficiently intense that IBHE dropped the approach. For the 1996 fiscal year, IBHE planned to reward institutions doing the best job by giving them a larger share of new program money, in the hope that this would not cause so much trouble in the legislature. Also to dispel concerns raised in the previous year, additional money was provided to all institutions under a new "undergraduate education" bonus category. This more cautious approach proved its merit when the chair of the House Appropriations Committee asked a legislative representative for IBHE at one of the early budget hearings, "Are there any blatant things in this budget like the PQP bonuses?"

At the time of our study, IBHE planned to consider indicators for academic productivity as the next stage of PQP. In a public meeting, the chair at that time described what he called a "10 percent rule": at least 10 percent of the programs any institution offers at any given time are probably of low quality and in need of review. The PQP should be seen, he said, as a continuous initiative to improve quality. He said that the easy program decisions were made in the first stage and now institutions face more difficult choices. "We are not about saving dollars," he said. "We are trying to use dollars to transform what we do. In the next phase PQP must consider the role of the faculty and how they spend their time."

The early stages of the PQP process received high praise from virtually every political leader we contacted, with the exception of some Democratic legislators. We were told by an assistant to the lieutenant governor that the process took an onerous burden off legislators in determining which programs ought to be closed to free resources in the current environment of constraints. A budget office representative said that PQP had given legislators the impression of accountability and that it had helped keep institutional budgetary requests within the 5 percent range that is reasonable in state budgeting. We were also told that PQP was appreciated by the legislature because it departed somewhat from the consensual processes the board had followed in the past.

A senior senator described PQP as the first step toward accountability for IBHE. At the same time, he criticized the board for the timing of their 1992 report, noting that it was released after the board had asked universities to evaluate their programs, but before universities had provided the results of their internal evaluations. A Democratic senator who was particularly concerned about problems at Illinois State University and believed that PQP contributed to them, said that communications about the process and overall goals were not clear.[13] A house Democratic staff member, while acknowledging the usefulness of IBHE's attempts to set priorities, told us that during the worst budget years, "PQP raised howls from the campuses and from legislators because IBHE had recommended cuts to some of the sacred cows like the Northern Illinois Law School and the Illinois State Agricultural Program." He continued, "These programs were not eliminated because the IBHE does not have the power to do so." At the time of our study, however, the legislature was no longer Democratic and was much more supportive of PQP than its predecessors.

Institutional representatives, while generally positive about the impact of PQP on efficiency, were more qualified in their praise than political leaders. Some suggested that the impact of the initiative varied widely by institutional type. A senior administrator for UI thought that other institutions had "stonewalled the IBHE." A faculty union representative argued that UI probably did not pay any attention to it. We were also told that the board of governors praised it publicly but probably did not do much about it and that the board of regents (particularly Illinois State) defied IBHE. One respondent suggested that many program reductions involved little more than getting rid of "catalog clutter, stuff that's been around for a long time and people knew shouldn't be offered but was still there for one reason or another." A prominent example given was an inactive Ph.D. program in mining at the UI Urbana campus that was ultimately abandoned after an unsuccessful effort to keep it in the catalog.

A faculty member suggested that the IBHE executive director and chair were, in fact, "scapegoats to take the heat off institutional leaders who did not want to confront their faculty." Supporting this perception were the comments of a senior university administrator who suggested that PQP provided his campus administration with the camouflage it needed to do the things that needed to be done. He added, "The administration almost leaped for joy at the board's PQP initiative." A faculty labor representative described the focus of the board on academic programs as "mistaken," arguing that the board should have focused its efforts on administrative expenses and costs. An official of one of the discontinued system boards said that building political support has been an important outcome of the PQP exercise.

Finally, the process clearly worked better in some areas than in others. Intercollegiate athletics did not go through the same type of discussion that characterized the other programs identified by IBHE. Ultimately, IBHE abandoned its effort to redirect to academic programs those state-appropriated funds spent on intercollegiate athletics.

Whatever the magnitude of savings, IBHE improved its reputation for effectiveness. A K–12 representative described the PQP process as the closest thing to reform in higher education he had seen, adding, "PQP has given IBHE more muscle and made them more vigorous in their view of the state-level leadership they might provide." A member of IBHE said, "Board reputation has been enhanced because the board has been able to reallocate funds to institutions from the PQP process." A reporter told us that PQP had a positive effect on institutions.

System Articulation

Encouraging institutions to work together across segmental boundaries is one of the functions a coordinating board might easily be expected to address, and it is one of the action items on the IBHE agenda. There are, however, widely divergent perspectives on the effectiveness of IBHE in encouraging the diverse institutions that comprise Illinois higher education to think of themselves as an integrated system.

We were told by a senior IBHE administrator that articulation and transfer between two- and four-year institutions have been on the agenda for almost 100 years—because Joliet (the first public two-year college in the nation) was founded in 1910 and current initiatives will be fully implemented in 2010. From his long-term perspective, IBHE and ICCB decided to address transfer and articulation cooperatively—as a statewide initiative that would develop a systematic process for improvement. As with other consensus-oriented projects, IBHE started with system academic officers and involved faculty in leadership positions on the campuses. To date, the initiative has produced a new general education core acceptable at all public institutions and 10 area panels for high-demand majors that jointly encompass 75 percent of the students who transfer. Panels include high school faculty members as well as faculty representing universities and colleges. The Illinois Board of Higher Education planned to have a fully articulated program in nursing by fall 1996. An IBHE staff member told us that Illinois has made more progress in articulation and transfer than most other states.

In contrast, an ICCB staff member told us that IBHE has studied articulation for 26 years. When the topic once again came before IBHE recently, staff suggested that it should be studied some more. The ICCB member who sits on IBHE rejected the recommendation and used information about the 3,000 annual reverse transfers to show a senior UI administrator what would happen if community colleges decided to reject their credits. A comprehensive university president described the new general education core as "a way of backing the UI into a corner so they can be less snooty about taking general education courses from transfer students." The same president described the board's approach as "nonsubstantive but tactically effective." The ICCB staff used the information system to show that in the final analysis very few students transfer to the UI.

A staff member from ICCB was even more blunt in his assessment of IBHE leadership. While acknowledging the transfer and articulation effort as "useful," he said it was about four or five years behind most progressive states. He added, "The place where articulation is worse is with UI and that is where IBHE should have and could have done the most, but hasn't. IBHE has stepped in and grabbed the agenda and taken credit for progress that has essentially been accomplished through individual community colleges and the ICCB." Characterizing IBHE transfer and articulation efforts as "not cutting-edge," he concluded, "There is a lot more rhetoric than actual change."

The reality of Illinois articulation probably lies somewhere between these contrasting viewpoints, as suggested by the closing comments of the IBHE staff member referenced earlier. He told us, "Articulation . . . must constantly be on the agenda. Once you have a general education core, institutions change their approach to general education, so the process must constantly be attended." His description of enforcement procedures for the transfer initiatives and core curriculum reflected the weak statutory authority of IBHE as well as its consensus mode of operation. Colleges, he said, will submit their requirements to IBHE and the outcome will be an Internet list maintained by someone not yet identified.

The IBHE role with respect to relationships between the private and public sectors seems much more straightforward, though not less controversial. A public university president said IBHE's role is to "compromise the public institutions so they would not trample on the privates." He saw this as a great source of strength for IBHE in the political context of Illinois. From a different perspective, the chair of IBHE told us that the board has a role in preserving good relationships between the public and private sectors. He continued, "Every once in a while a head of steam builds up to take money away from the private sector because public higher education has so many problems." He said that as a chair, he has tried "to nip such efforts in the bud."

The "not-so-veiled resentment" that characterizes the reactions of many community college representatives to IBHE is mirrored in the comments we heard from K–12 respondents. For instance, IBHE ignored the K–12 board in its discussion of admissions requirements during the 1980s despite the fact that the K–12 board was involved concurrently in looking at outcomes. We were also told, "There needs to be some way of linking higher education and basic education efforts. With respect to minority student achievement, higher education takes the moral high ground, but efforts at the institutional level in absence of pressures from the state have been pretty meaningless. Nothing much happens." The IBHE affordability study was described as another "strain on the conversation" because the board never considered the impact on elementary and secondary school costs. Rather, IBHE sent the message that, "If you would do a better job of preparing students, our costs would go down." One source concluded, "No matter what happens, seems like the ball rolls downhill."

Concurrently, we were told by IBHE representatives that the relationship between higher education and K–12 is becoming more important. The arrival of a new superintendent and the activities of a joint board of education and IBHE Education Committee were identified to us as "promising developments." From our K–12 respondent's perspective, however, the joint education committee is "a wonderful idea without authority, a very ineffective group" where meetings exemplify the gulf: "They sit on one side, we sit on the other." Most of the good things that have occurred involving cooperation between schools and universities, we were told, have happened at the local level.

CONCLUSION

While no one constituency is completely satisfied with higher education in Illinois, all recognized the ability of the state to assert and implement its priorities. Through a strong statewide coordinating board and a system with many built-in checks and balances, the system is able to maintain a healthy tension between institutional and market forces, and to alter the balance among these forces when necessary. A strong statewide coordinating board with responsibility for all four of the key work processes helps to steer the system in the direction of state priorities. A strong and highly regarded private sector has sacrificed some of its independence in return for the state's willingness to create and preserve a vital role for private institutions in higher education planning in the state.

NOTES

1. WICHE and the College Board, *The Road to College: Educational Progress by Race and Ethnicity* (Boulder, Colo., July 1991), pp. 7–8.
2. K. Halstead, *State Profiles for Higher Education 1978 to 1996: Trend Data* (Washington, D.C.: Research Associates of Washington, 1996), p. 25.
3. Unless otherwise noted, data in this paragraph are from *Chronicle of Higher Education Almanac* 43, no. 1 (September 1996), pp. 54–55.
4. J. M. Burns, J. W. Peltason, and T. E. Cronin, *State and Local Politics, Government by the People* (Englewood Cliffs, N.J.: Prentice Hall, 1990), p. 113.
5. R. C. Richardson, Jr., "Illinois," in *Charting Higher Education Accountability*, ed. S. S. Ruppert (Denver, Colo.: Education Commission of the States, June 1994), pp. 40–51.
6. "Illinois Higher Education: Summary Information: Enrollments, Tuition, Student Aid and State Support" (Springfield, Ill.: Illinois Board of Higher Education, 1996), not paginated.
7. Ibid.
8. *Chronicle of Higher Education Almanac*, pp. 54–55.
9. Ibid.; and Halstead, *State Profiles*, pp. 25, 28.
10. Task Force on State Policy and Independent Higher Education, *The Preservation of Excellence in American Higher Education: The Essential Role of Private Colleges and Universities* (Denver, Colo.: Education Commission of the States, 1990), p. 35.
11. The minutes of an IBHE meeting held September 6, 1995, report concerns about unnecessary duplication raised by a board member about a request by the Teacher's Union to establish a private graduate school for teachers in Chicago. The board member was informed that this was not a criterion for the approval of programs offered by private schools. Ultimately, IBHE approved the request unanimously.
12. Illinois Board of Higher Education, "Public University Program Review: Statewide Analyses, Board Agenda Item 5A," IBHE Board Meeting, Springfield, Ill., July 1995, p. 1.
13. During our study, the president received a no confidence vote from the faculty and subsequently resigned.

CHAPTER  9

Policy Environments, System Designs, and System Performance

I n chapter 1, we suggested that performance in state higher education systems is influenced primarily by the policy environment and the system design. We also noted that leadership is an important factor in under-standing system performance. States can shape policy environments by selecting policy roles that balance deference to professional values and the use of market forces. The role of the market has become increasingly important "in almost every nation state as governments seek, through more targeted regulation or through systematic deregulation, to harness the market as a means of higher education reform."[1] Many governments now believe that markets have more to offer than regulation as a means of improving performance, just as most came to the conclusion at mid-century that regulation brought a better return on the dollar than simply providing resources.

System design also contributes to system performance. Most states design higher education systems by choosing bureaucratic or federal principles to structure the relationship between government and institutions. To perform effectively, systems should be designed to be compatible with the policy environments in which they function. The role of state as regulator, for instance, works at cross-purposes with the deference to professional values that characterizes the most segmented systems. The regulator role is consistent with more centralized bureaucratic models, including the unified model. Yet central planning, which is often a feature of more unified structural models, does not fit well with increasing emphasis on the market.

States may design or restructure governance arrangements without considering the degree to which effective operation depends upon the incentives and disincentives of the policy environment. Conversely, policy environments can change over time to the point where governance structures designed for a different era no longer work very well. States in which the policy environment and structural design are mismatched create unnecessarily contentious circumstances that make leadership difficult. Systems with good leadership can at times overcome many of the constraints of poor design or incompatible state policy environments, and systems with poor leadership are likely to fall short of their potential under the best of circumstances. As Clark Kerr suggests, "Human beings often triumph over poor policies and bad structures. This human element can and does sometimes transcend seemingly impossible constraints of policy and structure as personal ability and personal relations make a system work better than seems possible."[2] Well-designed systems operating in compatible policy environments with good leadership have the best chance of performing in ways that satisfy policy priorities.

Table 9.1 provides information about the policy roles and system designs of the seven states in our study. While there tends to be one policy role that is dominant in each state, all states exhibit some characteristics of each of the four policy roles.

TABLE 9.1

STATE POLICY ROLES AND SYSTEM DESIGNS

| | System Design | | |
State Policy Role	Segmented	Unified	Federal
Steering			Illinois
Consumer Advocacy		Georgia	
Regulating	Florida		
	New York*		
	California*		Texas*
Providing Resources	Michigan		

* These states have incompatible state policy roles and system designs.

Michigan's policy role, which emphasizes providing resources, matches its highly segmented system design. The incentives in this arrangement emphasize deference to professional values. Illinois also has a match between a steering policy environment and a federal system design, but here the incentives focus on responding to the environment and to market forces. While many academics might argue that Michigan has by far the best of the two arrangements, our perspective is shaped by the belief that transformations such as "global capitalism"[3] will call forth responses from higher education that must transcend the preferences of academics.

Whereas Michigan has a highly segmented system, Florida, New York, and California have variations of segmented systems—in which Florida's system approaches a more unified design, and New York and California lie between Florida and Michigan on the continuum of more unified to more segmented structures. Florida operates in a state environment that emphasizes regulation with overtones of consumer advocacy. The California policy environment varies by segment. For the University of California (UC), the state operates mainly as a provider of resources because of the system's constitutional status. For California State University (CSU) and the community colleges, the state role remains significantly regulatory, although for the community colleges there is a disconnect between the state policy environment and the local districts. In New York, the state policy role remains highly regulatory.

Texas, New York, and California provide examples of mismatches between policy environments and system designs. All three systems are contentious and difficult to lead. Texas's federal design could respond effectively to steering, yet the legislature is committed to regulation. New York has a bureaucratic system operating under heavy state regulation. Not surprisingly, its public institutions are responding slowly to policies that insist upon the importance of the market. Californians no longer agree about the viability of the self-regulating 1960 Master Plan for Higher Education. Disagreements have led to policy drift and "public policy by anecdote."[4] Access to inadequately funded community colleges remains open and low-cost, but student charges at public four-year institutions rose rapidly in the first half of the 1990s, based on institutional needs.

Georgia's unified system design and central planning may also become a mismatch for the market emphasis that has been produced by the introduction of the HOPE scholarships in the state. Present strong leadership along with constitutional status for the entire system may give Georgia more latitude for coping with mismatches than other states confronting this issue.

The following section provides a more detailed discussion of the relationship between the policy environments and design of the seven systems. We then compare the performance of the seven systems on five sets of outcome variables. The chapter concludes with an assessment of ways in which policy environments and governance structures influence the strategies that appointed and elected leaders choose in efforts to influence performance.

THE POLICY DIMENSION: HISTORICAL AND CONTEXTUAL INFLUENCES

The character and history of state governments—including the constitutional strength of the governor, the legal or constitutional status of institutions, and voter initiatives—affect the balance between institutional values and market forces. Voter initiatives in California and Florida, for example, limit the alternatives available to public officials and may limit their interest in trying to change higher education. A strong private higher education sector and collective bargaining also influence the balance of forces.

Table 9.2 provides a summary of some of the constitutional factors that influence state policy environments.

TABLE 9.2

CONSTITUTIONAL FACTORS AFFECTING STATE POLICY ENVIRONMENTS

	Predominant State Role	Constitutional Strength of Governor*	Institutions with Constitutional Status
Illinois	Steering	Strong	None
Texas	Regulating	Weak	None
Georgia	Consumer Advocacy	Moderate	University System of Georgia
Florida	Regulating	Weak	None
New York	Regulating	Strong	None
California	Regulating	Strong	University of California only
Michigan	Providing Resources	Strong	All public four-year institutions

* From J. M. Burns, J. W. Peltason, and T. E. Cronin, *State and Local Politics: Government by the People* (Englewood Cliffs, N.J.: Prentice Hall, 1990), p. 113.

The relative powers of the governor and legislature are important aspects of the policy environment in each state. In Illinois a coordinating board interprets and implements the priorities of a constitutionally strong governor. In Texas a similar governance structure serves more as a scapegoat for the conflicting priorities of a part-time legislature that sees all issues as "local." A Georgia governor with less authority than his Illinois counterpart achieves similar outcomes by relying on direct interaction with a system chancellor and a unified governing board that he appoints. The Florida legislature relies on interactions with a strong chancellor to pursue priorities for four-year institutions. To a lesser degree, constitutionally strong governors in New York and California pursue their priorities for public four-year institutions through direct interactions with subsystem chief executive officers and appointed governing boards. Only in Michigan and to a lesser degree for the University of

California do higher education institutions negotiate with elected leaders almost as equals, except for the power of the purse.

The state's policy environment for higher education is also influenced by the presence or absence of constitutional autonomy for institutions. California, Georgia, and Michigan have conferred constitutional status on some or all higher education institutions. In Georgia and Michigan, such status was granted as an antidote to political intrusions. Constitutional status seems most controversial in California, where it has created different state relationships for UC and CSU. While constitutional status is a significant influence on system design in all three states, Georgia and Michigan are almost at opposite ends of the continuum in terms of state roles. In Michigan, constitutional status poses a barrier to state-institutional collaboration. In Georgia, that barrier does not seem to exist.

The relationship between the state and higher education faculty is another important aspect of the policy dimension. Collective bargaining laws and/or academic senates strengthen the influence of professionals in Michigan, California, New York, and Illinois. Faculty involvement in system-wide decision processes is much more in evidence in the more segmented states than in Illinois. Faculty members in the most prestigious institutions in California, Illinois, and Michigan have not organized, preferring to trust their fortunes to strong faculty senates and institutional leadership chosen with significant faculty involvement. In New York State, the effects of a strong collective bargaining law are blunted for the State University of New York (SUNY) by arrangements that require negotiations directly with a representative of the governor. Faculty play a much stronger role in the City University of New York (CUNY), where a strong senate augments the equally strong influence of a faculty union that negotiates directly with CUNY's governing board. Less prestigious institutions in all four states have organized for bargaining, often after a history of significant conflicts between administrations and faculties. Only California has mandated shared authority in addition to collective bargaining. The combined effects of the two complicate institutional leadership at CSU and, according to many, make effective leadership impossible at the community colleges. The states of Texas and Georgia lack enabling legislation for collective bargaining. University senates are not particularly strong in either of these states. A weak collective bargaining statute limits the influence of the faculty union for Florida's State University System.

The policy environment also includes decisions about chartering and financing private institutions. The shape of higher education in New York and Illinois has been influenced significantly by strong private sectors. The structural arrangements in Illinois have produced better integration of the private sector and significantly less inter-sector conflict. Florida, Georgia, and California also have strong private sectors, but they are overshadowed politically by dominant public institutions. Efforts to take advantage of private sector capacity in all three states are of relatively recent origin. In California, use of the private sector is inhibited by a constitutional prohibition against direct support to private entities. Despite the fact that private institutions in Georgia enroll more students overall (20 percent) than either Florida or California, the governing board for the University System of Georgia has not viewed private institutions as collaborators and there is little evidence of efforts to involve them in planning activities. In Michigan, where baccalaureate work is dominated by public universities, private institutions receive grants from the legislature for degrees awarded to Michigan residents. Private higher education does not seem to have sufficient capacity in either Michigan or Texas to be a major player in meeting state higher education needs.

THE STRUCTURAL DIMENSION: SYSTEM DESIGN

No common set of design principles guided the evolution of the case study systems. Each came to its current governance arrangements partly as a consequence of geography, political culture, and historical accident, but also partly because of the timing of state efforts at system reform. Table 9.3 provides an overview of similarities and differences among the higher education governance systems of the seven states.

TABLE 9.3

CHARACTERISTICS OF THE DESIGN OF STATE GOVERNANCE STRUCTURES

Type	Representative States	General Characteristics
Federal	Illinois Texas	There is a state agency that is neither state government nor higher education that acts as an interface between state government and institutions. This agency is responsible for all four of the key work processes. Institutions or systems have individual governing boards.
Unified	Georgia	All degree-granting institutions are governed by a single governing board that is responsible for all four key work processes.
Segmented	Florida New York California Michigan	All or most institutions have individual governing boards, or institutions are grouped into subsystems with their own governing boards. There is no meaningful state agency to which the state has delegated responsibility for the work processes.

The system surviving longest without significant modification, Michigan, is also the most segmented. Its 1963 constitution contains evidence of an effort to blunt the effects of segmentation by assigning coordinating and planning responsibilities for all of higher education to the state board of education. Board efforts to exercise these responsibilities were systematically nullified during the following decade by a series of court cases initiated primarily by the University of Michigan. A community college board in Michigan that is advisory to the state board of education has minimal statewide information-gathering and reporting responsibilities. Michigan's community colleges, like their four-year counterparts, have a voluntary coordinating and lobbying organization.

The University System of Georgia took its current form in the 1930s and 1940s when the state was much smaller and more rural, and when large bureaucracies were widely regarded as the most efficient and effective organizational forms. A similar type of state governance for four-year institutions in Florida dates to 1906. All four-year institutions in Florida are governed by a system-wide governing board; two-year colleges have local governing boards and a statewide coordinating agency. The Georgia system is different from the Florida system in two essential ways. In Georgia, two-year colleges operate under the same governing board as their four-year counterparts, and the entire system is shielded by constitutional status from direct intervention by elected politicians. These differences contribute to significantly less intrusion from state government and higher levels of collaboration between two- and four-year institutions in the Georgia system.

The two large bureaucracies that govern all public higher education institutions in New York evolved between 1926 and 1948. Institutions are placed in SUNY or CUNY based on geographic location. New York assigns community colleges outside the city of New York to SUNY for coordinating purposes. Within the city, the CUNY board governs both two- and four-year institutions. Apart from the greater complexity of an additional university system, governance arrangements in New York look very much like those in Georgia, with three fundamental differences. First, in New York a board of regents that primarily focuses on K–12 education also provides limited oversight for higher education on issues related to program quality, teacher education, and comprehensive planning. Second, neither of the New York subsystems enjoys constitutional status, thereby increasing exposure to political intrusions of the sort observed during the study. Finally, New York can and does rely more heavily on market influences because of a strong private higher education sector that enrolls more than 41 percent of the undergraduates in the state.

The California system, according to one of its surviving founders, was developed through the 1960 master plan as a "treaty among the constituent parts of higher education . . . that would, at the same time, be acceptable to the governor and the legislature."[5] Because the master plan created a system out of preexisting institutions, the results resemble arrangements in Florida, with the key difference that research universities in California are organized into a separate segment and that segment has constitutional status. Like Florida, California requires that a majority of first-time students enter the higher education system through community colleges. In the 1974 revisions to the master plan, policy makers tried to incorporate stronger statewide arrangements for planning, coordination, and information management. As in Michigan, resistance from the professional community first limited the delegation of state authority to a coordinating body and later attenuated the exercise of the limited authority that had been delegated. In California, the combined impact of system design, collective bargaining, and shared governance inhibits better coordination by allowing professionals to determine, without much involvement from outsiders, the appropriate responses to public perceptions of state needs.

The Illinois system was intentionally designed along federal lines in 1961.[6] Later in the same decade, Texas adopted similar arrangements. In both systems, sufficient state authority was delegated to an interface agency that was "neither higher education nor state government" to allow for professional management of the four key work processes. Both systems are overseen by a lay board that is not under an obligation to also serve as advocates for a particular set of institutional interests. Open-access community colleges in Illinois serve all geographic regions, but the state leaves decisions about attendance to students who may also enter relatively open-access four-year institutions. Community colleges in Texas provide extensive but not comprehensive geographic coverage. The coordinating board for community colleges in Illinois operates under the oversight of the coordinating board for all of higher education. The Texas coordinating board also provides coordination for community colleges, but there is no separate statewide community college board. Differences in the way the two systems operate are the result of variances in policy environments rather than in structural dimensions. Differences also can be attributed to variances in the relative strengths of the governors and legislatures.

Management of the Work Processes

A key component of the structural dimension is the use of the four key work processes: information management, budgeting, program planning, and articulation. The work processes are particularly important for purposes of policy analysis, as they provide a set of operational tools or levers for policy makers. The seven states differ significantly in the way they use these work processes.

Federal Systems

In Illinois and Texas, coordinating boards were created to improve statewide planning. The boards provide credible and timely information on system needs and system performance to elected officials, to institutions, and to the public. The boards use program approval and program review authority to limit duplication and to encourage quality. They reduce some of the inherent conflicts in the budgeting process and link resource allocation to state priorities. They design and implement articulation initiatives. In Illinois, the coordinating board involves a large and influential private sector in planning to achieve state priorities. In Illinois and Texas, the state legislature keeps a watchful eye on the balance between professional values and the market for educational services, intervening when the interests of one are threatened by the overzealous application of another.

Unified Systems

In Georgia's unified structure, the four work processes are managed by executive leadership at the system level. While the Georgia system provides less information on performance than states using a federal model, there is effective communication with the governor and legislature as long as the chief executive of the system—who is the single contact between the state and the system—has credibility. The system plans strategically and relates budget development to planning priorities. With strong executive leadership, the planning and program approval process prevents mission creep, ensures program quality, and guards against unnecessary program duplication. The inclusion of two- and four-year institutions in the same system provides a way to address articulation and transfer. The system board has not considered the inclusion of Georgia's private sector in meeting state goals as part of its responsibility.

Segmented Systems

In the more segmented state systems of Michigan, Florida, New York, and California, institutional or subsystem boards define and manage the work processes with little attention to the activities of other sectors or segments. Government agencies are often involved directly with governing boards, and the legislature provides most of the coordination between institutions or subsystems.

In New York and Florida, each institution or subsystem provides its own data, leading many elected officials to suspect that all such information has an "institutional spin." Reports provided by the California Postsecondary Education Commission are also suspect because that agency must rely on data provided by the segments. Michigan institutions do not provide information that permits comparisons or judgments about performance except as required by the legislature as a condition of the budgeting process.

In these four states, each institution or subsystem negotiates its own budget with the governor and the legislature. In Florida, the legislature dominates the higher education budget process, using it as a powerful instrument of state control. In New York, budget cuts have led to increased student aid, magnifying the impact of market forces on SUNY and CUNY. In California, the governor has used the budget process to negotiate directly with heads of the four-year subsystems. Because of constitutional status, budget negotiations are virtually the only way for state government to influence institutional priorities in Michigan and in the University of California.

None of the more segmented systems engaged in significant statewide strategic planning during our study, though all except Michigan have some coordinating structure charged with that responsibility. Michigan higher education institutions lack any capacity for statewide planning except through voluntary consensus. Institutions determine their own missions and decide which programs they will offer and where. Voluntary program review processes in the state serve to allay some policy concerns, but they have not prevented determined institutions from offering whatever programs they choose.

In New York, where two- and four-year institutions are part of the same heterogeneous subsystems, governing boards attend to articulation issues. In Florida and California, where subsystems are homogeneous, legislators assume responsibility for statewide articulation and transfer protocols. In Michigan, each institution is left to its own devices on matters of articulation within the general framework of a voluntary agreement negotiated in the late 1970s by the state admissions officers and registrars, but never accepted by the state's most prestigious public university. In all four of the more segmented states, legislators bear most of the responsibility for devising ways of including the private sector.

SYSTEM PERFORMANCE

We found relatively little disagreement across states about what elected leaders want from their systems of higher education. Whether implicit or explicit, all states hope their systems will provide access, equity, quality, efficiency, and reasonable choice. They hope that higher education will contribute to state goals for economic development and that institutions will remain affordable. They want institutions to demonstrate reasonable productivity and give priority to state residents. They also want undergraduate opportunities that satisfy students and encourage them to earn degrees, certificates, or competencies within a reasonable period. The following five sections summarize evidence from the case studies and from available national data on differences in performance among the seven case study systems.

Responding to Contextual Change

While all of the study states faced similar fiscal pressures, not all confronted contextual changes of equal magnitude. All states faced changes associated with the global economy, technological developments, and internal demographic shifts. Illinois, Georgia, and Michigan faced modest changes in enrollment growth, along with relatively stable and healthy economies at the time of our study. Texas, Florida, New York, and California faced stronger enrollment pressures and less certain revenue projections.

Coherent statewide strategies for responding to contextual change were most apparent in those states where some combination of market influence and system design provided incentives and mechanisms for effective responses. Statewide boards in Illinois, Texas, and Georgia monitored contextual change and institutional performance, and developed strategies to reduce gaps between performance and needs. The legislature performed a similar, if shorter term function in Florida.

In marked contrast, elected leaders working with segmented systems in Michigan, California, and New York generally lacked the information needed to assess institutional performance. They did not communicate clearly defined priorities, and typically had at their disposal only weak mechanisms for system-wide planning or for encouraging collaboration across institutions and subsystems.

Responsiveness to State Priorities

While all seven systems responded to state priorities in some fashion, the nature of a system's response was clearly influenced by environment, design, and leadership. The more segmented systems (Michigan, California, and New York), operating in policy environments where market influences were limited by constitutional status or state regulations, responded in ways that protected professional values, often at the expense of other stakeholders. Such systems were highly resistant to public priorities. Georgia (a unified system) and Illinois (a federal one), operating in more market-oriented policy environments, responded in ways that took into account public priorities, sometimes at the expense of professional values. Institutions in Florida (a less segmented system) and Texas (a federal system), operating in regulatory policy environments, resisted state priorities that conflicted with professional values when it was safe to do so, and looked for creative ways to respond the rest of the time.

In Texas, the coordinating board served as a referee for the public forum in which higher education issues were played out. As is often true for referees, the board's role was both contentious and unenviable.

Elected leaders in Illinois, Texas, Georgia, and Florida identified and communicated priorities to their higher education systems. Not surprisingly, these systems were perceived to be more responsive than those in New York, California, and Michigan, where elected leaders relied more on the budget to shape institutional behaviors. While elected leaders in Illinois were sometimes impatient with the pace of change, most believed that higher education was doing a good job of responding to state priorities. In Texas, there was general satisfaction with the higher education system, although there were some concerns that it was "messy" and irrational. Policy makers in Georgia believed that higher education had been responsive to state priorities, particularly through the strategic planning process then underway. Elected leaders in Florida believed that the State University System stalled and resisted legislative initiatives. While Florida's community colleges were seen as more responsive, leaders wanted more and better information from both segments.

The New York State system did not appear to have priorities other than the implicit ones of access and quality, and the governor's explicit calls for greater efficiency. There was general satisfaction with system performance on access and quality. The governor's appointment of "activist" trustees to SUNY and CUNY suggested dissatisfaction with efficiency. California established no priorities for higher education beyond those that could be inferred from the master plan or from the governor's budget compact. Although elected leaders believed that the system's recent responses had been satisfactory, they were concerned about the future. Policy makers in Michigan were satisfied with the performance of higher education, although they conceded that the system was inefficient and incorporated too much program duplication. Their biggest concern was affordability as institutions continued to increase tuition.

Balancing Public and Institutional Interests

The Illinois federal system, operating in a steering environment, did the best job of balancing public and institutional interests. The federal system in Texas achieved reasonable balance, but the process was less predictable and more contentious than in Illinois because of a regulatory policy environment and the presence of two large and powerful university subsystems with long histories of ignoring or contesting coordinating board authority, often with the tacit support of the legislature. Aided by constitutional status applied to a unified system, Georgia also did a good job of balancing statewide and institutional interests, but was clearly dependent on strong leadership from the office of its chancellor to keep institutional interests from predominating. The combination of constitutional status and segmentation in Michigan and for the University of California favored institutional interests at the expense of larger statewide concerns. In contrast, statewide priorities overshadowed institutional concerns where constitutional status was missing in the regulatory policy environments of the State University System in Florida, the California State University, and the City University of New York. The absence of strong and stable leadership in the bureaucratic State University of New York—along with a regulatory policy environment that protected less efficient institutions and programs—probably favored institutional over public interests, although not in ways that were very visible to outside observers during the study.

The Illinois Board of Higher Education balanced institutional and public interests and enforced peace between the private and public sectors. When legislators believed the board had been too heavy-handed in promoting system-wide priorities, they intervened to preserve institutional independence. In one instance, the legislature altered board-adopted admissions standards. In another, they limited board options in rewarding institutions for their responsiveness to the Priorities, Quality and Productivity (PQP) project. The breakup of the "system of systems" can also be seen as a legislative response to a perceived lack of balance between centralized coordination and institutional flexibility, with the intent of shifting more leverage back to the institutions.

In Texas, coordinating board members were strong advocates of the public purposes of higher education, and served as a countervailing force to some of higher education's parochial interests. As in Illinois, the Texas legislature ensured that institutional interests were not overlooked in coordinating board decisions. In Georgia, system-wide priorities were balanced with those of institutions by a strong chancellor. Under weak leadership, institutional interests tended to prevail and there was mission creep. Florida used a strong regulatory environment to ensure responsiveness to what legislators perceived as the public interest. Florida's elected leaders showed little deference to professional values.

In New York, the capacity to balance statewide and institutional interests depended upon leadership in each of the two systems. In SUNY, the only identifiable focus during our study was articulation. In contrast, a unified board and strong chancellor in CUNY imposed such priorities as collaboration, productivity, and efficiency. The response of faculty professionals, reflected in the actions of the faculty senate and in lawsuits filed by faculty unions, deflected or deferred many of the chancellor's change initiatives.[7]

In California, each segment was assigned an almost exclusive set of responsibilities in the 1960 master plan under the assumption that their aggregate response, along with the contributions of the private sector, would equal statewide needs. The California Postsecondary Education Commission (CPEC) served as a neutral meeting ground for issues the segments were willing to discuss.

Since there was no statewide planning nor any specified priorities in Michigan, legislators had to assume that the sum of the actions of individual institutions reflected state priorities and needs. While in-state observers often described the arrangement as a "market model," the baccalaureate market was for all practical purposes limited to heavily subsidized public institutions.

Cost, Access, Equity, Affordability, and Retention

As can be seen in table 9.4,[8] the seven state systems achieved different results for cost per student, access, equity, affordability, and retention. Only in the case of affordability, however, does there appear to be a strong link between governance structures and performance.

Affordability seemed to fare best in states where some public entity (coordinating boards in Illinois and Texas, a governing board in Georgia, and the legislature in Florida) was given or took responsibility for representing the public interest in decisions that affected the prices institutions charged. In California the emphasis on access in the 1960 master plan contributed to the state's high ranking on affordability. However, the affordability of four-year institutions in the state, especially UC, has been seriously eroded by tuition increases that outpaced available financial aid. In New York, affordability was addressed through a need-based aid program that was essentially structured as an entitlement. Georgia's low rank on the adequacy of need-based aid is somewhat misleading because its extensive HOPE scholarship program is awarded on the basis of high school and college performance rather than need.

Higher cost systems did not achieve discernibly better results on these measures than their lower cost counterparts. The highest cost state, Michigan, tied for third on access, ranked last in equity (measured by performance of minority students relative to white students), last in affordability, and fourth on retention. The lowest cost state, Florida, ranked last in access and retention, but was first in equity and third in affordability. Larger states should in theory achieve economies of scale. Yet Georgia, New York, and Michigan exceeded the national average for operating costs. Florida and California had the lowest operating costs per FTE student. Both of these states limited student choice through a system design that required a majority of first-time freshmen to matriculate in low-cost community colleges. The outcomes provided in this chart reveal no evidence that federal or unified systems are more expensive because of the costs of supporting interface agencies, as some observers have argued.

TABLE 9.4

Performance Measures for Study—States and the U.S. Average

	IL	TX	GA	FL	NY	CA	MI	U.S.
Cost Per Student*								
(1995-96)	$6,524	$6,540	$7,312	$5,386	$7,528	$5,876	$9,057	$7,020
State Appropriations								
per FTE Student	$5,223	$4,783	$5,577	$4,121	$5,068	$4,798	$5,163	$4,801
Access† (fall 1994)	63.9	50.4	57.6	48.4	70.2	60.6	60.6	57.3
Equity§ (1994-95)	94	95	100	108	104	97	93	100
Affordability‡								
(1994-95)								
Family Share of								
Total Funding	19.9	26.9	23.7	23.5	32.7	18.4	43.0	31.6
% Change in Family								
Payment Effort,								
1985–1995	72.22	(10.42)	17.02	5.71	34.15	54.00	16.33	40.82
Median Income/								
Two-Year Tuition	109	167	115	97	55	358	91	100
Adequacy of								
Need-Based Aid	1.04	0.09	0.05	0.20	1.55	0.31	0.37	0.50
Retention**								
(1994-95)	131	83	124	67	103	116	110	100

* The cost per student is the total of state appropriations to the public sector, plus public tuition charges, divided by the number of FTE students in the public sector. Under this heading we also report state appropriations to the public sector divided by the number of FTE students in the public sector, to provide a measure of state support through direct funding to institutions.

† Access is the proportion of high school graduates starting college anywhere.

§ Equity (termed equitable opportunity by Halstead) is an index of the degree to which minority students graduate from high school, enter state colleges, and graduate relative to the retention of white students as a state standard.

‡ Affordability is the family share as a percentage of total funding, and the change in family payment effort (tuition relative to median income of households). Under this category we also show the relationship between median income and two-year college tuition, and the ratio of available need-based aid to the amount required for a needy youth to enroll at an in-state public four-year college.

** Retention is the ratio of the starting rate for high school graduates to the retention rate for first-time freshmen indexed to the national average.

Sources: K. Halstead, *State Profiles: Financing Public Higher Education 1978 to 1996: Trend Data* (Washington, D.C.: Research Associates of Washington, 1996); and K. Halstead, *Higher Education Report Card 1995* (Washington, D.C.: Research Associates of Washington, 1996).

The three southern states did least well on access, with only Georgia exceeding the U.S. average. Florida and Texas, however, were two of the top three performers on equity, measured by the performance of minority students relative to white students. Both states supported large, historically black public universities. The same two states performed least well on retention and rank, well below the national average.

Choice

Choice is influenced heavily by the strength of the private sector. Also important are such aspects of the policy environment as emphasis on the market to determine user charges and the availability of aid to offset prices charged to students. System design contributes through the role assigned to community colleges and the degree to which the private sector is included in statewide planning.

Illinois provided wide choice by supporting a variety of four-year institutions with differing programs, environments, clientele, and admissions standards. A comprehensive array of well-funded and well-regarded community colleges, a strong and well-integrated private sector, and an extensive program of need-based aid added to options available in public four-year institutions. Information about institutional performance was available to the public and competition between the public and private sectors was closely monitored.

Texans did not say much about the choices their system provided. Higher than average numbers of students attended public institutions. Relatively few went out of state or attended private institutions, despite the existence of need-based tuition equalization grants. In Georgia, the HOPE scholarships acted as a mechanism for public choice. The HOPE program did not, however, provide greater choice for low-income students who already received money through the Pell or other federal grant programs, because the HOPE scholarship to each student was reduced by the amount of federal money received. The HOPE program increased the award for students choosing private institutions, but it did not cover full tuition—as it did in the public sector.

In Florida a very large proportion of students began college in public institutions, and more than 80 percent were required to attend community colleges. A student aid policy that supported choice produced below-average outcomes. New York provided a full range of choices through an array of public institutions with widely varying missions, and a strong independent sector. Extensive student aid helped students take advantage of independent sector offerings.

In California, only the top 12.5 percent of high school graduates were allowed to attend UC and only the top one-third CSU. Those who succeeded in community colleges were guaranteed a place in some baccalaureate program, but not necessarily one of their choice. Rapidly increasing tuition at UC (and to a lesser extent at CSU), weak transfer programs in some community colleges, and faculty resistance to curriculum changes limited the realistic range of choices, especially for poor and minority students.

Michigan provided many options in the public and private sectors, although high tuition narrowed the effective range for many students. A tuition equalization plan helped needy students attend private institutions, and capitation grants provided an incentive for private institutions to graduate Michigan residents. Limited capacity in private institutions curbed the private sector's influence in the provision of baccalaureate and graduate programs.

POLICY ROLES, SYSTEM DESIGNS, AND LEADERSHIP

State policy roles and system designs, which include the allocation of responsibility for the four key work processes, establish the range of strategies available to elected and appointed leaders in their relationships with higher education institutions. In the states we studied, unified or federal systems that operated in a steering or consumer advocacy environment tended to identify priorities, shape institutional responses through all four of the work processes, and use information to communicate progress. Those states with segmented higher education systems—whether the policy environment was predominantly providing resources or regulating—generally lacked the information needed to assess institutional performance. These states often failed to communicate priorities effectively and typically had only weak mechanisms for system-wide planning or for encouraging collaboration across institutions and subsystems. Successful examples of statewide strategic and/or adaptive leadership in our study were limited to states where system designs included an interface that made use of all of the four key work processes.

System designs based on bureaucratic authority (segmented and unified) exhibited different strengths and weaknesses than those that exhibited a federal form. Bureaucratic designs were more susceptible to both good and bad leadership. States with bureaucratic systems were more likely to engage in planning and less likely to provide the information that supported such planning to those outside the system. The federal model was more likely to include the private sector as an explicit element of the design, and more likely to provide formal arrangements for specific representation of the public interest in decision processes. Both bureaucratic and federal approaches left higher education institutions and systems open to interventions from governors and legislators in the absence of the constitutional status enjoyed by the Georgia system, the University of California, and all public four-year institutions in Michigan.

In federal systems, coordinating boards typically built consensus among institutions and segments rather than relying on their statutory or regulatory authority, which was often weak. The use of consensus building was particularly evident in the budgeting, program review, and articulation processes used in Illinois, as well as in the development of the formulas used to distribute state appropriations in Texas. Institutions and systems sometimes relied on coordinating boards to make difficult program decisions that might otherwise have threatened cohesion among members. In the Illinois PQP project, presidents saw the actions of the coordinating board as strengthening their hand in dealing with faculty resistance to curriculum reform. Leaders for the University of Texas system were content to defer to the Texas coordinating board the responsibility for choosing between two campuses that wanted to offer the same doctoral program.

In segmented structures, relationships between professional leaders and state government were frequently tense, particularly where the state played a regulatory role. In California, strong leadership expanded the boundaries of discretion at California State University, but it could not entirely overcome the regulatory inclinations of elected officials and state agencies. Strong system and segmental leaders in California and Florida typically provided institutional heads with considerable latitude on internal decisions while enforcing strict discipline in relationships with state government, largely to preserve a united front for budget negotiations. The segmented design models used in California, New York, and Florida achieved collaboration within higher education segments, but not across them—except as provided by gubernatorial or legislative mandates. The lack of collaboration across segments seemed particularly problematic where institutions were grouped by mission, as in California, and when changes in external circumstances called for responses not clearly within the mission of any specific segment.

Our data do not support conventional wisdom that coordinating and unified governing boards constrain institutional autonomy. Institutions in the federal systems seemed freer from regulation than many of their counterparts in more segmented arrangements. This was particularly the case in Illinois, where the coordinating board operated in a steering policy environment. In both Illinois and Texas, the legislature kept a watchful eye on coordinating boards to be certain they did not overstep their authority. In Texas, where the state role was predominantly regulatory, the legislature intervened on behalf of institutions to reject a policy on performance funding that it had previously mandated. Institutions in Georgia, subject to the oversight of a system-wide governing board, did not seem significantly less independent in making internal decisions than their counterparts in states not subject to a statewide governing board. Constitutional status gave the Georgia system the breathing space it needed from state government to develop the strategic planning that was used to respond to a policy environment that was tilted toward consumer advocacy.

Different designs attracted different kinds of leaders. Entrepreneurial leaders who enjoyed operating in the interface between state government and institutions, and who preferred to be free of system constraints, were drawn to Illinois, Texas, and Michigan. Institutional leaders in the remaining states devoted more of their attention to institutional concerns and had to be prepared to collaborate and compromise in those instances in which institutional aspirations conflicted with system or subsystem priorities. None of the leaders we interviewed in either setting expressed significant dissatisfaction with the arrangements under which they worked, perhaps because institutional leaders seek settings that are a reasonable match for their preferences. Satisfaction among leaders does not, therefore, appear to be a particularly useful criterion for distinguishing among the policy roles and system designs among these seven states.

Some of the leaders we interviewed argued that success was primarily a matter of leadership and that good leaders could make any system design work. Such an argument can be seductive if a system is performing well. The corollary to this argument, however, is that good leadership is rare in contemporary higher education, since most systems are currently the focus of considerable criticism. We reject the "good leaders overcoming all" argument. Our research suggests that some of the leaders we observed were operating in system designs or policy environments that were a mismatch for what they were being asked to accomplish. We return to this concept of a match between system design and policy environment as we explore the policy implications of this research in chapter 10.

NOTES

1. D. Dill, "Markets and Higher Education: An Introduction," *Higher Education Policy* 10, no. 3/4 (September-December 1997), p. 164.
2. C. Kerr, "A Critical Age in the University World: Accumulated Heritage Versus Modern Imperatives," *European Journal of Education* 22, no. 2 (1987), p. 185.
3. L. Thurow, *The Future of Capitalism: How Today's Economic Forces Shape Tomorrow's World* (New York: Morrow, 1996).
4. See W. H. Trombley, *Public Policy by Anecdote* (San Jose, Calif.: California Higher Education Policy Center, 1993).
5. C. Kerr, "The California Master Plan for Higher Education: An Ex Ante View," *The OECD, the Master Plan and the California Dream: A Berkeley Conversation*, ed. S. Rothblatt (Berkeley, Calif.: Regents of the University of California, 1992), pp. 54–55.
6. Interview with L. Glenny conducted by R. C. Richardson, Jr., January 10, 1996, San Jose, Calif.
7. After completion of the case study, CUNY board members attacked the chancellor and, when she resigned to accept another position, they replaced her with an administrator more acceptable to system professionals.
8. For further explanation of these quantitative measures, see appendix B.

CHAPTER 10

Policy Implications

This chapter is about the future. It is about public policy. The earlier chapters presented our empirical research, describing and analyzing systems of higher education in seven states, as we saw them in the mid-1990s. Although empirical research can inform policy choices, the number of these choices that will determine the future is legion. Even had we studied the extant structures in all 50 states we would not have exhausted the possibilities. The leap from description and analysis of seven state systems to their policy implications for all states is a long and risky one—but necessary. State policy leaders now face—or soon will encounter—critical decisions about their colleges and universities. We believe, somewhat presumptuously perhaps, that the policy implications of our research have useful lessons for them.

State and higher education leaders face difficult decisions for two reasons: First, the success of American colleges and universities over the last half-century has given rise to high societal expectations. Second, unprecedented challenges to higher education are emerging from the substantial demographic, technological, economic, and organizational transformations in our society. Past successes suggest that continuity provides us with one option, an option that offers the advantage of organizational stability and predictability, but also the possible disadvantage of failing to meet new needs in a rapidly changing environment. The pace of societal transformations, on the other hand, suggests that organizational changes are needed. Yet these changes have the possible disadvantages of organizational instability, and of unintentionally discarding hard-earned lessons of the past. The tension between continuity and change will characterize the early decades of the next century. For colleges and universities, a large part of this tension will surface in attempts to find a new policy consensus between academic professional interests and the public interest. Problems and solutions will be difficult to identify; framing them for purposeful policy adaptation will be even more challenging.

In the first section below, we discuss the role that public policy has played in meeting past challenges, and we briefly describe six impending major challenges facing higher education. The second section poses the fundamental questions that frame state and public expectations of higher education and the latter's capacity to meet them. A third suggests that states can improve their responses to impending challenges through policy analysis performed at three levels. Our concluding section returns to the theme of balance among institutional and market forces.

THE CONTEXT: CHANGE AND UNCERTAINTIES

The world of higher education has changed dramatically since the state and national policy debates in the 1960s and 1970s. And it is still changing. What are the public purposes of higher education? What do states and the nation need from higher education? What will they need 10 or 20 years from now? How adequate for the next century are the public policies and system designs that have been adopted and refined by states over the past half-century? What policy changes—and what continuities—in structure, governance, finance, and accountability will facilitate adaptations to new circumstances and expectations? These questions are overarching ones that public policy must address.

The Changing Public Policy Environment

On the threshold of the twenty-first century, public policy decisions are complicated by a wide variety of far-reaching changes that are taking place in society. Six of these will, we believe, have serious impacts on colleges and universities.

1. *Higher Education and Social Stratification.* Is the gap between the rich and the poor widening and hardening? Evidence is accumulating about income inequalities in America—about the contrasting life expectations of those with college degrees and those without.[1] More so than at any previous time, education and training beyond high school are necessary conditions for middle class life. For individuals and for society, public policy must assure the development of human talent, and higher education is more critical than ever to such development.

2. *Increasing Enrollment Demand.* After more than a decade of relative stability, the nation's high school graduating classes will begin to grow dra-

matically in the late 1990s, and continue to grow at least until 2008. Some sunbelt states will experience increases as large as 51 percent. Only four states and the District of Columbia are expected to have declines. Overall, the high school graduating class of 2008 is projected to reach an all-time high of 3.2 million students, 26 percent more than in 1996. This growth will occur when classrooms are already overflowing with students in many of the most impacted states, and it will be greatest in states that are also experiencing changes in the ethnic composition of their younger populations.[2] Only recently have the implications of this tidal wave of potential college students for college opportunity been recognized by policy leaders.

3. *Pressures of Cost Containment.* The last major expansion of higher education was in response to the baby boom cohort. It took place when public budgets were rapidly growing. The next dramatic increase in student numbers will coincide with projected federal and state fiscal constraints and growing public resistance to tuition increases. Competition from other social services—the public schools, health services, welfare, and corrections—will require colleges and universities to tighten their belts. In this difficult financial context, state governments will revisit policy commitments to instruction, research, and public service—the broad array of benefits historically associated with higher education. For states faced with growing demand for college opportunity, whether from high school graduates or older citizens or both, new patterns of public investment and cost containment are likely to be needed.[3]

4. *Erosion of Consensus on Financial Support.* Earlier national consensus on the allocation of financial responsibility for higher education has eroded substantially. In the 1980s and 1990s, without any explicit policy decision, the nation drifted into a policy of heavy reliance on student debt financing of college, implicitly treating higher education as a private benefit for which recipients should shoulder ever larger shares of the costs. An economy that demands more and better educated citizens operates at cross-purposes with public policies that make access more difficult and more expensive.[4]

5. *Growing Concerns about Quality.* Although access and cost appear to be the public's main concerns, those who are most supportive of higher education's purposes and most knowledgeable about its functions are increasingly critical of how well it works. The competence of some college graduates and their capacity to function effectively in an advanced economy is no longer taken for granted. Interviews and focus groups with leaders in communities across America show a concern about higher education's effectiveness. Public policy does not—and should not—specify the content and design of instructional programs. But policy should include responsibility for seeing that higher education performance meets public needs, and for recognizing and supporting quality assurance mechanisms.[5]

6. *The Powerful but Unpredictable Impact of Electronic Technologies.* Technology has already revolutionized research and has had a major impact on college and university administration. How will technology affect the quality and accessibility of instruction on- and off-campus? Technology is already stimulating greater competition and the entry of new providers of higher education. And technology threatens the efficacy and relevance of many policies that are predicated upon geography, such as institutional service areas, regional accreditation, and, some would say, state boundaries themselves.

These wide-ranging challenges are not trivial. So daunting are they that in 1997 the Commission on National Investment in Education found them "a time bomb ticking under the nation's social and economic foundations."[6] The challenges are particularly daunting because so many are at the heart of public policy, where both governmental and individual aspirations intersect with the resources available to realize them.

The Role of Public Policy

As serious as the challenges facing higher education are likely to be, they can be met. A major strength of American higher education is that college and university operations are not centrally managed by either state or federal governments. Yet public policy—not governmental management—has played, and continues to play, a major role in shaping the responses of the higher education enterprise to public needs. State governments determine the governing structures of public higher education, and some states have established mechanisms for coordinating public and private institutions. Historically, public policy has been critical during the major transitions that have shaped modern American higher education—that is, the creation of land-grant universities in the nineteenth century, the development of the American research university, the establishment of community colleges, and the expansion of access and participation in the post-World War II era.

In the international context, the American system of higher education has been appropriately characterized as "market driven." This feature has been particularly emphasized by scholars who have contrasted it to the roles that European central governments play in relation to their systems of higher education. They cite the decentralized character of our national system, the existence of a non-governmental private sector, and diversified funding sources. These and the federal government's emphasis on policies that strengthen market strategies—need-based student financial assistance and competitive research funding—sharply differ from the centralized and bureaucratic models of governance and funding that represent historical patterns elsewhere.[7]

While public policy concerning higher education in the United States can be distinguished by its market-like characteristics, states have been much less market-oriented than the federal government in supporting higher education.

States have, it is true, delegated extensive authority to lay boards, and most academic and internal resource allocations are institutional prerogatives. Nonetheless, the major emphasis of state public policies is on the institution, not the market. In fact, one effect of decentralization and lay governance at the state level, especially when augmented by constitutional status, has been to insulate colleges and universities from both state regulation and market influences. In this context, most states have selectively asserted public policy priorities through regulation statutes and varying, centralized structures for governance. Much the same can be said of state higher education finance: state appropriations to public colleges and universities are based largely on workload measures or across-the-board, incremental adjustments to prior year budgets. The bulk of research funding provided by states is not allocated on the basis of competition or peer review, but supports reduced teaching responsibilities for all regular faculty in public research universities. A very small portion of state financial support of higher education is devoted to portable student financial assistance. In these respects, the state emphasis has been mainly on institutional capacity-building and on maintaining institutional assets. One might characterize the state role as a counterweight to the market emphasis of federal policies. On a spectrum that ranges from institutional strategies at one extreme to market strategies at the other, most states have taken an approach to public policy that has been much more closely aligned with institutional strategies.

This institutional focus notwithstanding, there are considerable variations among states in the ways that system designs and policies have combined to balance institutional and market forces. These variations are important, and they influence the performance of higher education, as discussed in chapter 9. In the 1990s, market forces both within and outside the control of state policy altered the higher education landscape. In the first half of the decade, states reduced subsidies for higher education, shifting costs to students.[8] Federal and state student financial assistance, primarily in the form of loans, increased significantly. Technological transformations, new providers of higher education, and new federal tax policies increased competition among institutions and offered new choices for many students. Federal tax legislation in 1997 gave states an incentive to further reduce institutional subsidies by shifting costs to the federal government through higher tuition. In addition, although it is too early to identify any pattern of response, statewide governance systems are coming under increased scrutiny and pressure. Legislators in several states, including one of the seven states we studied, have adopted reorganization plans for higher education.[9] Legislators in other states have experimented with new approaches to the public finance of higher education.[10]

Public policy has been a major force in setting the course of colleges and universities in the past. And it will be an equally important factor impeding or supporting American higher education's adaptation to new public needs in a changing policy environment.

STATE EXPECTATIONS: ASSESSING PERFORMANCE

Many of the environmental conditions we have outlined are national or international in scope and have implications for higher education in every state. Others, such as growing enrollment and increased student diversity, will affect states differently. The challenge of finding appropriate responses will be complicated by the diversity of current state systems. As is apparent from the states in our study, higher education systems are structured in a variety of ways. Each state system offers different tools and opportunities to those charged with leading it, and some are more attuned to conditions that are likely to dominate the future than others. Less obvious, but equally real, are the differences in incentives, explicit and implicit, offered by each state to assert its policy priorities.

Differing combinations of policy roles and system designs result in differing capacities to meet future challenges. Some states may be well prepared for the future; others may not. Each state has the responsibility to its citizens to assess the capacity of its colleges and universities to respond to the substantial changes that the next several decades are likely to bring. The probability of seminal change in higher education is sufficiently great, we believe, for concerned policy leaders to *assume* that new issues and problems will arise and to take steps to explore that assumption. To prepare for this, each state should ask three fundamental sets of questions about the state as a whole, not about particular institutions or their organization.

First, what does the state need and expect of its colleges and universities, including public and private institutions? What factors—economic, demographic, and technological, for example—are likely to influence future needs and expectations? How well prepared are the state and its colleges and universities to meet projected future needs?

Second, how well does the current performance of colleges and universities meet state and public needs and expectations? Are there gaps in program offerings? In accessibility? In quality? Are there realistic plans for filling these gaps?

And third, if there is a gap between higher education performance and state needs—or if it appears that projected needs cannot be met without major changes—what options do state government and the institutions have to remedy the situation?

Implicit in these broad questions about expectations and performance are much more specific concerns about:

- *Educational Attainment.* Does the educational attainment of the state's citizens match the state's plans or aspirations for enhancing individual opportunity and economic development? In what areas is such attainment adequate? In what areas is it lacking?
- *Enrollments.* How many students will be expected to enroll in the years 2000, 2005, and 2010? In which institutions? How do these expectations match the capacity of existing institutions? How, if at all, will the economic, geographic, and ethnic composition of the enrollment pool differ from that at present? If the differences are substantial, what are their implications for programs?
- *Costs.* What are the present costs of educating college and university students, and how do these differ across types of institutions? How are these costs distributed between the state and the student? Based on state revenue projections, are these costs sustainable for the foreseeable future?
- *Institutional and Programmatic Adequacy.* Are the types of institutions sufficiently diverse in programs and locations to serve all people in the state? Is the state taking advantage of the capacity and programs of private institutions? How well are the state and its institutions of higher education prepared to utilize the new electronic technologies to address access needs and the improvement of quality and productivity? Is the current mix of programs that has evolved from past needs—graduate, professional, baccalaureate, technical, and occupational—appropriate for the future?

In a few states, much of the information needed to answer these kinds of questions may be readily available. In most, however, answers will not be so easy to find, and this is particularly true for questions regarding state and regional needs and costs. Because the state policy emphasis has been focused so heavily on institutions, institutional projections and aspirations are more likely to be available than aggregated information about whether the totality of current and future institutional efforts can meet current and anticipated needs. State costs of student financial aid, a noninstitutional cost, must be factored in, and program cost analyses should be disaggregated by level—that is, lower division at community colleges, and undergraduate and graduate at four-year institutions. Information on the qualitative dimensions, particularly on the performance of the system, is extremely difficult to find. Despite increasing state use of performance indicators, there is little agreement on criteria for measuring institutional performance.

An initial assessment, particularly if it is based on expert opinion, may support the conclusion that higher education performance is meeting public needs, responding to state policy priorities, and poised to address foreseeable future needs. Policy leaders—governors and key legislators—should review such findings with care. Elected and appointed higher education officers and their staffs in most states are, as we and others have found, reasonably satisfied with the status quo, and are likely to prefer it over any proposed alternative. This bias toward the "devil that is known," can keep leaders from asking hard questions that produce unwanted answers and may suggest the need for difficult action *now* to resolve a problem that will arise only in the *future*.[11] Even more troublesome for college and university faculty and administrators is the prospect of confronting adaptive problems requiring responses that lie outside the system's existing repertoire. Clark Kerr notes:

> One must be impressed with the endurance and the quiet power of the professoriate, and particularly of the senior professors, to get their way in the long run—and that way at all times and in all places is mostly the preservation of the status quo in terms of governance and finance.[12]

As we learned from our study, current faculty and administrative leaders may argue that all problems can be resolved with adequate financial support while concurrently believing that needed resources will not be forthcoming.

In many states, an initial assessment of higher education performance and projected challenges is likely to reveal several issues we found among the states we studied. More students are expected than can be accommodated by existing institutions as they currently operate. Or employers believe that job applicants lack sufficient skills and that existing institutions do not offer them. Or the mix of state-subsidized programs may be skewed toward the preferences of the most prestigious institutions—that is, toward overinvestment in graduate programs and research and away from undergraduate and occupational needs. There may be an overabundance of less-than-distinguished graduate programs. Or there may be evidence of such problems, but insufficient information to define their seriousness with precision. Many states that face this gap in information are unable to assess the capacity of their state's public and private higher education in relation to current and future public needs—or even to agree on the appropriate information on which to base such an assessment. Such a finding in itself suggests the existence of policy or design problems, or both.

NEXT STEPS: CONNECTING PROBLEMS WITH SOLUTIONS

Many problems that arise at the intersection of state government and higher education are technical issues that are routinely, often informally, resolved. The *policy* issues with which we are concerned here, however, center on the strategic or adaptive capacity of a complex *system* to respond in the *future* to societal needs that neither fit neatly into the current pattern of institutional responses nor reflect the preferences of most academic professionals. These issues are not routine. They require the attention and response of a state's highest policy makers, not by imposing simplistic answers, but in creating conditions that marshal the knowledge and influence of educational leaders and experts to help the public reach informed judgments about the shape and direction of their future interests.

If an initial assessment of the performance of and projected challenges facing higher education suggests an absence of capacity (as reflected in unmet needs or insufficient information), deeper probing becomes essential. In chapter 1, we suggested two areas for such probing: the incentives and disincentives present in the state policy environment, and the allocation of responsibilities as determined by system design. For the purposes of this chapter, it is helpful to separate the tools available through the key work processes as a distinct and third level of concern. If a higher education system is to accomplish more than its aggregated campuses could do individually, it is in these three areas that help will be found. In examining higher education's performance relative to present and future state needs, problems and solutions appear at one or more of these three levels of analysis, and in the interactions among elements of all three.

Three Levels of Policy

Each state that we studied exhibited three levels at which policy direction had an impact on performance, and the substance and influence of these levels varied across the study states. System design—that is, the structure of a state higher education system—can be viewed as the middle of three levels of state policy: (1) the macro-policy level or the policy environment; (2) the system design level; and (3) the work processes level.

Each of the three encompasses a different aspect of the interfaces between society, government, and institutions of higher education. At each level, public policy seeks to balance the influences of the market and the influence of institutions in ways that promote the general welfare. Societal and institutional interests are not necessarily inimical. Most of what is valued by institutions and academic professionals serves the public welfare—academic freedom, high-quality instruction, competent graduates, and excellent research, for example. But educational professionals and institutions have their own interests that may not always reflect the common good. Derek Bok says it well:

> No good book was ever written on command, nor can good teaching occur under duress. And yet, conceding this, the fact remains that left entirely to their own devices academic communities are no less prone than other professional organizations to slip unconsciously into complacent habits, inward-looking standards of quality, self-serving canons of behavior. To counter these tendencies, there will always be a need

to engage the outside world in a lively, continuing debate over the university's social responsibilities.[13]

The interests of institutions are usually articulated in views of quality that are expressed primarily in terms of *inputs*—staffing ratios, funding and salary levels, selectivity in admissions, support of research and graduate programs—and *processes*, such as shared governance. The public interest may well encompass many of these inputs and processes, but it lies primarily in the *outcomes* or *performance* of colleges and universities, and in the impact of these on both individuals and society.

The goal of state policy, then, is to use state authority to achieve public priorities by *balancing* the interests of institutions and educational professionals with broader societal concerns. Balancing these interests does suggest the presence of tension. Human societies are dynamic and the social structures that serve them must change as well. States that uncritically preserve policies and systems that were created to respond to a different set of priorities may be indulging either the self-serving tendencies of institutions or the most immediate demands of the market at the expense of emerging needs of greater long-term consequence.

As state policy makers attempt to strike an appropriate balance between institutional interests and market forces, they have a wide array of options to achieve their objectives, as outlined by the four policy roles described in chapter 1: providing resources, regulating, consumer advocacy, and steering. For instance, states can restrict or encourage competition; they can create new providers, such as the Western Governors' University; they can offer incentives to new or existing private or nonprofit programs of higher education; or they can seek to protect the student markets of existing institutions by impeding the entry of new providers. States can fund students directly on the basis of merit or need or both, or they can fund institutions. They can support institutions on a "maintain the asset" basis, on the basis of performance, or on the basis of performance and competition. They can act as principal owners and operators of institutions (the maintenance approach). Or they can act as consumers in the marketplace, purchasing instruction and research from the public and private institutions that meet their access, quality, and cost requirements. They can create centralized or federal governance structures, or they can leave each college and university to the exclusive guidance of its own board. They can regulate or create systems and agencies to manage and administer colleges and universities; they can have procedural accountability through extensive rules and control mechanisms; or they can hold institutions accountable for results and outcomes.

While all of these options can be observed in some form somewhere, most states employ a particular combination of options that has resulted from *ad hoc* responses to economic conditions or political problems that appeared at an earlier time in the state's history. Few states explicitly use policy to balance market and institutional interests to assure the right combination for the priorities that the state currently confronts. We believe that awareness of options among the three levels of policy direction can lead to the more intentional use of public policy to pursue specific priorities, as well as to more systematic and useful policy analysis.

1. The Macro-Policy Level or the Policy Environment

The state policy environment—or the macro-policy level—encompasses the relative authority of the executive and legislative branches of state government, the capacity of the state to support higher education, the proportion of state budgets devoted to higher education, the status of institutions that are constitutionally protected or are exempted from taxes, prohibitions against direct financial support of nonpublic educational institutions, the relative state emphasis upon appropriations to institutions versus direct state support to students, the existence and roles of private as well as public colleges and universities, and the ways public finance may be shaped by the initiative process, including constraints upon tax revenues or expenditures. Even less malleable elements at this level are the state's political culture and traditions, as well as demographic and economic factors that affect higher education, government, and the market.

The structural or governance aspects of the policy environment may influence the direction of state policies toward institutional preferences or toward responsiveness to external forces, which have been characterized in this study as the market. Constitutional status, for instance, substantially insulates some institutions from state procedural controls, as well as from the market. Another example might be state policy that dedicates substantial portions of state financial support to portable grants to students. Such a policy would direct the state to strengthen the influence of the market and the responsiveness of institutions to students.

Constitutional status in Georgia, California, and Michigan insulates some or all institutions from state procedural controls. A state policy like the Georgia HOPE scholarships allocates major financial support to students, and strengthens both the impact of the market for educational services and the responsiveness of institutions to student demands. Georgia combines a governance model that is characterized by constitutional protection, with student financing that seeks to stimulate market sensitivity. Its strategy balances institutional and market influences to encourage performance that is responsive to its policy priorities.

2. The System Design Level

The system design level includes the decisions a state makes about the shape and capacity of its higher education system, the assignment of specific responsibilities for achieving higher education goals, and the lines of authority and accountability between state government and institutions. The system design level of policy direction interacts with and is partially shaped by the macro-level (or state policy environment) above, which includes constitutional limitations on revenues or appropriations and institutional or system constitutional status. The system design level also gives shape to the work processes or policy direction level below it, including defining who is responsible for collecting and reporting information about performance, prescribing the framework for budgeting, allocating responsibilities for monitoring program quality and redundancy, and specifying arrangements for collaboration across institutional boundaries.

Historically, each public college or university had its own governing board, and each dealt directly with state executives and legislatures. Over time, the number of campuses increased, as did the number and seriousness of statewide issues. Likewise, state governments grew and became more bureaucratic (we do not use the term pejoratively). As the task of control became more complex, most states established system designs to simplify and rationalize that task by aggregating or consolidating individual campuses. For the seven states in this study, we have characterized the system designs resulting from this rationalization as *segmented, unified,* or *federal.*

In 23 states (Georgia is the example in our study), rationalization took the form of a *unified* state system—that is, aggregation of all public campuses for governance by a single statewide board. Other states maintained institutional boards, but all except a very few interposed a state higher education agency between the colleges and universities on the one hand and the governor and legislature on the other. In these states, some, but not all, institutions may be grouped under a multicampus board. Depending largely on the state policy environment and the use of the four work processes, these state higher education systems may be characterized as *segmented* or *federal.*

Segmented state systems are usually found where the state policy environment tends to favor academic professional interests and to isolate higher education from market forces and from government regulation. In two states in the study—California and Michigan—institutions have constitutional status. In these and two others—Florida and New York—the state agencies' authority over work processes appears insufficient to affirm those market forces that are seen as adverse to the interests of higher education institutions. The Michigan higher education system provides the primary current example of virtually total segmentation.

In the two states in this study that have *federal* systems, Illinois and Texas, the state agencies appeared to have sufficient authority over all four of the work processes to achieve reasonable balance—on an ongoing basis—between the interests of the institutions and the imperatives of the market.

System design is affected by the number and type of public institutions, it includes the missions assigned to each, and it affects the use that is made of the private sector. States such as California and Florida, where large numbers of students are required to complete their first two years of postsecondary study in a community college, achieve significant operating efficiencies over such states as Georgia, where two-year institutions are less effectively used. Evidence on the efficiency of utilizing the private sector is less certain, but including the private sector in higher education planning, as in Illinois, enhances student choice and limits the tensions that can otherwise flare between public and private institutions, as in New York. Where two- and four-year institutions are components of the same system, as in New York and Georgia, governing boards attend to articulation concerns. Where they are not, as in Florida and California, legislatures must find ways of requiring institutions with different missions to work together. Federal systems such as Texas and Illinois have the capacity to address articulation issues, but they may use that capacity reluctantly in the interests of avoiding confrontations with influential state and higher education leaders.

3. The Operational or Work Processes Level

The work processes include the important day-to-day practices and procedures of governance and administration: information management, budgeting, program allocation, and articulation and collaboration. These provide operational tools or levers of public policy through which elected and appointed leaders can strengthen either market or institutional influence.

Information Management. The lack of information about a system of higher education—particularly about institutional and overall statewide performance—weakens both market and state influence, and renders accountability difficult. Information can be collected and made available in ways to strengthen market forces if it is directed toward clients or consumers and their decisions—as in Illinois. Or information can be collected for purposes of regulation, as in New York, which may be in the interests either of the market or of some or all institutions.

Budgeting. The methods a state uses to allocate financial support of higher education can be nearly as important as the amount of that support. Block grants or base budgets that are uniformly adjusted for all colleges and universities are the most deferential to institutional, academic interests. On the other hand, budgets that are adjusted on the basis of institutional performance (e.g., student retention or achievement of specified outcomes) seek to influence institutional behavior in the direction of public priorities. And budgets that require institutions to compete for public support on the basis of explicit public policy objectives seek to stimulate greater market responsiveness. In the latter cases, the market is structured by state-established priorities and by public dollars that flow to support those priorities. State student financial aid programs represent the most aggressive market strategy because these programs move the locus of decision-making that determines the flow of state dollars outside the institution. There are many variations and combinations of these approaches.

Program Planning. How are the missions and programmatic allocations of colleges and universities established? How much choice is available for students? What, if any, are the constraints against redundancy and unnecessary program duplication? Is the use of private institutions or out-of-state institutions encouraged or discouraged? How is the match between public needs and available programs determined and by whom? The policy mechanisms to respond to these questions can, at one extreme, be market driven, encouraging competition. Or, at the other extreme, they can be institutionally driven, encouraging proliferation of high-cost programs that reflect faculty preferences (often characterized as mission creep). Most states regulate the establishment of new programs, and some extend this control to termination of existing ones. States can authorize or refuse to authorize institutions to operate within their boundaries, including private, nonprofit institutions. Some differentiation of mission—a regulatory function—is probably needed to assure a range of choices in the student marketplace. Yet excessive regulatory power can stifle competition, encourage cartel-like behavior, raise prices and costs, and diminish student choice.

Articulation and Collaboration. States can defer to institutions on matters of collaboration and articulation, or they can establish policies, incentives, and accountability to facilitate these processes. The absence of actions fostering collaboration tends to restrict student mobility and discourage institutional cooperation. Ineffectual articulation policies defer to the preferences of those who ultimately grant degrees, primarily faculty of baccalaureate-granting institutions.

Consistency within and Alignment across Policy Levels

Neither problems nor solutions are usually found exclusively at any one level of policy direction. At each level, state policy makers respond to incentives and disincentives using whatever tools they are given by the system's design and associated work processes. In the *short term*, it is relatively easy for governmental and higher education leaders to influence matters at the work processes or operational policy level. This is one reason why solutions at this level are attractive—for example, revising a budgetary formula or giving a state agency additional authority. Tools at the operational policy level are legitimate and important ones that should be employed when appropriate. But it is essential that all work processes are informed by an appropriate system design and consistent policy directions. If they are not, inconsistency among the work processes can produce policy frustration and gridlock. Over the *long term*, it is the alignment of the four work processes with the state policy environment and with the system design that makes them effective or ineffective in leveraging performance.

Compared to the operational level, the system design level is more difficult to employ as an element of policy direction. We have already noted that higher education leaders almost uniformly prefer their current system design, however configured, over any possible alternative. The same can be said of most legislators. Changing a system design inevitably creates winners and losers. A number of programs and campuses of the State University of New York, for instance, would have been losers had the system been forced to respond effectively to the governor's budget cuts. Ultimately, the New York State Senate made sure all campuses survived. At the City University of New York, professional values and the unions that represented them were outraged by the chancellor's strategic endeavor to reduce the number of duplicative programs, and to align faculty numbers in specific fields with student interests. In California, a changing environment for higher education has so far evoked only those campus-replicating responses that each public segment had long held as a normal part of its individual repertoire. Cross-segmental responses were conspicuous by their absence.

To say that changing a state's system design is difficult is not the same as arguing that it is impossible. Illinois partially dismantled its "system of systems" during our study as part of its effort to free individual institutions from what policy leaders saw as excessive and unnecessary regulation. Texas altered its institutional alignments to give several smaller, more isolated colleges and universities the protection and political clout of belonging to a large and powerful university system. Missions were also changed in Texas to allow Hispanic-serving institutions to offer a wider range of graduate programs. We do not believe that it was just coincidental that our examples of design change came mostly from the federal systems. Segmented and unified systems incorporate many principles of bureaucracy, especially tendencies to disregard environmental change and to focus on stability. Federal systems such as those in Illinois and Texas are designed to be more dynamic. To a greater extent than segmented and unified systems, federal ones incorporate concerns for the societal environment and expectations of change.

One of the most difficult problems for state public policy is inconsistency or misalignment of the three policy levels. Misalignment may arise from state attempts to solve a problem at one policy level by measures more appropriate to another. Tools appropriate at the operational policy level—for example, tinkering at the margins of budgetary formulas—would not achieve the desired result if the problem were at the system design level. Nor would they be effective in the presence of constitutional constraints that perpetuate inadequate funding. Misalignment may also result when state government adapts policy incentives aimed at enhancing the influence of market forces without altering the design of a higher education system that has grown accustomed to heavy regulation. Although faculty members are at the leading edge of scholarly and scientific inquiry, their institutions have sometimes been shielded from both the marketplace and state regulation by independent governing boards, sometimes bolstered by constitutional status. One rationale for institutional independence was based on a long-held consensus that professional academic interests and the public interest were identical. Under this consensus, American higher education prospered and served the nation and states well for much of its history.

But recently, evidence of the erosion of this consensus is apparent in controversy over the costs and prices of higher education, student qualifications for admission, the appropriateness of institutional partnerships with corporate interests, and the appropriate role of technology in the delivery of instruction. With the erosion of consensus, states are increasingly at risk of having policy environments, system designs, and work processes out of synchronization and at cross-purposes. At the work processes level, for example, a state may offer financial incentives to encourage institutional responsiveness to the instructional needs of a more diverse group of students while the macropolicy and system design levels encourage a continuing professional and institutional quest for traditional symbols of prestige. States that fail to address the systemic issue of alignment will approach higher education reform through a series or package of discrete endeavors. Such approaches run the risks of misalignment and inconsistency. And, of great practical importance, they are unlikely to achieve the desired system performance.

CONCLUSION

It is difficult to convey a sense of urgency without sounding like an alarmist. But it is urgent—very urgent—that state leaders carefully assess the current and prospective performance of their higher education systems against their state's needs and policy goals. The societal environment of colleges and universities in the next century will be very different from that of the past. Responding to its challenges while preserving the best of higher education's legacies will require leadership of the highest order. It will also require, we believe, higher education policies and structures that recognize the tension between the external forces—characterized here as the market—and the interests and values of higher education institutions and academic profession-als. Absent such considered assessment, both states and the colleges and universities will act in a policy vacuum, and they will be at the mercy of short-term and short-sighted political pressures that so often lead to unforeseen, negative consequences.

Depending on the results of assessment, state policies can tilt the balance between the market and institutional interests one way or the other. There is no magic in the strategies that they can use. The appropriate role of states is to use the policy tools at their disposal at each level—policy environment, system design, and work processes—that will most likely result in the desired educa-tion performance. And desired performance is more likely to be reached if policies and strategies are adopted with explicit understanding of these three levels of policy, of the tools available at each level, and of the need for coherence or alignment within and among the tools and the policy levels.

Issues of continuity and change underlie the tensions between the market and institutional or professional values. Change is implicit in policies that restructure decision-making and finance with the aim of making institutional behavior more sensitive to external forces, such as student demand, economic development needs, and state policy goals. Change is implicit also in policies that decentralize, deregulate, encourage competition, or provide financial support to students or to institutions based upon specified performance or outcomes. In these instances, market forces "steer" institutional behavior toward change. On the other hand, continuity is represented by policies and structures that insulate institutions from external demands and short-term pressures, promote constitutional protection, use central authority to buffer campuses from societal pressures, and finance colleges and universities based on institutionally defined needs and priorities.

State policies continually, almost always implicitly, balance change and continuity. From time to time, however, it is necessary to revisit the balance or mix deliberately and explicitly. It is at these times that finding the appropriate balance challenges policy makers. Market-oriented strategies can promote responsiveness to societal change and ward off some of the dangers of "pro-vider-driven" institutions that are responsive primarily to their own interests at the expense of service to society. Institutionally focused strategies, on the other hand, can protect the enormous asset that higher education represents in each state, and can sustain areas of scholarship and instruction whether or not they are currently in vogue.

Each historical era may call for a different balance. The institution-building period benefited from structures and policies that insulated colleges and universities from external forces, and asserted public interests through regula-tion and centralized structures. Our research suggests that this institution-building period is closing. In contrast to it, the conditions of the early twenty-first century may call for state policies that make greater use of public investment to structure market forces, forces to which institutions, system designs, and work processes will be expected to respond.

The search for balance between continuity and change will be wide-ranging over the coming decades. States and colleges and universities will face a subset of that search as they seek to balance market forces and academic professional values. Some help in the latter search can be found in the experience of other states. But the balance must be struck one state at a time in the context of that state's unique needs and capacities. We are confident that this balance can result in an array of colleges and universities that will be responsive to society's changing needs. These institutions may or may not look like those of today. But however they are governed or structured, they can be responsive to societal change, continuing to support America's place in the new world economy and educating all of its motivated and qualified citizens. At the same time, they can continue to perform their core functions, preserving knowledge of the past, passing it on to the present, and creating it for the future. We are optimistic about what state higher education systems *can* be, but warn that what they *will* be depends on the present foresight and initiative of state policy leaders—our governors and legislators.

NOTES

1. See Executive Office of the President of the United States, *The Economic Report of the President* (Washington, D.C.: United States Government Printing Office, 1997); and U.S. Department of Education, National Center for Education Statistics, *1997 Digest of Education Statistics* (Washington, D.C., 1997), pp. 421–22.
2. *Knocking at the College Door: Projections of High School Graduates by State, Race/ Ethnicity 1996–2012* (Boulder, Colo.: WICHE Publications), as cited in L. Reisberg, "Size of High School Graduating Class Will Hit 3.2 Million," *Chronicle of Higher Education* (March 27, 1998), p. A48.
3. See California Higher Education Policy Center, *Shared Responsibility: Strategies for Quality and Opportunity in California Higher Education* (San Jose, Calif., 1996); and Commission on National Investment in Higher Education, *Breaking the Social Contract: The Fiscal Crisis in Higher Education* (Santa Monica, Calif.: RAND Corporation, 1997).
4. See J. Immerwahr, *The Price of Admission: The Growing Importance of Higher Education* (San Jose, Calif.: National Center for Public Policy and Higher Education, 1998).
5. See Wingspread Group on Higher Education, *An American Imperative: Higher Expectations for Higher Education* (Racine, Wis.: Johnson Foundation, 1993); J. Immerwahr with J. Boese, *Preserving the Higher Education Legacy: A Conversation with California Leaders* (San Jose, Calif.: California Higher Education Policy Center, 1995); U.S. Department of Education, National Center for Education Statistics, *National Adult Literacy Survey* (Washington, D.C.: National Center for Educational Statistics, 1992);

and J. Harvey and J. Immerwahr, *The Fragile Coalition: Public Support for Higher Education in the 1990s* (Washington, D.C.: American Council on Education, 1995).

6. Commission on National Investment in Higher Education, *Breaking the Social Contract*, p. 2.

7. See B. R. Clark, *The Higher Education System: Academic Organization in Cross-National Perspective* (Berkeley, Calif.: University of California Press, 1983), pp. 136–81.

8. P. M. Callan and J. E. Finney, eds., *Public and Private Financing of Higher Education: Shaping Public Policy for the Future* (Phoenix, Ariz.: American Council on Education and The Oryx Press, 1997), pp. 30–55.

9. R. T. Garrett, "Patton's Reforms: Kentucky Governor Brings Change to Postsecondary Education," *National CrossTalk* 5, no. 3 (fall 1997), p. 1+; W. Trombley, "Mega Merger in Minnesota: Anticipated Gains in Savings and Efficiency Prove to Be Elusive," *National CrossTalk* 5, no. 3 (fall 1997), p. 3; and A. C. McGuinness, "The Functions and Evolution of State Coordination and Governance in Postsecondary Education," in *1997 State Postsecondary Education Structures Sourcebook* (Denver, Colo.: Education Commission of the States, 1997), pp. 1–48.

10. See W. Trombley, "Performance-Based Budgeting: South Carolina's New Plan Mired in Detail and Confusion," *National CrossTalk* 6, no. 1 (winter 1998), p. 1; and A. Serban and J. Burke, *Meeting the Performance Funding Challenge: A Nine State Comparative Analysis* (Albany, N.Y.: Nelson Rockefeller Institute, 1997).

11. The State of Washington's "2020 Commission," established by the governor in 1998, is a notable exception. In this case a commission was appointed to probe the future of a state system that is generally believed to be successful.

12. C. Kerr, "A Critical Age in the University World: Accumulated Heritage Versus Modern Imperatives," *European Journal of Education* 22, no. 2 (1987), p. 186.

13. D. Bok, *Universities and the Future of America* (Durham, N.C.: Duke University Press, 1990), p. 111.

APPENDIX A

National Advisory Committee

STATE STRUCTURES FOR THE GOVERNANCE OF HIGHER EDUCATION

Chair

Robert Atwell, President, American Council on Education

Vice Chair

Virginia Smith, Director, Futures Project, A Consortium of California Independent Colleges

Members

Julie Davis Bell, Education Program Director, National Conference of State Legislatures

Carol A. Cartwright, President, Kent State University

Richard Chait, Director, Center for Higher Education Governance and Leadership, University of Maryland, College Park

Lyman Glenny, Professor Emeritus, University of California, Berkeley

Paul Goren, Executive Director, Policy and Strategic Services, Minneapolis Public Schools

Alan Guskin, Chancellor, Antioch University

D. Bruce Johnstone, University Professor and Former Chancellor, State University of New York

Richard W. Jonsen, Executive Director, Western Interstate Commission for Higher Education

Richard Licht, State of Rhode Island Board of Governors

Anne-Marie McCartan, Vice Chancellor, Virginia Community College System

Eleanor McMahon, Distinguished Visiting Professor, A. Alfred Taubman Public Policy Center, Brown University

Kenneth P. Mortimer, President, University of Hawaii

Barry Munitz, Chancellor, California State University

Donald Phelps, W. K. Kellogg Regents Professor, Community College Leadership Program, University of Texas, Austin

Piedad Robertson, Superintendent and President, Santa Monica Community College

Guillermo Rodriguez, Executive Director, Latino Issues Forum

The National Advisory Committee served from 1995–1996. Titles and organizational affiliations reflect positions held at the time of the study.

APPENDIX B

Quantitative Measures

There are a limited number of quantitative indicators available to compare outcomes across states. One of the most respected experts concerning national indicators is Kent Halstead of Research Associates of Washington. The California Higher Education Policy Center, now The National Center for Public Policy and Higher Education, commissioned Halstead to develop a series of measures for this analysis of seven states, and these measures are used in chapter 9. Brief definitions of the various indicators are provided below.

While the Halstead indicators provide valuable comparative information on performance, they have limitations. First, most of the data include public institutions only; the exclusion of independent institutions in these measures distorts the performance of states such as New York and Illinois, which have a substantial number of students in the private sector and provide significant financial support for students attending independent colleges and universities. Second, in providing data for each state as a whole, Halstead combines support for and performance of all types of institutions; this confuses the picture somewhat in states such as California, which have very large, inexpensive community college systems and large, expensive university systems.

Despite these limitations, the Halstead measures are among the best and most current national comparative data available. These data have been supplemented in the case studies with individual state data on enrollment, tuition, state appropriations, graduation rates, and other relevant indicators. Because state data are not comparable across states, we have used them only in the individual case studies and not in the cross-case comparisons found in chapter 9.

Following are definitions of Halstead's measures used in this analysis:

- *State Appropriations plus Tuition per FTE* (identified in chapter 9 as cost per student) is a measure of the total of state appropriations plus tuition divided by the full-time-equivalent (FTE) student enrollment in the public sector.
- *Percentage of High School Graduates Starting College Anywhere* (identified in chapter 9 as a measure of access) measures the percentage of high school graduates that go on to college, be they public, independent, or out of state.
- *Equitable Opportunity* is an index of the degree to which minority students graduate from high school, enter state colleges, and graduate relative to the retention of white students as a state standard.
- *Family Share of Total Funding* is a measure of tuition as a percentage of total funding (appropriations plus tuition).
- *Change in Family Payment Effort* is a measure of the 10-year change (1985-86 to 1995-96) in tuition relative to the median income of households.
- *Relationship of Two-Year Tuition to Median Income* is the ratio of median household income to state average tuition at public two-year colleges, indexed to the national average.
- *Adequacy of Need-Based Aid* measures the ratio of available aid to the amount required by potential enrollment of needy resident youth at in-state public, four-year institutions.
- *Balance of Retention to Starting Rates* (identified in chapter 9 as retention) is the ratio of the starting rate (ratio of all public first-time freshmen to recent resident high school graduates) to the retention rate (ratio of FTE public enrollment to all first-time freshmen), indexed to the national average.

INDEX

by Linda Webster

coordinating boards for, 3
in Florida, 90, 91, 93, 94, 95, 98–101, 104, 198
in Georgia, 111, 112–13, 198
in Illinois, 144, 148, 149, 174
in Kentucky, 10
in Michigan, 25, 26, 27, 28, 31, 34–35, 39
in New York, 72, 77
in Texas, 130, 131, 174
Connally, John, 134
Consolidated governing boards
in Florida, 90
in Georgia, 19–20, 106, 107
in state systems of higher education generally, 3, 7, 9
Constitutional autonomy
of California higher education institutions, 8, 50, 170, 171, 196
of Georgia higher education institutions, 106, 170, 171, 196
of Michigan higher education institutions, 8, 25, 29, 32, 34, 39–40, 170, 171, 196
Consumer advocate role of state government, 14–15, 20, 89, 168–69
Coordinating boards
in California, 3, 7–8, 45
in Illinois, 3, 7, 19–20, 144, 148–65, 179
in New York, 3, 8, 72, 76, 79–80
in state systems of higher education generally, 3, 5, 7, 8
in Texas, 3, 7, 19–20, 125–26, 134–36
Costs. See also Budgeting; Financial support
containment of, 188
per student, 180–81
questions on, 192
CPEC. See California Postsecondary Education Commission (CPEC)
CSAC. See California State Aid Commission (CSAC)
CSU. See California State University (CSU)
CUNY. See City University of New York (CUNY)
Cuomo, Mario, 74, 80

Dalglish, T. K., 8
DeKalb College, 111, 123
Delaware, 3
Design of state governance structures. See Structure
Dewey, Governor, 74

Education Roundtable (California), 54, 59
Educational attainment, 192
Electronic technologies, 189
Emory University, 113
Engler, John, 26, 33, 35
Enrollments
in California, 45, 48–49
in Florida, 95, 100–101, 102
in Georgia, 110, 111
in Illinois, 148
increasing enrollment demand, 187–88
in Michigan, 27, 28
in New York, 76
state expectations on, 192
in Texas, 126–27
Equity, 180–81

Faculty. See Unionized faculty
Federal Higher Education Act amendments of 1972, 8–9
Federal systems of governance
description of generally, 17, 20, 172
in Illinois, 144, 148, 168, 172, 174, 175, 198
and leadership, 183–85
and system design, 172, 174, 198
in Texas, 125, 168, 169, 172, 174, 175, 198
and work processes, 175
Ferris State University, 40
Financial aid programs
in California, 54–55
in Florida, 96–97
Georgia's HOPE scholarships, 19, 96, 106–7, 108, 113–14, 116, 117, 169, 180, 182, 196
in Illinois, 149
in Michigan, 32, 36
in New York, 73, 80
Financial support. See also Budgeting
in California, 47–48, 62–65